Fine and Dandy

Vicki Ohl

Fine & Dandy

The Life and Work of Kay Swift

Yale University Press   *New Haven and London*

Published with assistance from the Louis Stern Memorial Fund.

Designed by Rebecca Gibb. Set in Monotype Fournier by Duke & Company. Printed in the United States of America by Vail-Ballou Press.

Library of Congress Cataloging-in-Publication Data
Ohl, Vicki, 1950–
    Fine and dandy : the life and work of Kay Swift / Vicki Ohl.
        p.   cm.
Includes list of works (p.   ), bibliographical references (p.   ), and index.
ISBN 0-300-10261-5 (clothbound : alk. paper)
1. Swift, Kay, 1897–1993. 2. Composers—United States—Biography.
3. Women composers—United States—Biography. I. Title.
ML410.S972045 2004
780'.92—dc22
2003020226

A catalogue record for this book is available from the British Library.

The paper in this book meets the guidelines for permanence and durability of the Committee on Production Guidelines for Book Longevity of the Council on Library Resources.

10 9 8 7 6 5 4 3 2 1

To my parents, Ferris and Dorothy Ohl

Contents

Foreword   *Allen Forte*

Against the extraordinary background of the American Musical Theater in the 1920s and 1930s, Katharine (Kay) Swift's fabulously colorful life, tinged with sorrow and disappointment, unfolded. Vicki Ohl's beautifully crafted biography, rich in sensitively interpreted detail, provides a remarkable view of the complex career of this complex woman: composer, pianist, mother, lover, and charmingly gregarious woman whose associations with prominent figures of the time—most notably George Gershwin—are legendary.

Of the very few women composers in the popular music field at that time (one thinks of Dana Suesse, Ruth Lowe, and Ann Ronell), Kay Swift occupies center stage not solely, as Vicki Ohl takes pains to point out, because of her many connections with prominent individuals, not least among whom was her husband James Paul Warburg, scion of the famous banking family, but because of her own finely honed musical talents, best exemplified by her musical, *Fine and Dandy,* the first full-scale musical comedy written by a woman.

As a biographical study, the present work is artistically intelligent, cogently presented, and solidly grounded in a deep and comprehensive study of source documents, as well as first-hand reports of interviews with persons closely associated with Kay Swift, primarily those with her granddaughter and namesake, Katharine Weber, whose beautifully preserved recollections provide a splendid mosaic upon which the author draws.

The author's extensive—I am tempted to say exhaustive—bibliography is a goldmine for scholars and energetic readers whose interests lie in this amazing period of American popular music of 1920–1950, a time perhaps never to be matched, and one in which Kay Swift played a vital role both as a musician in her own right and as consort of George Gershwin. I cannot imagine a more comprehensive and illuminating study of this extraordinary individual than the one presented in this volume.

Preface

Kay Swift is often remembered as George Gershwin's able assistant, his trusted associate and adviser, and the woman who came closest to becoming his wife. Yet Kay Swift was an accomplished musician in her own right, a pianist and a composer who had far more education and a greater musical pedigree than George Gershwin. She was the first woman to write a complete Broadway show, an accomplishment that seems to have been overlooked. How their lives and careers intersected and intertwined is of great interest to Gershwin fans. But how Kay Swift lived her ninety-five years, fifty-five of them after Gershwin's premature death, is an equally intriguing story that I have had the privilege of re-creating.

My interest in Kay Swift, sparked by a lifelong attraction to Gershwin's music, was aroused in 1995 during a summer seminar of the National Endowment for the Humanities at Yale University. Directed by Professor Allen Forte, "The American Popular Ballad, 1925–1950," steeped us in the music of Irving Berlin, Jerome Kern, George Gershwin, Richard Rodgers, Cole Porter, and Harold Arlen, as well as some of the lesser-known Broadway composers of the time. This was Kay Swift's niche, although she held a more prominent position among the "others" because she had lived until 1993 and her papers had just been deposited in the Music Library of Yale

University. A woman who earned a living in a career dominated by men, she was talented, lucky, and determined.

Born at the end of the Victorian era to parents of modest means, Katharine Swift was blessed with intellect and musical gifts that her parents, grandparents, and dedicated teachers nurtured carefully. Her musical tastes were shaped at the Metropolitan Opera House, developed at the Institute of Musical Art, and realized on Broadway and at Radio City Music Hall. Ever curious and open-minded, she did not hesitate to mix styles in the music she appreciated or in the music she wrote.

Kay Swift was also a New Yorker. Born and raised in Manhattan, she absorbed the hurried pace, diverse ethnicities, and varied musical cultures that surrounded her. She spent most of her life in the city, convinced that nowhere else could be as stimulating or satisfying. Only once did she leave the city for an extended period, escaping the memories and routine of a life that was not to be. Her time in the West may have been therapeutic, but it could never have been permanent.

For Kay Swift loved New York City, its glamour, and its culture, thriving under the pressure of deadlines and the challenge of competition. She was a survivor, never daunted by obstacles. Her creativity, determination, and sense of humor helped her cope with difficult times, a gift she recognized as a "disappointment adjustant." Swift was a woman who lived for the moment, experiencing joy and tragedy to the fullest.

It is Kay Swift's unique story that I have chosen to tell here, with the aid of diaries, interviews, newspaper articles, Gershwin biographies, and her own music. She was indeed a close friend of George Gershwin and one of his most reliable associates. But she was also a woman making her way in a male-dominated profession, balancing her talents, desires, and ambitions with society's constraints. In the end, we not only treasure her wonderful music but admire her style, perseverance, wit, and class.

Kay Swift died two years before I began my research, so I have had to rely on the memoirs and memories of those who knew her well. Gracious thanks go to her granddaughter Katharine Weber, who with her husband, Nicholas Fox Weber, is co-trustee of the Kay Swift Memorial Trust. Not only has Katharine regaled me with touching and humorous anecdotes about her grandmother for the past eight years, but she has provided me with information, advice, contacts, photographs, recordings, and more than two hundred pages of Kay Swift's unpublished memoirs. In short, she has offered invaluable assistance; without her help, this biography would not have been as complete or as colorful.

The National Endowment for the Humanities Summer Seminar I attended at Yale University in 1995 created the impetus for this book, and I am thankful for that profound experience and the friendships formed during that summer. I am most grateful to Allen Forte, who not only introduced me to the Kay Swift Papers but offered encouragement and advice while my interest evolved into a dissertation, conference presentations, and now this volume. His wisdom, inspiration, and support have never wavered.

Librarian Kenneth Crilly of the Yale University Music Library and his efficient staff, especially Suzanne Eggleston Lovejoy, have been patient and accommodating over the past eight years. Also appreciated are the efforts of Richard Warren, curator of Historical Sound Recordings at Yale; Diane Joust of the Radio City Music Hall archives; Ray White, Wayne Shirley, and Betty Auman of the Performing Arts Division at the Library of Congress; and Jane Gottlieb at the Juilliard School. I would also like to acknowledge Michael S. Strunsky, trustee of the Ira and Leonore Gershwin Trust, for funding the cataloging of the Kay Swift Papers; James Leve, for undertaking and completing that task; orchestrators Russell Warner and Larry Moore, for restoring her musical, *Fine and Dandy;* and Tommy Krasker, for producing the new recording with PS Classics.

I appreciate the candor of the other family members whom I had the opportunity to interview: April Gagliano, Swift's eldest daughter, and Shippen and Lee Swift, her nephew and his wife. A cousin, Nancy Tatnall Fuller, generously sent me her thorough history of Joseph Swift and his family. I recognize that biographies are intrusive, and I have done my best to capture Kay Swift's spirit and her accomplishments while respecting the family's privacy as much as possible.

I am grateful to Robert Kimball, artistic consultant to the Ira and Leonore Gershwin Trusts, for his input. His expertise in the area of musical theater and friendship with Kay Swift have informed and improved this book. Equally appreciated and informative were interviews with friends and colleagues William Bolcom and Joan Morris, Bobby Short, Esther Leeming Tuttle, Russell Warner, and William Zeffiro, who offered glimpses into Swift's personality and professionalism. Three interviews conducted by others were particularly valuable to my research. James Leve, who cataloged the Kay Swift Papers, interviewed two of Swift's closest friends, Louise Carlyle and Alfred Stern, in 1995. Both have since died, and I am thankful that he captured their thoughts and memories on tape. Last, Vivian Perlis had the foresight to interview Swift herself in 1975 as part of the Oral History American Music Project at Yale. Swift's wit and philosophies are apparent in these conversations.

I owe deep thanks to my dissertation adviser at Bowling Green State University, Professor Jack Santino, whose insight and perspectives guided my early research. He and committee members Lillian Ashcraft-Eason, William E. Grant, and Rosalie Politsky offered me their enthusiasm and support. I also thank my colleagues Ann Sears, Charlotte Greenspan, Ben Sears, Brad Conner, and Jan Younger for their views, advice, and encouragement.

I thank Heidelberg College for its support and flexibility: an Aigler Grant in 1999 financed a research trip to New York City and travel funds allowed me to make several conference presentations. My Music Department colleagues Elizabeth Blades-Zeller, Jennifer Hilbish Schuetz, Daniel Schuetz, and Gregory Rike (now at the University of Mississippi) offered their time and talents to perform numbers from *Fine and Dandy*. And the Faculty Research Symposium twice gave me a forum to share my research about Swift with the Heidelberg community.

I have grown to know Kay Swift well; my appreciation for her as a musician and as a woman continues to grow. I have enjoyed telling others her anecdotes—both humorous and heartbreaking—and performing her music. Now it is time to share her story with a wider audience.

Fine and Dandy

CHAPTER 1

Prelude

April 27, 1897. A quiet moment in the late afternoon gives me an opportunity to open this book after a long interval. I had not realized it was so long and now I have an important and joyful record to make, no less than the birth of our first grandchild, a dear little girl to be named Katharine Faulkner, after one of Nell's sisters. It was born on the nineteenth of April (Easter Monday) and is a large fine child, with good features and called by others as well as its partial Grandma a lovely baby. . . . Nell is getting along well and Sam is both proud and happy and we are all deeply thankful.—Gertrude Horton Dorr Swift

The entry in the diary of Gertrude Horton Dorr Swift announces the birth of her first grandchild to her son, Samuel, and his wife, Ellen Faulkner Swift, with the pride, reverence, and formality typical of a late Victorian woman of culture. For more than seventy years Gertrude Swift kept a diary, and it reveals her to be an educated woman who loved music and was devoted to church and family. Through her journal we glimpse the culture, behavior, and family relationships that shaped young Katharine Swift, nurtured her musical talents, and encouraged her development as a pianist and composer. That Katharine would study music is not remarkable. That she

1

would pursue composition as a profession in a time when few women did is a testament to her musical abilities, her family's support, and her personal strength.

The Swift family originated in the British Isles but had lived in America for several generations. Samuel's great-grandfather Joseph Swift was born in Bristol, England, in 1731. He immigrated to the United States, bringing his Anglican traditions to the New World, and married Margaret McCall in Philadelphia in 1759. Glasgow, Scotland, had been the McCall family's home. The ancestors of our diarist, Gertrude Horton Dorr, they had resided in the northeastern United States since the early 1700s, moving from Connecticut to New York, Pennsylvania, New Jersey, and Delaware.[1]

More than a century later, Katharine Swift's grandfather Joseph Swift was residing in Roseville, New Jersey. He had married Gertrude Horton Dorr on June 18, 1868, in Newark, New Jersey, and was employed by the family business, Swift and Courtney, which manufactured safety matches (later the Diamond Match Company). Gertrude wrote with admiration that Joe was highly respected by all who knew him and that he had been president of the Athletic Club, a testament to his civic involvement. They began their family immediately but lost their first two children in infancy. The first baby to thrive was Katharine's father, Samuel Swift, who was born January 19, 1873. The Swifts would eventually bring twelve children into the world, though only six lived to adulthood. Samuel was raised with his five sisters, Frances (Fanny), Mary, Elizabeth (Elsie), Eleanor, and Gertrude.[2]

Music was an important component in the children's lives, as it was in the homes of many cultured families. Mother Gertrude had an organ and a Steinway piano in her home. She not only played both instruments but composed hymns, art songs, and parlor songs. All of the children took lessons in voice, piano, or violin, and the family often sang hymns before going to bed. Samuel studied piano as well as organ. His mother proudly reported on his musical progress in March 1886: "Sam is getting on very well, having a good clear touch, which with more practice would become brilliant as well as sympathetic. He has a great deal of musical feeling, and his voice, although scarcely settled yet has every promise of a fine baritone." All indications were that Samuel was a typical American youth, a source of both joy and consternation to his ambitious mother. Several months later she continued, "He has developed a beautiful taste for music and begins to make fine harmonies in extemporising, but does not practice sufficiently to improve as he ought in execution." Despite her concern for his diligence, his mother was extremely proud of her only son: "a great blessing to us, being thoroughly reliable, gentle, earnest, and conscientious, attentive to his religious duties and very creditable in his conduct at school and standing high in his classes. Joe and he play games together. . . . With me, there is the great bond of music. . . . He is still my pupil." She must have been pleased that he persevered with his music study, evidently improving his practice habits—as a young man he served as organist for various churches and taught Sunday school.[3]

In 1889 Joseph retired and moved his family to Wilmington, Delaware, to be near his brother, William, who had also been with Swift and Courtney. Gertrude's parents, Horatio and Adeline Van Nostrand Dorr, resided in Wilmington as well, so the family members were near one another. The same year, Samuel enrolled in the University of Pennsylvania, where he concentrated on musical activities. He joined the University Glee Club, studied voice and harmony at the Philadelphia Musical Academy, took organ lessons from David Wood in Philadelphia, and was organist at Calvary Church and Christ Church. He earned his bachelor of science from the University of Pennsylvania in 1894.[4]

After graduation, Samuel sailed to Europe for several months with the Reverend H. Ashton Henry, rector at Trinity Episcopal Church in Wilmington, where Samuel then substituted as organist. On the return voyage he met a young English woman, Ellen Mary Faulkner, and became infatuated with her. Once home, Samuel returned to his position as organist in Wilmington. Ellen went to live with her sister, Frances Faulkner, a schoolteacher in Philadelphia. Shortly thereafter, Gertrude's brother, Robert Dorr, publisher of the evening newspaper the New York *Mail and Express,* offered Samuel a job as music critic, a position that would offer him more opportunities in his chosen field and a chance to live in New York City. He accepted with enthusiasm.[5]

Ellen Faulkner had been born and raised in Leicestershire, England. Two years older than Sam, she had a great appreciation for art, music, and literature. Katharine Swift later described her parents in her memoirs. She remembered her mother as

> a strikingly pretty, vivacious Englishwoman . . . with pink cheeks, soft chestnut hair, and large hazel eyes. She was lively and full of fun . . . a ready, brave person who could rush in and try anything, generally bringing off whatever project she had in mind. My father, equally brave, was patient, even-tempered and of a relentlessly high standard. Mother was witty, mercurial and a 'good sport,' to quote a phrase much in use at that time. She was good for my father, urging him on and taking nothing too seriously, and he was equally helpful to her, as he held her back when she dashed ahead rather recklessly in any direction. . . . My mother adored him.[6]

Katharine's positive memories of her parents and their relationship signal a secure and happy childhood. It was one that would help her to develop confidence in herself and her abilities.

Samuel Swift and Ellen Faulkner corresponded for more than a year, and they announced their engagement in January 1896. Gertrude confessed that Ellen was "a very charming, bright, fresh-faced girl, very well educated. . . . [She] has charmed us all." They were married on June 8 at the home of Philadelphia friends, Mr. and Mrs. Rufus Shapley, since Ellen's sister, Frances, was not feeling well and was making plans to return to England for a visit. Only relatives were invited to the wedding, and John Van Nostrand Dorr, Samuel's cousin, was his best man. Four small girls, including Samuel's sisters Gertrude and Eleanor, served as bridesmaids, and the Reverend Henry, the Swifts' family pastor, officiated. Samuel and Ellen settled in New York City in a fifth-floor walk-up apartment at 200 West 96th Street. Their daughter, Katharine Faulkner Swift, was born on April 19, 1897.[7]

Both Samuel and Ellen Swift played the piano, and music filled their apartment. Swift's assignments as music critic necessitated his frequent attendance of performances at the Metropolitan Opera House. In preparation, he would familiarize himself with the works by playing them on the piano with his wife. Years later, Katharine Swift remembered these sessions. Her mother, she recalled, "read any musical score at sight, with plenty of bravado and several clinkers, a great help to my father, who played beautifully by ear and read slowly. They always went over new scores that my father was about to review." It was into this cultured, intellectual home, "unburdened by wealth of any kind," that Katharine had been born. Ellen and Samuel Swift shared their musical interests and talents, a collaboration that benefited the entire family and made a lasting impression on their young daughter. By 1901, Samuel was appointed to critique both music and art and, by the next year, was a contributor to *Harper's Weekly Magazine*.[8]

Gertrude Horton Dorr Swift kept her diary until 1916 and often recounted visits with her son and his family. These visits always included trips to concerts and operas. In February 1898, she and her husband, Joseph, visited Sam, Ellen ("Nell"), and the baby, when Katharine was less than a year old. During this time, they attended three Wagnerian operas and Gioacchino Rossini's *Barber of Seville,* in addition to a "charming morning concert at the 'Astoria' Hotel conducted by [Anton] Seidl, which featured a Tschaikowsky symphony (the Pathetique) and a violin concert of Bruch played by Miss Maude Powell." An entry in January 1899 describes a short visit to New York in which Katharine's grandmother heard "three operas splendidly given." The account describes the performers to a far greater extent than would a casual concertgoer, revealing a deep interest in the names of the singers and conductors.[9]

Thus raised by serious amateur and professional musicians, young Katharine did not disappoint her family. Grandmother Swift observed in June 1898, when Katharine was one, that her granddaughter "evidently has an excellent musical ear, recognizing little songs by the tune without the words and taking her own little part by filling out with the right word or gesture at the critical moment." She expected her to be a "remarkable musician." Several months later, she described singing Gilbert and Sullivan's aria "I'm Called Little Buttercup" to young Katharine so frequently that Katharine called her "Buppa-pa," her version of "Buttercup."[10]

As a young girl, Katharine accompanied her father to the opera so often that she memorized various lines and parts of Wagner's *Ring of the Nibelung* and developed aspirations of singing the part of Brünnhilde. Her grandmother's diary entry in September 1903 suggests the extent of six-year-old Katharine's talents:

> Katharine's musical achievements, entirely untaught, are wonderful. I believe she will become a remarkable musician by the time she is grown. She plays whatever she hears and works over the harmonies until she approaches in many instances the correct ones. Not only this, but her little compositions have a form and coherency that is almost marvelous in so young a child. Besides this she has great fluency and plays chords . . . without the least hesitation, using the pedal quite judiciously, although to do so involves her sitting on the edge of the piano stool.

Grandmother Swift's pride in Katharine's early accomplishments and in her potential as a musician is obvious. She did point out, however, that her granddaughter was a "genuine little child" who "climbs trees and swings with her cousin Joe." Katharine also enjoyed her baby brother, Samuel, Jr., who had been born in January 1903, when Katharine was not quite six. By 1904, Grandmother described young Sam as "a fine child, very merry, though with a strong will and somewhat pugnacious, but still very tender and affectionate."

In February 1905 the diary entries note that Gertrude Swift attended five operas and three concerts during her weeklong visit to New York, as well as "an afternoon tea and dinner party." She was very proud of her son and his position. "It was . . . so pleasant to go with my dear boy who takes such tender care of me when I am with him. It is such a pleasure too to know that he is so much thought of and liked by people of real worth and culture, and also to see him so happy with his dear wife and children." Though we cannot know who Gertrude Swift considered "people of real worth and culture," we can speculate that they included his friends who were present at tea or at dinner; or perhaps the famous musicians and artists that Sam met when he reviewed their performances and exhibitions. Earlier she had commented, "They have many delightful friends among refined and artistic people." It is important to note that this pride in his social status was balanced with the pleasure she felt as she noticed the attention and joy he shared with his family. Grandmother also noted Katharine's musical development at age seven: "Katharine's progress with her music is excellent and her love for it and appreciation is wonderful. She went with me to hear *Rheingold* and sat with unfailing attention through the two hours and a half, enjoying it most intelligently. She has heard it once before and knew the libretto perfectly."[11] Katharine's extraordinary memory would become legendary in her later years. This comment by Gertrude Swift establishes early evidence of her gift.

Such exposure to opera made a lasting impression on young Katharine. In her later years, Swift herself spoke of her love for opera in an unpublished memoir. This excerpt describes her natural musical talent, her intense involvement with music, and her vivid imagination.

> Starting at the age of just past four, nothing really mattered much
> to me except the opera. My father happened to be a music critic,
> and he played, often by ear, scraps of different operas on the piano,
> which whetted my imagination for a fuller hearing of these magical
> performances. As my father's assignments took him to the Metro-
> politan Opera House—the old Met on West 39th Street—he
> not unnaturally took me with him. . . . It was just then that a door
> swung open for me, into an enchanted land, in which I remained
> for ten years. Looking back, I am amazed at the forbearance of my
> mother and father during this total immersion of an otherwise ap-
> parently normal child into a world composed of fantasy. I not only
> played a game in which I half-believed the characters depicted in,
> say, Wagner's *Ring of the Nibelung,* were real people, friends who
> conversed with me and, by night, took me, in waking fancy, as well
> as in dreams, into their unreal world. Being a musician with positive
> pitch and almost total musical recall, from a very early age, I liter-
> ally lived in Wagner's opera world. As soon as I could read music
> —which was when I was six—I memorized parts of the scores.
> Without understanding German, I learned several of the operatic
> roles.[12]

While this passage emphasizes the creative fantasies that opera awakened in the young Katharine, it also attests to her remarkable gift of memory— both for music and for language patterns—and to an intellect that could grasp the complex Wagnerian plots at age six.

In another section of the memoir, Swift describes her youthful friendship with Eleanor Hyatt, whose mother, Mabel Hyatt, was an opera singer.
Katharine accompanied Eleanor to productions in which her mother sang,
and she became enthralled with this art form. "Shining vistas opened up
before me, dreams of backstage at the Metropolitan Opera House; all these
dreams came true, and we had magnificent times, learning most of the music of several operas by heart, and singing them together. Sometimes Ellie's
father, who was a composer of songs, accompanied us. Sometimes Daddy
did, or Mother (who could sight-read much more easily than could Daddy,
although she didn't play nearly as well as he played by ear)."[13]

With humor, Kay Swift recalled a "maddening phase" she went through,
of imitating the chromatic laugh given by Brünnhilde's sister Valkyries in
act 3 of *Die Walküre:*

> This difficult laugh started on a high note I could hardly reach and
> descended on a chromatic scale. I tried to time myself, saving the
> dread cackle for a moment when I would have laughed anyway,
> but the result was a maniacal sound. My parents suffered during this
> dreary period, which was terminated at last by my father. He told
> me that he had fallen in love with my mother, whom he had met on
> board a ship returning from her native England, when he first heard
> her happy, natural laugh. This was true and the telling of it proved
> a brilliant ploy, which stopped me cold, in mid-hoot.[14]

Another close friend of young Katharine was Louise Homer, Jr., daughter
of the renowned Met contralto, Louise Homer, and her husband, composer
Sidney Homer. Madame Homer sang with the Metropolitan Opera from
1900 to 1919. The girls often attended opera productions, after Louise had
summarized the plots for Katharine. They learned bits of the operas and
sang duets. Katharine especially remembered the production of Engelbert
Humperdinck's *Hänsel and Gretel.*

> When *Hänsel and Gretel* was produced at the opera house, Mme.
> Homer played the part of the witch. She wore a horrible false chin
> and a huge, hooked nose through which she sang in a predictably

nasal fashion. Louise Junior and I fell in love with the opera, and immediately learned almost all of it, Louise playing Hänsel (she was a little older and bigger) and I, Gretel. The Homers often had a free box on the second tier, so we must have seen nearly every performance of Humperdinck's masterpiece. One night, a short, rosy Santa Claus of a man in the next box turned out to be the composer, Engelbert Humperdinck himself, so we met him, which was a great thrill.

Opera was a passion for Katharine that sparked creative play, a sense of drama, and musical foundations that she remembered and used throughout her life.

Education and Values

Young Katharine attended Miss Veltin's School for Girls from age seven to seventeen. Housed in a five-story building on New York's Upper West Side, the small private school graduated twenty young women in 1915. Memories from the alumnae indicate that it was a closely knit class, all of whom cherished their years at the school. In 1978, Swift reminisced:

> Who among us could ever forget the Assembly room with its beautiful proportions, the fine reproductions of the Parthenon frieze around three walls and the raised platform on which Miss Veltin sat, queenly in her white or pastel dresses, with the smooth grey pompadour above her fine face? I can hear her mellow voice in my mind's ear, reading a psalm, and then, after all two hundred and fifty of us had chanted the Lord's Prayer and sung a hymn, the gentle exhortation she gave us, in which she often urged us to exert self-control at all times during our lives. The organ, which was a fine instrument, [was] well-played by a thin man whose back was always to the room, directly behind Miss Veltin.[15]

Other students remembered the "Tiffany glass amber-colored windows" in the assembly hall; Miss Veltin's "handsome, intellectual face, which radiated contentment"; the 11:15 A.M. break for crackers and milk; and the Friday afternoon "spreads" in the gymnasium, with a potluck lunch followed by basketball and dancing. Miss Veltin's was, indeed, an institution that reinforced civility and manners in these young ladies as well as academics. Years later, Swift learned that her attendance at this fine school had been made possible by a generous scholarship.[16]

After Katharine's brother, Samuel, Jr. (Sam), was born, the family moved to a larger, fourth-floor walk-up at West End Avenue and 101st Street. Katharine welcomed her younger brother, and she vividly recalled the "Big Boy Beds" that she and Sam slept in as he grew older, which "magically, to us, folded into a couch by day." Sam was "dark-eyed, strong, and could clown around. I adored him, putting up with some hard kicks in the shins, which must have been fun for him." The Swifts shared the floor of the apartment building with the Bryson and Edith Burroughs family. The Burroughses were artists, a painter and a sculptor, a circumstance that further encouraged Katharine's appreciation of the arts. The Burroughses had two children, Alan and Betty, and Katharine and Sam often played with them.[17]

In the summer of 1905, Samuel Swift, Sr., served as the *Evening Mail and Express* art and music correspondent in England and France. This assignment gave the family the opportunity to visit the Faulkner relatives when Katharine was eight years old and young Sam was two. They grew to know the extended family and their English heritage, as well as a culture that would always be a part of Katharine's life and work. In a letter to Adeline Dorr, his eighty-four-year-old grandmother in Wilmington, Katharine's father marveled at the beauty of the towns along the coast, as well as the "hedges and green pastures [around Moira] that make the land look rich," where he had taken "some capital bicycle rides." He also confessed to becoming "motor mad," for he had traveled eight hundred miles over English and French roads in a car owned by their London friends.[18]

Music critics were poorly paid, and Samuel Swift had a difficult time meeting his family's needs. In 1907, he left full-time newspaper work and, with the help of his father, Joseph, purchased a business in New Haven, Connecticut, the One-Lock Adjustable Reamer Company, which he hoped would offer a more promising financial future. He kept the New York apartment for his family so that the children's school and Katharine's music lessons would not be interrupted. This meant a two-hour commute each way to work. To supplement his income and to maintain his contacts in the music world, Samuel continued to review musical performances in New York three times a week, thus compounding an already strenuous schedule. Returning home from New Haven by seven o'clock in the evening, he "dressed in a tuxedo (as all critics did in those days) and hurried off, after a hasty dinner, to an opera or concert." Swift sought extra work assisting critics from other newspapers, such as W. J. Henderson, H. E. Krehbiel, and Richard Aldrich, or filling in for them "so they didn't have to go out every night."[19]

Swift was from 1907 to 1909 the assistant music critic for the *New York Tribune* and, from 1909 to 1910, critic for the *New York Sun*. Unfortunately, the One-Lock Adjustable Reamer Company failed to make a profit, and in late 1910, Samuel sold it "at a serious loss." He returned to New York to join his wife and son, while Katharine spent three months with her Aunt Frances, her mother's sister, now in Dedham, Massachusetts, and attended school there. Her grandmother reported that Katharine "showed a great desire to help her father by doing some work in the school there for which she would be remunerated. At thirteen it showed much character." Ellen Swift eventually took up interior decorating to supplement the family income. Although the Swifts experienced financial hardships and Samuel's newspaper assignments interrupted time spent with his family, Katharine had vivid and loving memories of him and his work in music. Fondly, she remembered, "My mother did a lot of research for him, because when a new opera or a new symphonic work was about to be played, Mother got a copy and read it [at the piano] with him. . . . That was very happy to see such a good team. They were such a happy couple." Gertrude Swift observed that both Sam and Nell were "delightful, ready to help others, and so cultured and such cheerful companions."[20]

In spite of these financial constraints, the Swifts seemed to maintain positive outlooks on life. Faith provided a means for coping with adversity and was an important element in Katharine's childhood. Grandmother Swift was very active in her Episcopal parish in Wilmington, and she composed and published several hymns. Samuel Swift, Sr., had taught Sunday school in his church for several years while in high school and served as organist for several area churches before his marriage. He and his young family observed the Christian traditions they had learned as children, and Grandmother Swift admired the way Katharine could "follow the service in her little prayer book" at a young age. Katharine received religious instruction at Miss Veltin's, and her mother read Bible stories to her. She vividly remembered the tale of "the man who hid his talents under a bushel. I had no idea what a bushel might be, but I did get the idea that the talents referred to were probably for writing music, painting, or some similar occupation. So this gave me the guilts . . . whenever I wasn't turning out any work." In her memoirs, Katharine wrote of the solid faith her parents shared. Ellen Swift firmly believed in an almighty being, from whom she drew strength. While Samuel Swift grew away from the traditional church in his later years, he led a life of stewardship and kindness. On Sam's fortieth birthday, his mother wrote, "His religious views have changed somewhat in the last few years, and it is a grief to me that he does not feel as he used about our dear church, but he assures me that he is traveling in the same direction, and if his earnestness of life and unselfishness and consideration for the interests of others account for the Christian life, I am sure he is leading it."[21]

Ellen Swift was also somewhat of a mystic. On occasion she had the gift of "second sight," or the ability to foretell coming events. As she grew older, Katharine believed that she had inherited some of this perception, for she, too, sensed impending events from time to time. One of her granddaughters, Katharine Weber, who with her husband, Nicholas Fox Weber, serves as co-trustee of the Kay Swift Memorial Trust, does not remember that Kay Swift was deeply religious or devoted to a particular denomination, although she did observe Christmas and Easter. She recalled her grandmother's nontraditional faith, which included an interest in metaphysics, as well as "clairvoyance, séances, ouija boards, spells, signs and the power of prayer over plants." She was a faithful attendant at the Church of Truth, which met at Carnegie Hall, and whose leader, Dr. Ervin Seale, was a renowned scholar of metaphysics. Weber accompanied her grandmother to one of these services. Swift seemed to believe in a higher power and in sharing her talents and gifts with others but, like her parents, chose a less traditional mode of worship than her grandmother.[22]

An unlikely passion in Katharine Swift's young life was baseball. When she was eleven her father took her to see the New York Giants play the Chicago Cubs at the Polo Grounds, and she "was instantly hooked." She began clipping pictures of her favorite players out of the Sunday supplement of the *New York Times* and hanging them on the walls of her room, replacing the opera divas with her new baseball heroes. She described going with her grandfather daily to TriState League ballgames in Wilmington when she "was a lumpy twelve-year-old."

> Nothing he or anyone else could have done would have given more
> pleasure. We always sat in the same seats, right behind third base,
> and soon knew some of the players—not really, but enough to call
> out loud greetings to them as they took the field. . . . [W]e all sec-
> ond-guessed the managers, exhorting them to take out the pitchers,
> or to leave a man in—when he was being replaced and took that
> sad, long walk back to the bench. Gramp was a handsome man,
> six feet two, with silver hair and mustache. I was proud of him, and
> delighted when he lent me a beat-up old brown felt hat that kept
> slipping down over my eyes. The sun beat relentlessly on us, but
> we loved every moment of the games.[23]

Her brother, Sam, was to become a fine athlete, boxing ably and serving as co-captain of both the football and baseball teams at Milton Academy in Milton, Massachusetts. Swift recalled that a Boston sportswriter described him as being "the best schoolboy first baseman he'd ever seen." Sam played first base and pitched with a semiprofessional team under the name Tim Cassiday so that he could retain his amateur status. He was offered a try-out with the Cincinnati Reds organization after high school and played in a semiprofessional league in Worcester for one summer. Baseball became another activity that brought the Swift family together, increasing Katharine's competitive spirit and her appreciation for excellence and professionalism. She attended Giants and Yankees games but became a life-long Brooklyn Dodgers fan, cheering for the team even after it moved to Los Angeles.[24]

The Swift family was close and happy. They nurtured Katharine's intellectual and artistic creativity while providing a secure, loving environment for her emotional and spiritual growth. Her imagination, confidence, and self-expression thrived as she developed the qualities that contributed to her extraordinary life.

Music Lessons

Samuel Swift's contacts with influential figures of the classical music world enabled young Katharine to study with some of the most gifted and exacting instructors available. Her first piano teacher was August Spanuth, a music critic for the German newspaper *Staats Zeitung*, who volunteered to give her lessons. Katharine apparently made fine progress, for Grandmother Swift commented in February 1905, "She plays a little piece of Reinecke with spirit and clear notes, singing it in German, and playing the accompaniment in a most spirited manner." Spanuth lost his patience with young Katharine, however, "when I added several variations of my own in the middle of a little piece by Carl Reinecke, explaining that it sounded better that way. . . . I'd done the same in pieces by Handel, and Mr. S. kicked his own piano (instead of me, probably) and called off future lessons."[25]

More productive study began when the Institute of Musical Art in New York opened its doors in 1905. The precursor to the Juilliard School of Music, the institute was conceived by founders Frank Damrosch, James Loeb, and Paul and Nina Warburg as an institution to create "complete musicians" —amateurs as well as professionals. Ear training, music theory, and history were to be studied in conjunction with private lessons. Damrosch was its first director. Although not himself a performer, he was the son of renowned conductor Leopold Damrosch and the brother of New York Symphony Orchestra conductor Walter Damrosch. It was his inspiration for a broad music education that drove the curriculum and led to the nickname "the Damrosch school." James Loeb, a partner at the Wall Street firm of Kuhn, Loeb and Company, provided major funding for the school. Loeb's first passions were archaeology and the classics, which he had forsaken to carry on the family financial business. His interest in the institute was a means of both pursuing his creative instincts and establishing a memorial to his mother, Betty Gallenberg Loeb, who had died in 1902. She had had aspirations of becoming a concert pianist before her marriage and was always a strong supporter of the arts. Solomon and Betty Loeb had had four children, Morris, Guta, James, and Nina, and all were given music lessons. Nina Loeb married Paul M. Warburg, and they, too, made significant financial contributions to the school. Paul served on its board of trustees, as did other Warburg family members. Damrosch was passionate about his mission, and he devoted much time and effort to the facility. These founders would hold more than a little significance for Katharine on both personal and professional levels. Samuel Swift was good friends with both Walter and Frank Damrosch, and it was Frank Damrosch who recommended her for a scholarship. And later she would marry James Loeb's namesake, Paul's only son, James Paul Warburg.[26]

These interesting connections meant little to young Katharine in 1905 as she and her mother rode the horse-car across town to the institute. Her piano teacher was Bertha Fiering Tapper, who served on the faculty at the institute from 1905 until 1911. Tapper had studied with Agathe Backer-Gröndahl in Norway, Theodore Leschetizky in Vienna, and Carl Reinecke and Louis Maas in Leipzig before coming to the United States. She was a friend of Edvard Grieg and edited two volumes of Grieg's piano works. From 1889 to 1897, she taught at the New England Conservatory, and in 1895 she had married Dr. Thomas Tapper. Her husband was hired as a music historian on the staff at the institute and wrote a music history book with Percy Goetschius. One of Tapper's piano students was Leo Ornstein, who immigrated to the United States from Russia in 1907 and earned a degree from the institute in 1910. Ornstein had a successful, though brief, concert career, wrote modernist compositions, and in 1920 founded the Ornstein School of Music in Philadelphia. Although he had also studied at the St. Petersburg Conservatory, he called Tapper "the strongest single influence on [my] life in music." A strict and demanding teacher, Bertha Tapper was a dominant force in her students' lives.[27]

Tapper recognized Katharine's ability and that first summer took her to the Tappers' summer home in Blue Hill, Maine, for extensive coaching. A resort town near the coast, Blue Hill was the vacation spot of several prominent musicians, including members of the string quartet anchored by Franz Kneisel, first violinist and well-known teacher at the Institute of Musical Art. Tapper often played Beethoven piano quintets with the quartet in the evening. Kneisel encouraged his students to visit Blue Hill and play chamber music. Eventually an auditorium was built and named in his honor, and the tradition he started became the Kneisel Hall Summer Music Program at Blue Hill.[28]

Bertha Tapper instilled a rigorous practice ethic in her young, undisciplined student. Swift recalled those months at "boot camp," where she had to place corks between her fingers for two hours at a time "to stretch the gaps between them." Swift became much more focused that summer and had nothing but admiration for Tapper, whom she called "Mor," Norwegian for mother. "Everything went with it," she recalled, "not only music. She taught me to swim and dive. There was a discipline that went with it. I had to make my bed; I had to do everything by the clock, which was splendid. I practiced in the morning only on a clavier, or dumb piano, which I used to call it, with clicks. It made the weight stiffer and stiffer. And then in the afternoon [I practiced] on a piano, so it was dessert to practice the piano after doing the exercises. . . . I was an undisciplined child. I was hard to teach because I did not keep track of time and didn't do things at a certain time of day, so Mrs. Tapper really gave me something that I have remembered always."[29] Katharine studied with Tapper for ten years. She was enrolled at the institute from 1905 to 1908, after which she took lessons at Tapper's home and continued to play in student recitals. Grandmother Swift reported attending one of Swift's piano recitals in May 1909, at which Katharine, aged twelve, and another student played Robert Schumann's Andante and Variations, a duo-piano piece that requires fairly advanced technique and musical understanding. Swift recalled that every lesson with Mor "was a stimulating, happy occasion. It was impossible not to feel the excitement generated by this special, vital lady. Her standard of excellence was never dropped for an instant. . . . But with Mor, there was no nonsense. I can still hear her saying, 'There's only one right way to do a thing.'"[30]

The Swift family began to spend part of each summer at Blue Hill, sharing a cottage with their friends, the Terrys, near Tapper's home. Another musician who summered in Blue Hill was Horatio Parker. One of the most esteemed American composers of the time, Parker had been a professor of music theory at Yale since 1894 and was appointed dean of the Yale School of Music in 1904. Grandmother Swift proudly wrote on September 8, 1907,

"When I put it on record that Mr. Parker is writing down one of Katharine's original songs, it will indicate what he thinks of her musical ability."[31]

When in New York, Tapper held monthly studio classes in her apartment on Riverside Drive, where selected pupils played. "Each of these occasions was treated with all the formality—and the accompanying nervousness by the students—of a recital at Carnegie Hall," Swift recalled. Katharine was nine when she attended her first studio class. "The first time I attended one of these, I took off my hat and coat, strode to the Steinway piano and sat down. 'Get up,' said Mor. 'You'll play, but later, when I tell you.'" During the first few years of Katharine's lessons, most of Tapper's students were eighteen or twenty years old and were very advanced. "Then Leo Ornstein, the first male among us, arrived on the scene. He played brilliantly, with a dazzling technique and so much dramatic impact that it was hard to realize he was only half a dozen years older than I." A photograph of 1908 shows Bertha Tapper with her students. Flanking her are Katharine Swift and Leo Ornstein. Also identified in the photograph are Pauline Mallet-Provost, who later married Ornstein, and Claire Raphael, who as Claire Raphael Reis became a tireless promoter of new music as well as executive director of the International Composers' Guild and, later, of the League of Composers.[32]

Tapper ensured that all of her students followed contemporary trends in music as well as learning the classics. Claire Raphael invited writer Waldo Frank and Paul Rosenfeld to hear Leo Ornstein play in 1914. Ornstein played a program of Maurice Ravel, Claude Debussy, and Isaac Albéniz, as well as some of his own compositions, which Frank remembered as "a voluminous, cacophonous broadside of chords that seemed about to blow the instrument in the air and break the windows. Chaos spoke." Although there is no record of Swift's attendance that particular Saturday, she was still Tapper's student. Her father, too, was a supporter of contemporary music; he was a member of the MacDowell Club and a founder of the New Music Society of America. Given that commitment, he was likely to have exposed his talented daughter to new musical styles whenever possible.[33]

Katharine Swift began to study composition with Arthur Edward Johnstone when she was twelve. A friend of her parents, Johnstone had written an overture, piano works, and songs and had published a book on instruments. He lectured in the summers at Washington University in Saint Louis.

Johnstone encouraged Swift to compose away from the piano. She later explained, "When one writes at the piano, one is limited by one's technique, especially if one turns to orchestra. It is much better to hear it in your head right away, which is what I do now and have for years." Among his many works, Johnstone wrote books of songs that used a limited range of pitches for children to sing and play. He assigned Katharine to write several of these using only five notes. She recalled: "It's a wonderful discipline. It keeps one from doing the thing that otherwise I'm sure he would have done, which is write in a terrific range, so the singer has very difficult things. Mr. Johnstone was very strict and would say, 'Every note you come to rest on has to be like a drink of water, and harmonically, it should have that effect, too, so that you don't get tired hitting on the same note. Coming back to it becomes anticlimactic.' All these things were splendid discipline." Swift credited Johnstone as having the greatest influence on her writing "because he covered so many fields," among them theory, counterpoint, and composition. "As he was so strict, it made me more critical than I would have been of my own work, because one has to like it or one throws it away, and I've been more careful ever since."[34]

Johnstone and his wife, Clara, had lost a daughter who was Katharine's age and shared the same name. "They told my parents that it comforted them to have me around. So I visited them for several months, walking to school from their apartment in the morning and returning to lunch. . . . I had daily lessons that were stimulating." Her early compositions were often songs with piano accompaniment, inspired by poetry. One of her earliest, "My Thoughts Are Like the Little Birds," is based on a poem by Grace H. Duffield. Twenty-four measures long, it is in the tradition of a nineteenth-century parlor song, with secondary harmonies and chromatic inner voices (ex. 1.1). The first twelve-measure section (three four-measure phrases) modulates from G to C major. The second half, a modified repetition, remains in G but introduces more chromatic chords, particularly toward the end. There are subtle changes in register and in melodic elaboration as well. Katharine was probably twelve or thirteen when she wrote the song. Another student work, "Boots," dated 1911, sets the famous poem of Rudyard Kipling.[35]

Swift was especially fond of Johnstone and his friend Harvey Worthington Loomis. Loomis, "a zany, gifted man," was also a composer and a distant

1.1 "My Thoughts Are Like the Little Birds," measures 1–8

cousin of Swift and boarded with the Johnstones. To celebrate her fifteenth birthday in 1912, Katharine had two requests. "First, I longed to see the opening game of the New York Giants' baseball season; second, I wanted Mr. Johnstone and Harvey Loomis to come to dinner. Both wishes were granted by my understanding parents, and I remember that the Giants won their game and Johnstone, Loomis and brattish Swift played the piano far into the night."[36]

Another outlet for Swift's artistic expression was dancing, a "special passion" of hers. She took ballet as a young girl and as a teenager had the opportunity to dance for Ruth St. Denis, an innovator and performer in modern dance who was also a friend of the Swifts. St. Denis noted that Katharine had talent but criticized her absence of a "feeling of the outdoors" in her dancing. Katharine thought that this deficiency was logical since she had been born and raised in the city. She had, however, managed to feature the sounds of nature in her compositions, probably because she had been setting poems of classic writers, which frequently contained references to nature. "Only my dancing had been urban in character." After St. Denis's remarks, she tried to incorporate "something of the wind, the sea and the trees into my thinking while I danced." At fourteen Katharine was able to study ballet with Madame Marie Bonfanti, whom she later described as "an aging ex-ballerina who had danced at the Metropolitan Opera." Actually, Bonfanti had been a prima ballerina throughout her long career in the United States, which had begun in 1866. On her retirement from the stage in 1897, she opened a dancing school and taught many students from prominent New York families.[37]

Katharine's young life had been blessed in many ways. Her family had offered tremendous support for her creative interests and provided her with fine teachers. Her mother possessed artistic as well as musical talent and a spirit of adventure, encouraging Katharine's experimentation. Her grandmother, a pianist and composer, served as a model for the budding musician. Most particularly, her father's role as a music and art critic contributed to her fine education. The many concerts and operas she attended with him exposed her to a wide repertoire of music. He may also have shared some of his insights about the performances with her, attuning her to specific aspects of compositions, performers, and conductors. She was proud of his career and proud to share a love of music with him. And of course life in New York City exposed her to many cultures and artistic trends, all of which introduced her to a variety of ideas, people, and situations. The rich and full musical culture of the Swift household offered Katharine many opportunities for growth.

CHAPTER 2

Professional and Personal Choices

July 21, 1914. Sam died this morning. That I should live to write it. . . .
God pity us all and help us to bear it.—Gertrude Horton Dorr Swift

Katharine's father died prematurely and unexpectedly on July 21, 1914, from complications after two gall bladder surgeries. Although he had seemed to recover from his first surgery in November 1913, he never fully regained his strength. Without benefit of antibiotics, minor complications apparently led to his death. After visiting his parents in Wilmington in early June, Swift suffered another attack of gallstones that lasted six weeks. Young Sam was sent to spend some time with his great aunt in Valley Forge, Pennsylvania, and Katharine remained with her mother. A second surgery was finally deemed necessary and was performed on July 20. When it became apparent that Swift would not live, Katharine, her mother, and her father's cousin John Van Nostrand Dorr gathered in his hospital room. Dorr, a distinguished chemical and metallurgical engineer, had been Swift's closest friend during their youth. Katharine recalled, "A strong, handsome man with a beard, I shall never forget him standing with Mother, two doctors and myself in the hospital room where Daddy lay dying. My father said calmly, 'Is this the pilgrimage?' Neither doctor replied, but John Dorr walked up to the bed and said simply, 'Sam, I'll look after them.' Daddy died, then, peacefully."[1]

The death of her father was a terrible loss for Katharine. She was just seventeen and she identified strongly with her father. "It was a shock from which none of us ever fully recovered," she later admitted. She claimed she "could hear him playing 'The Death of Asa,' from Grieg's *Peer Gynt Suite,* every night for weeks after he died. I can still remember exactly how it sounded, unbearably sad." Yet in her diary her grandmother noted Katharine's mature manner in dealing with her father's death. For her part, Ellen, though initially distraught, managed her husband's death with a strength and dignity that helped the children endure the loss. Swift later wrote, "Thank the Lord, both my father and mother had a strong quality of faith. They believed in a central Power to whom we can turn, and in the continuity of life. Even during the fearful days and nights following my father's death, Mother never relinquished her conviction that he was nearby, and that they would eventually meet again. . . . My parents had been married eighteen years, and to date I have seen pitifully few marriages that approach theirs for sheer love, mutual admiration and compatibility."[2]

Ellen Swift had been working as an interior decorator, one of the first women in a relatively new field, and Katharine taught lessons in piano and dance to help support the family. She took on piano students who were not advanced or serious enough to study with Bertha Tapper. (She and her mother referred to these pupils rather indelicately as "spit-backs . . . an unattractive phrase used to describe the half-eaten chocolates sometimes found in a box.") She was paid to accompany a group of women in the Thursday Club, whom she described as "some eager amateur ladies, middle-aged and rich," who got together to sing for each other. Sometimes they rehearsed with the accompanist before the event, sometimes not. Katharine's sight-reading skills were stretched, for the club expected perfection from her during their efforts. Katharine used her dancing skills to choreograph several amateur shows and to teach ballet and social dancing. This helped to pay for her continuing ballet lessons with Madame Bonfanti. Her change in status from a dependent to a wage-earner must have influenced her self-perceptions and increased her sense of worth as she tried to combat the void left by her father's death.[3]

Gertrude Swift appreciated the many tributes to Sam's "beautiful life and character" that she had received and which appeared in the newspapers. She eased her grief by writing an anthem, "In Heavenly Love Abiding," which was published in 1914, three months after Sam's death. She commented that a small check she received for the publication of "the High School song" was turned over to Nell "for the fund for a stone for our dear boy's memory." The Swifts were struggling financially, and Katharine's sense of grief would probably have been compounded by anxiety over the family's income.[4]

John Van Nostrand Dorr kept his promise to his cousin to look after the family. Cousin John, or "C. J.," sometimes stayed at their apartment, brought ice cream on "scorching August afternoons," and contributed to all their expenses. The following summer, in 1915, he led a family party of ten on a trip to the western United States. He took Ellen, Katharine, young Sam, and four of their cousins along with his own two daughters to Colorado and California. The group rented two cars, with Katharine, her mother, and brother in the car driven by John Dorr. The travelers spent a month in Denver with Dorr's sister and her family, where the highlight for Katharine was visiting a ranch near Colorado Springs. There "we rode spirited but well-broken horses across long stretches of plains and winding roads at the foot of the Rockies." Once in California, Katharine, her mother, and Sam spent a month in San Francisco as guests of the Torreys, the family of an art dealer. Their daughter, Dorothea, "a radiantly beautiful creature," was several years older than Katharine, and the two became friends. Katharine recalls visiting the naval base, where Dorothea "cast an understandable spell over a few midshipmen from Annapolis whom I'd known from the dances at the Naval Academy to which I'd been 'dragged.'" They also visited the World's Fair in San Francisco that summer, and she and Sam took "ten successive rides" on "the addictive, though terrifying roller coaster." She played the piano frequently at the Torreys', while Dorothea, "who was an accomplished drummer, played her various percussion instruments during the more spirited 2/4 tunes."[5]

On their return trip, Katharine, having inherited some of her mother's prescience, sensed another tragedy. "On the way back, during the train trip, a horrible presentiment came to me that something dire must have happened.

I wept without quite knowing why. On returning to New York, we learned that Mor had just died, after a brief illness." Within a year, Katharine Swift had lost two important role models. They had prepared her well, however, and she began to search for her own strength and direction.[6]

Katharine was graduated in 1915 from Miss Veltin's School for Girls. She enrolled in the Institute of Musical Art during the year 1915–16, following the regular piano course. She now studied piano with Anna Lockwood Fyffe, a member of the institute faculty since 1905. Additional courses included ear training and dictation with Franklin Robinson, music theory with Percy Goetschius, lectures on music history with Waldo S. Pratt and music critic Henry Edward Krehbiel, and attendance at lectures, rehearsals, recitals, and concerts. Her name appears on several programs of students' recitals at the institute that year, both as a pianist and as a composer. On November 20, 1915, she performed the Prelude, Fugue, and Variations of César Franck. She accompanied Pauline Michel, violinist, in a performance of Beethoven's Sonata in C Minor, op. 30, no. 2, for violin and piano, on January 29, 1916. On April 16, 1916, Swift performed the Prelude and Fugue in A Minor by J. S. Bach. These works in the standard repertoire of music literature signify that her technical and musical development was outstanding. In addition, she was one of seven students selected to play for a reception recital in honor of composer Percy Grainger on February 19, 1916, when she repeated Franck's Prelude, Fugue, and Variations.[7]

Swift also received recognition when several of her pieces were performed on the recital of student compositions on May 13, 1916. Two of her songs, "Le Ciel est par-dessus le toit" and "Impression fausse: Dame souris trotte," on texts by Paul Verlaine, were sung by Hazel Penniman. Claude Debussy had written two song cycles setting poems by Verlaine, *Ariettes oubliées* (1888) and *Fêtes galantes* (1892–1904), and Swift may well have studied those cycles before composing her own songs. "Impression fausse: Dame souris trotte," a song with piano accompaniment, is one of the few manuscripts from this period that are preserved in the Kay Swift Papers. It features some of the impressionistic characteristics Debussy employed, such as parallel chords and extended triadic harmonies used in a nonfunctional manner. The song is in an ABCA' form that begins and ends in E minor. It features many chromatic pitches and explores a variety of key areas. Other characteristics of Debussy that Swift employed in this piece include whole-tone passages, thick-textured chords in extended ranges, rolled chords, and parallel harmonies.

Swift performed her own composition for piano, Fuga per moto contrario, and accompanied Charles Vardell in his Double Fugue for Two Pianos. Although the fugue does not survive, Swift is identified as being a Level V composition student, signifying that she was proficient in advanced counterpoint. The regular piano course normally took three years to complete, but with her extensive background, Swift completed it in one. For that she credited her study with Arthur Edward Johnstone. "He was a meticulous musician . . . and the limitations he imposed on me . . . helped me beyond measure. It was entirely due to his teaching that, later, I was able to complete the course at the Institute of Musical Art in one year instead of six, returning for a second year only to brush up on orchestration." She received a certificate of graduation on June 1, 1916, along with six other students. The concert and commencement exercises at Aeolian Hall were attended by her mother, her brother, Sam, and her grandparents Gertrude and Joseph Swift. For the graduation concert, Katharine performed the Prelude and Fugue in A Minor by Bach, as well as the Double Fugue for Two Pianos written by classmate Charles Vardell. Grandmother Swift reported that "Katharine played beautifully at the concert and received her diploma and also to our great gratification, she was awarded a scholarship which means another year at the Institute and an artists' course. This is the highest honor that the Institute confers and there was only one other given. There are six hundred students." Gertrude Swift continued, "The second night was devoted to Class Day exercises, which were very amusing and in which K. also distinguished herself, composing two original choruses, and also dancing charmingly. She is a lovely girl, most charming in her manner and disposition and so talented in many ways. How proud and happy dear Sam would have been. Perhaps he knows about it."[8]

The scholarship allowed Katharine to remain at the institute the following year for what was considered postgraduate work, but she did not follow the artists' course, as her grandmother had indicated. Instead she registered for the piano teachers' course, which may have been a practical decision, since her family needed the income it would have brought. Swift also played accompaniments "at two dollars an hour, for anyone who needed my services." This led to some unusual assignments, as she recalled.

> One singer, a middle-aged lady with a goiter, said she could not rehearse [for a recital in Williamstown, Massachusetts], which was understandable, but went through her whole program . . . whistling her songs. When the day came and we traveled by train, the singer . . . did manage to make a sound, but the whistling had been superior. . . . On the train, Mme. Goiter . . . showed me a very poorly copied manuscript [of a song with an Indian theme], smudgy and far from clear. . . . She told me that it would be begun by her, unaccompanied, offstage. "Then I'll walk in, continuing to sing." I had put on a pair of moccasins in traveling, and I noticed Mme. G. eyeing them. "Would you mind if I borrowed them for the Indian number?" Of course I said, "No, not at all," and she did take them. . . . The first part of the program sounded so dreadful that I felt ashamed, especially as I heard a man behind me say to his wife, "Isn't this appalling? We really should get our money back." Then, even worse, came the Indian number. The note that poor Mme. Goiter hit, offstage, turned out to be a fourth lower than the one indicated on that messy copy on the piano, and I had to transpose the whole dire ditty. In a way, that kept me from looking too closely at the unfortunate lady, who entered wearing a head-band with a feather. . . . My moccasins were supposed to lend authenticity to the costume, but she wore the same evening dress that had graced the opening numbers.

Swift was rapidly developing expert skills in diplomacy and adaptability, in addition to musical skills of sight-reading and transposition. Fortunately, many of her accompanying experiences were with fine musicians, and she had the opportunity to learn advanced standard repertoire. "At one time, I played for all of Franz Kneisel's pupils. . . . They were all highly accomplished, Kneisel being impatient with amateurs and teaching no beginners. . . . I hated tearing into concertos (concerti?) hitting a dozen mistakes ('clams,' we call them now) but I did, faking along in the correct tempo, as best I could." When it came time for performance, however, Swift was meticulous in her preparation and in her mastery of the music. Bertha Tapper's high expectations were ingrained in her approach to the piano. Even as a child, "I loathed playing any piece for which I wasn't prepared by recent, thorough practice."[9]

During her second year, Swift again appeared at students' recitals as both a pianist and a composer. School records show that on December 2, 1916, she performed four short impressionistic pieces, Debussy's "Mazurka," "Danseuses de Delphe," and "Valse," and Ravel's "Pavane pour une infante defunte" for a recital presented to the members of the auxiliary society. On January 20, 1917, she and violinists Frances Goldenthal and Marianne Kneisel performed the Suite for Two Violins and Piano, op. 71, by Moritz Moszkowski. For the commencement exercises on June 4, 1917, in Aeolian Hall, she presented her own "Chaconne and Finale on Negro Themes." There were thirteen graduates, two of whom received artists' diplomas in singing and violin, and eleven of whom received teachers' diplomas in piano, violin, or singing.[10]

While at the institute Katharine became close friends with cellist Marie Romeat, and the two joined violinist Edith Rubel to form the Edith Rubel Trio. The three traveled and performed Brahms and Beethoven trios for a year and a half. They coached at Blue Hill with Henry Krehbiel before their New York debut and played concerts in and around the New York area and in New England. This work generated additional income for the Swift family. One of the trio's performances in the summer of 1917 was at the home of Isaac and Guta (Loeb) Seligman in Upper Saranac Lake in the Adirondacks. The Seligmans' daughter, Margaret Lewisohn, was a friend of Katharine's, had heard the trio elsewhere, and hired the group for her family to enjoy. At the Seligmans', Katharine met Margaret's cousin, Bettina Warburg, daughter of Paul and Nina (Loeb) Warburg. Bettina liked Katharine and invited her to her summer home in nearby Hartsdale. There she met Bettina's brother, James, an introduction that would change her life. The trio began to play occasionally at Woodlands in Westchester County, the summer estate of James's uncle, Felix Warburg. Katharine and James became sweethearts and were engaged in the fall of 1917.[11]

Even after receiving her teachers' diploma in 1917, Swift enrolled in the institute the following year, studying piano with Carl Friedberg and Anna

Fyffe. For the annual recital in commemoration of the birthday of the late Betty Gallenberg Loeb (the maternal grandmother of James Warburg, to whom Katharine was now betrothed) on January 16, 1918, Swift performed the Bach Concerto in A Minor for Violin, Flute, and Piano Solo with the accompaniment of string orchestra. Joseph Philip Fuchs and Edward Victor Meyer were the other soloists. That year she also continued her study of theory and composition with Percy Goetschius, writing a fugue each week. Chamber music was the focus of her composition that year as she presented "Pantomime," a Sonata Allegro for Pianoforte, Violin, and Violincello, with Samuel Gardner and Marie Romeat, at a students' recital on March 16, 1918. Swift was then designated a Level VII composer, the highest at the institute, which signified facility with larger forms, a complete sonata, chamber music, vocal forms, an overture, and orchestration.[12]

During these years at the Institute, Percy Goetschius commanded the highest respect. He had served on the faculty at the New England Conservatory and taught private students before he was hired to head the theory and composition department at the Institute of Musical Art, a post he held from 1905 to 1925. Swift remembered him fondly: "Dr. Goetschius was a strong influence. He fought anything that was the least unexpected, far from possessing the drink-of-water-theory that Arthur Johnstone had. He used to say that anything that was not predictable he would label 'quaint.' 'Well, it's quaint.' But he also taught me so much about counterpoint. And I loved that."[13]

While some complained that Goetschius was "not open enough" about new methods and styles, Swift responded, "Oh, of course not, not in the least. . . . He didn't pretend to be. . . . If you go to a dressmaker to have a dress made, you don't worry because you don't get a pair of boots, too." In spite of her traditional education, for her graduation recital in Aeolian Hall, Swift composed and performed a prelude and chaconne on the theme "Nobody Knows the Trouble I've Seen." In this piece she took a simple African-American theme and transformed it, perhaps following the model of Antonín Dvořák in his *New World Symphony* (1893), when he featured and reworked spirituals and folklike tunes. According to Dvořák, "The new American school of music must strike its roots deeply into its own soil." He conveyed this philosophy to his students at the National Conservatory of Music in New York when advocating the use of African-American spirituals and Native American songs in concert music. One of Dvořák's students was Harvey Worthington Loomis, the Swifts' distant cousin. Loomis later wrote a suite entitled *Lyrics of the Red Men* (1901) and could have easily conveyed Dvořák's message to Swift either directly or through her teacher Arthur Johnstone. Swift described her graduation piece: "It had a lot of . . . 'ragtime' in the fugue, and Goetschius didn't take exception to it at all. . . . I think it was because the fugue was in very strict counterpoint until the fughetta, or entry of all four voices, had been accomplished. And then I went into a free-flowing ragtime, jazz really, version of the theme. And it seemed to work out and nobody minded it."[14] Already Katharine Swift was displaying a sense of independence as she added a hint of jazz and spirituals to her solid classical education.

In the not-too-distant past of the nineteenth century, women commonly studied the piano and voice and learned rudimentary theory, but it was unusual for them to study advanced theory and orchestration. From the beginning, however, the Institute of Musical Art opened its doors—and all of its courses—to female students. Indeed, the majority of its students were female, although few played wind instruments. Eight women comprised the institute's first graduating class in 1907.[15]

It was still atypical for women to study composition in the early years of the twentieth century. Swift was fortunate, indeed, to have begun working at such a young age with Johnstone, who gave her a solid understanding of composition. Further study with Goetschius at the institute increased the depth of her education. This very traditional classical instruction determined Swift's basic style, technique, and discipline and shaped her sense of proportion and musical line in the tradition of Western European masters.

However thorough her teachers were, they were nearly all male. And although it was not unusual for young women to study and excel in music, it was unusual for them to advance later to public positions of authority. Here the Institute of Musical Art stands out: some highly respected women were on the faculty during Kay Swift's early years. Of fifty-one faculty members listed for the year 1905–6, nineteen were women, nearly 37 percent. However seventeen of the female instructors taught studio voice, piano, or harp—instruments considered more acceptable for women. The other two female instructors taught languages. Not surprisingly, orchestral instruments and all the more intellectual subjects—theory and composition, music history, and pedagogy—were instructed by men.[16]

The Warburgs

In the mid-1890s, brothers Felix and Paul Warburg were associates with M. M. Warburg and Company, their family's successful banking operation in Hamburg, Germany. A visit to Germany in 1894 by the German-American banker Jacob Schiff, who now headed Kuhn, Loeb in New York City, would change both of their lives. Felix Warburg fell in love with Schiff's daughter, Frieda, immigrated to the United States and married her in March 1895. He dutifully joined her father's bank, the very firm whose partner, James Loeb, had cofounded the Institute of Musical Art. Felix was carefree and engaging, differing dramatically from his stern, humorless father-in-law, who followed Jewish custom and law piously. Felix disliked the financial business and in time turned his attentions to philanthropic organizations, supporting the arts in New York and Jewish organizations worldwide.

Representing the Warburg family at Felix and Frieda's wedding in New York were Paul and their sister, Olga, Paul serving as best man. The maid of honor was Nina Loeb, Frieda's aunt and James Loeb's sister. Nina and Paul's mutual attraction was obvious, and Nina joined her new relatives Paul and Olga on their return voyage to Germany. Paul, who was far more serious and conservative than Felix, proposed to Nina on the ship. The couple married in New York six months later, so aunt and niece became sisters-in-law. This dual relationship cemented the Warburg association with Kuhn, Loeb, even though Paul and Nina lived in Germany for the next seven years. With another brother, Max, in Hamburg, Paul managed M. M. Warburg and Company, becoming expert in international investments. Two children were born to Paul and Nina in Hamburg, James Paul in 1896 and Bettina (named in honor of Betty and Nina) in 1900. In 1902, after the death of Nina's mother, Betty Gallenberg Loeb, Paul and Nina Warburg immigrated to the United States, and Paul became the second Warburg to join Kuhn, Loeb. Opposites though they were, Paul and Felix established themselves as successful partners and productive citizens. Paul's knowledge of central banking practices made him an instrumental adviser during and after the financial panic of 1907. He laid the groundwork for America's Federal Reserve System and was appointed by President Woodrow Wilson to the first Federal Reserve Board in 1914. Nina, the youngest of the four Loeb children, was well educated and had been tutored in music, dance, riding, and languages. A fall from a pony cart when she was a child resulted in a broken hip that never healed properly. Forever crippled by this accident, she was reserved and sweet, though firm in her intentions. And although Paul and Nina followed Jewish tradition out of respect for Jacob Schiff, they were not particularly devout. (Their son James termed them "twice-a-year Jews," those who attended synagogue on the Jewish New Year's Day and the Day of Atonement.) The couple raised their two German-born children to be American citizens with wealth, culture, power, and a sense of public responsibility.[17]

James, or Jimmy as his family called him, was far more flamboyant than his father. He was graduated from Harvard with honors at age sixteen and by 1917 was a pilot in the U.S. Naval Reserve, "with a mile-wide rebellious streak, a taste for experimentation, and few inhibitions." He was immediately attracted to Katharine's petite beauty, intellect, and musical talent. As he later recalled in his autobiography, "Kay was fun to dance with and even more fun to talk to. She had a lively sense of humor, brown hair worn in a chignon, brown eyes, and a provocative little figure." He did not seriously consider marrying her, though, for the United States had entered World War I, and he anticipated being sent into combat. "'This,' I thought 'is going to be my girl until I go overseas.'"[18]

As the war raged in Europe, anti-German sentiments grew in the United States. Felix and Paul had close family connections to Hamburg and emotional ties to their homeland, and the disintegration of relations with Germany before World War I was particularly difficult for them. In his collective biography of the Warburgs, Ron Chernow observes, "For Paul and Felix, the war exposed a cultural chasm that separated them from their children. Like other immigrant parents, they had encouraged their children's assimilation into American society, then were pained and surprised when they succeeded." James seemed to delight in his Americanization, sometimes forsaking his own German-Jewish heritage and adopting behavior and tastes that were more typical of the Christian traditions he had absorbed at Middlesex School, a prep school whose alumni frequently moved on to Harvard, as he did. His enlistment in the U.S. Naval Reserve in anticipation of war with Germany was a deep embarrassment for his father, who still felt allegiance to his homeland and concern for his parents and three brothers in Hamburg.[19]

In the fall of 1917, James Warburg discovered that his father, exercising some political clout, had intervened in his military career and asked Secretary of the Navy Josephus Daniels to keep him out of combat in Europe, "where I might have to drop bombs on my own relatives." (Indeed, Eric Warburg, Max's son, fought for the German army during the war.) James was furious, and his subsequent proposal to Katharine was in part a reaction to his father's meddling.[20]

In 1917, Katharine was twenty and at the threshold of her adult life. Europe was at war, and American society was undergoing rapid social and technological changes that would affect her and her family. As the United States prepared to enter World War I, armed combat suddenly became real for thousands of young men, including many of James Warburg's friends. Patriotism flourished, and all things German were out of favor, particularly on the East Coast. Women were campaigning for the right to vote, and increasing numbers of middle-class women were choosing to work in offices and department stores. Changes in popular culture disseminated the ideas, tastes, and fads of a new generation. An interest in sports and the outdoors was on the rise among both men and women, and women's fashions were changing to allow women freer movement. Henry Ford had announced in 1907 that he would "build a motor car for the great multitude," and by 1917 the Ford Motor Company was producing nearly 750,000 Model Ts per year, changing Americans' business and leisure habits. Many citizens were calling for Prohibition, protesting the use and abuse of alcohol; others were simply using and abusing it. As the Great Migration brought many African Americans to the North, jazz was making its way from the Deep South to New York and Chicago, where it would change popular music forever. Dancers Vernon and Irene Castle had opened their cabaret, Sans Souci, on Broadway and were transforming the art of ballroom dancing. Adapting dances from African-American sources, the Castles toned down what they perceived as exaggerated, sexually suggestive motions and made them acceptable to the white upper class. Movie theaters were becoming respectable places for young women to be seen, and new motion pictures starring Douglas Fairbanks and Mary Pickford reflected society's shift from the Victorian values of thrift, hard work, and denial to the modern values of leisure, youth, pleasure, and consumption. Fairbanks's healthy physique and heroic acts along with Pickford's vital spirit and wholesome image made them the All-American couple.[21]

On June 1, 1918, less than a year after they first met, James and Katharine were married at 4:30 P.M. in the Upper West Side apartment of Katharine's mother. Magistrate Robert C. Cornell, an old friend of the Swifts, performed the civil ceremony. The attendants were Katharine's childhood friend Louise Homer, daughter of Sidney Homer and Madame Louise Homer of the Metropolitan Opera Company, and James's fellow naval reservist Ensign Westmore Willcox. Giving Katharine away was John Van Nostrand Dorr, her father's cousin, who had pledged to take care of the family. The bride wore a traditional white gown trimmed with lace and a lace veil held with orange blossoms. The maid of honor wore pink satin and carried pink roses. Guests were limited to family and a few close friends and were seated by Ensigns Davison and Hutchins, also of the Naval Reserve Aviation Section. The *New York Times* reported that these guests included Mr. and Mrs. Felix Warburg; Mr. and Mrs. Jacob Schiff, Felix Warburg's in-laws; Mrs. Isaac (Guta) Seligman, who was James Loeb's sister and Paul Warburg's sister-in-law; and Mr. and Mrs. Samuel Lewisohn (Guta Seligman's daughter, Margaret, and her son-in-law). A reception and dance at the Cosmopolitan Club at 133 East Fortieth Street followed the ceremony.[22]

Paul and Nina Warburg loved Katharine. One of her granddaughters, Katharine Weber, suggests, "They were adventurous and thoughtful people, and they had that Warburgian sense of freedom, which was uncommon to people in their socio-economic position. . . . They felt that she was good for their son, . . . who was earnest, hardworking, and ambitious." Yet the marriage did raise concerns in the Warburg family. Although Paul and Nina admired Katharine's talent, culture, and spirit, they felt that the couple was immature. Katharine, too, had been raised as a Protestant, and even though her non-Jewish heritage was not an issue with them, it was a problem for some extended members of the Warburg family—especially Jacob Schiff, who revered his Jewish heritage and strictly observed its traditions. On the couple's wedding day, Schiff sent a telegram scolding James for "marrying out of the faith in view of its probable effect upon my own progeny." In addition, Swift "was an independent career woman . . . [who] lived in shabby-genteel poverty on Manhattan's Upper West Side . . . at a time when Warburg women only ventured outside the home to perform charity work." For James, perhaps, the attraction of Katharine may in part have been another means of defying the Jewish "Our Crowd" pattern that the Warburg clan followed. Katharine was not Jewish; she was not wealthy; and she was a well-educated, professional musician who planned to continue her career. She was probably more mature than James, having been forced to help support her family after her father's death. More recently, she had endured the loss of Bertha Tapper and her great grandmother, Adeline Dorr, in 1915, as well as the deaths in 1917 of her paternal grandparents, Joseph and Gertrude Horton Dorr Swift, to whom she had been close. Katharine's mother, Ellen Swift, was delighted with the marriage, encouraged by one of her visions. She had told James that her late husband had appeared to her in a dream and approved of the match. Warburg later admitted to his granddaughter that he felt he had been pressured into marriage "by a god-damned ghost."[23]

It is interesting to think of the extended Warburg family attending the ceremony in Ellen Swift's modest apartment at 309 West 101st Street. Perhaps a generation later Katharine and James might have considered holding the wedding at the expansive, luxurious Warburg home, which would have more elegantly accommodated the guests. Yet tradition dictated that the bride's family host the wedding, and Katharine's memoirs deny any indecision about the site. "Looking back, I can't imagine what made me think it was a good idea to be married in Mother's apartment, though it had been home to me for years. Jim's relatives turned out in full force, gallantly struggling up the five long flights on a broiling afternoon in June. A very pleasant justice of the peace, who had unfortunately taken a dose of calomel the night before, married us, probably in great discomfort."

Holding the ceremony in the Swifts' apartment may have helped James's efforts to establish independence from his parents' ways. A Jewish ceremony was not possible, since Katharine was not converting to Judaism, but a

Christian ceremony was equally unacceptable, considering the Warburgs' heritage. James's inclusion of fellow pilots in full dress uniform as attendants was a further reminder of his rebellious nature, since the military had been a source of conflict between him and his parents. Despite their concerns, Paul and Nina Warburg embraced Katharine and even established a generous trust fund for her. This fund paid her a monthly income so that she would never have to depend on James for "walking-around money."[24]

In the years before 1918, anti-Semitism was on the rise in middle-class America as more Jewish immigrants gained financial success and excelled in the fields of banking and entertainment—areas that would become central to Katharine Swift's life. America's entry into the war heightened these suspicions. The Warburgs were a respected banking family whose success led to their productivity, enabled their generous philanthropy, and placed them a step away from the inner circle of New York society. Yet with war in Europe, even their position was somewhat shaken. As James Warburg recollected in his autobiography, "Anti-German feeling on the eastern seaboard was perhaps more extreme than in Britain or even in France. Friends in New York and Washington had warned my parents against keeping on their faithful German servants. . . . Beethoven's music could not be performed in New York, while even in London an established English family changed its name from Battenberg to Mountbatten."[25]

There is no record of Kay Swift having been concerned about the ethnic or religious differences between their families, particularly since James had done his best to minimize them. And whether Katharine was aware of the subtle accusations about Paul Warburg's divided loyalties between Germany and America is not known. It would have been difficult, however, for her not to have recognized that such prejudices existed in 1918, especially when Paul felt obliged to resign from the Federal Reserve Board, his brainchild, after his term expired that year. To his chagrin, President Woodrow Wilson did not reappoint him. Katharine would likely have been sensitive to criticism of the Warburgs' religious and ethnic heritage on the eve of her marriage into the family.

After the wedding and a honeymoon at the Mohonk Mountain House resort, the newlyweds moved to Washington, D.C., since James was still an officer in the Naval Reserve. There he clerked for the Metropolitan Bank of Washington. That first year, he recalled, Katharine gave him lessons in harmony and he taught her to drive a car. Katharine was soon pregnant, and their first daughter, April, was born in April 1919. After the end of the war, James sought a position in banking but resisted going to work in his father's newly established International Acceptance Bank. He wanted to prove himself a capable banker, not just a Warburg, and took a position with the First National Bank of Boston in June. They moved to Cambridge, where James became an expert in textile finance.[26]

Katharine took advantage of the move to continue her musical training. She began piano study with Heinrich Gebhard, a German-American pianist who, like Bertha Tapper, had studied with Theodore Leschetizky in Vienna. Gebhard was now on the faculty at the New England Conservatory and had made a name for himself performing Charles Martin Loeffler's work for piano and orchestra, *A Pagan Poem*, op. 14 (1907). He later would teach Leonard Bernstein.[27]

While studying with Gebhard, Swift performed several recitals with her friend Louise Homer, accompanying the soprano on the piano and playing solos as well. One of these concerts was held at the Smith Opera House in Geneva, New York, in May 1920. A newspaper review evaluated Swift's playing as "artistic": "the delicate and musicianly manner in which she played quite elevated the audience. She played two groups responding to an insistent encore after the second one, when she played a Brahms Intermezzo. While perhaps there was vigor lacking there was much perfection of detail and caressing of tone that evinced a sympathetic understanding and appreciation of theme and feeling."[28]

Swift certainly played with sensitivity and musicality, if not great strength. An account of a recital featuring Louise Homer and "Mrs. Katherine [sic] Swift Warburg"—likely within months of the Geneva recital—appeared in Wilmington's newspaper. At this time, Homer, a solo recitalist since 1917, was preparing for a series of performances in spring 1921 with her famous mother, recently retired from the Metropolitan Opera. These concerts had been proposed after the pair had spontaneously performed an enthusiastically received duet as an encore at one of Homer's solo concerts. The recitals in which Katharine Swift accompanied Homer may have been in preparation for these performances. One of Homer's most popular numbers in the 1920 concert, repeated in the 1921 recitals, was "The Banjo Song," written by her father, Sidney Homer.[29]

Charles Martin Loeffler had retired from his violin duties in the Boston Symphony Orchestra in 1903 and had been composing for years when Katharine and James Warburg arrived in Boston in the summer of 1919. Swift admired Loeffler's music. Her piano teacher Gebhard arranged for Swift to meet Loeffler and study composition at his home in nearby Medfield. Swift describes the lessons that she then began with him:

> I went out there on a Saturday morning, taking some little remnants of something that I had, a manuscript, and I had to go out, the only train at that time got one there at 11:00, thereabouts, but I had to leave the house at 8:30. I lived in Cambridge, and he had me stay all day. There was lunch in the middle of the day with him and Mrs. Loeffler, and then I stayed until about 4:30 or 5:00. We worked all the time. It was wonderful; it was the most stimulating experience. And I always tried to have something for him ready that he hadn't seen before. . . . And I went every Saturday that way for a long time. I was so thrilled.[30]

After her lesson, Loeffler often took out his violin and the two would play sonatas by Gabriel Fauré or Vincent D'Indy and then read through some of Loeffler's music. "It was a tremendous experience, for I admired him so," Swift recalled. "He was in his early seventies, tall, slim and erect, with silver hair and moustache—handsome, distinguished and humorous."[31]

Loeffler had been born in Germany, but he had long since rejected German politics, customs, and traditions for French manners and tastes. His compositions reflected strong French and some Russian influences. This would have suited Katharine, who had played and studied many French piano works and whose early compositions tended to feature impressionistic sonorities and techniques.[32]

Swift later described his responses to her music, which were always phrased in positive terms. He never denigrated her work, instead suggesting "more interesting" alternatives. He was receptive to a variety of styles, and she felt comfortable showing him her sketches. Because her studies with

Loeffler were so soon after April's birth, she may not have been able to focus on composition as much as she might have wished. Swift's only extant pieces from this time period are a set of four Nursery Songs (1920–21) for voice with piano accompaniment entitled "Doggie," "Kitty," "Piggie," and "Sleep" —most likely intended for April. Although the songs are short (twenty-four to thirty-six measures) and the titles are juvenile, they more closely resemble art songs than folk songs. James Warburg provided the lyrics. Although these little songs are not important to her output, they show that she was composing and provide examples of her style. Chromatic triads and seventh chords support the melody of the last song, "Sleep." While parallel harmonic passages occur, the tonal areas clearly shift between C major and A major. Although this piece was probably never heard publicly, it does display melodic and harmonic characteristics that would pervade her writing.[33]

James Warburg supported Katharine's studies with Loeffler and sometimes accompanied her on social visits to his home. Warburg recalled finding a common interest with the composer, describing him as "a charming old gentleman, who, besides being a distinguished violinist and composer, was something of an authority on Asian cultures. . . . Occasionally we spent an evening there. The old gentleman showed a kindly interest in my translations of Greek and French poetry and, to my surprise and delight, asked me to try my hand at writing a libretto for an opera with a Hindu setting he was then composing. Many evenings of labor went into the attempt to fulfill this assignment. Loeffler liked my libretto, but unfortunately the opera, *Karma,* was never finished. The composer died before he could complete the score."[34]

Warburg clearly admired his wife's musical abilities and supported her interests. However, he and his family "thought the arts were good hobbies but not professions; she prized them more highly." The couple's decision to return to New York City in 1921 would allow Katharine to intensify and expand her musical activity while James advanced in the field of banking.[35]

CHAPTER 3

Highbrow/Lowbrow in New York City

In all this semi-serious play, the one unforgivable sin was to be found slow or dull-witted.—James Warburg

Paul M. Warburg's reputation as the father of the Federal Reserve System and his position on the Federal Reserve Board underscored his financial expertise and commitment to his adopted nation. Given these credentials, it is not surprising that three years after Katharine and James married, the federal government sought to use James's talent as well. In 1921, during Warren G. Harding's presidency, the new commerce secretary, Herbert Hoover, offered James the position of assistant secretary of commerce. This was a rare opportunity for a twenty-five-year-old, but James, exhibiting his strong spirit of independence, rejected the offer. He claims to have "had an instinctive negative reaction to both the proposition and Hoover." He apparently found Hoover's smug attitude annoying and declined the position partly out of personal dislike for the man. Paul, too, supported his son's apprehension, maintaining that James was too young and inexperienced for the position. James had a healthy respect for Paul's financial abilities and opinions, so he heeded this advice and instead joined his father's newly formed International Acceptance Bank. So in 1921 James and Katharine moved back to New York City with April, now two. James had a chance to work with his father, gaining from his insights and knowledge of international banking. The move also placed James and Katharine in a city of many cultural advantages and temptations.[1]

When the couple returned to New York, Katharine re-enrolled in the Institute of Musical Art, where she was listed as a student in 1921–22, studying theory with Percy Goetschius. She clearly intended to develop her musical talents further, even though she had already received diplomas from the institute in the regular piano course and in the piano teachers' course. She apparently had no intention of resuming her piano teaching, although she had the diploma and the experience. Instead, Katharine pursued the more private activities of composition and performance, occupations of a cultured woman. It seems likely that if Katharine Warburg had wanted to teach private students, she would have.

Although it would have been normal for a woman of Katharine Warburg's social position to pursue her interests in classical music during her leisure time, it was less likely that music would be the basis for a career. Katharine's study with Loeffler and recitals with Louise Homer extended her professionalism and independence. She was pursuing a profession, not simply an avocation, and this was a choice that did not correspond to Warburg tradition. Ironically, the circumstances of her marriage and family allowed her both the means and the leisure to pursue her ambitions. The Warburgs were wealthy and employed a large household staff, including a groomsman, a cook, a governess, a nurse, and Katharine's "lady's maid," who only helped with her clothing. Katharine did not have to spend much of her time on domestic duties or child rearing, and she was free to concentrate on her musical interests.[2]

Katharine remained active as a pianist, playing recitals with her longtime friend Louise Homer, and casual accompaniments with other friends. Cellist Marie Romeat Rosanoff, who had played professionally with Katharine in the Edith Rubel Trio before her marriage, continued to join her for informal chamber music sessions on occasional Sundays in Paul and Nina Warburg's home. Swift described another particularly memorable afternoon of chamber music with some remarkable musicians at the Warburgs':

They had invited Albert Einstein to lunch; also Felix Kahn,
who collected rare violins and brought along three beautiful Stradi-
varius specimens. After lunch, Willem Willeke (cellist of the then-
disbanded Kneisel quartet), Mr. Einstein and I played Mozart trios
all afternoon. I wished that I could have understood all the German
into which Einstein broke as he gaily took up first one "Strad"
and then, after perhaps thirty-two bars, another one, trying to find
tiny differences among them, carefully tuning each, and looking
as happy as I can remember seeing any man look while he played.
Actually he played uncommonly well.[3]

Records from the Institute of Musical Art indicate that Katharine was
also composing during this year. As a young mother she composed Songs
for Soprano, Flute, and Piano, entitled "Proverb" and "Nocturne," and
performed them with Nora Fauchald, soprano, and Arthur Lora, flute, on
the Students' Composition Recital at the institute on May 20, 1922. Perhaps
it is noteworthy that she selected one sacred and one secular title. She was
again pregnant, with a child due in September 1922. A proverb might offer
sage advice to a young mother or her child, and a nocturne would be an
ideal lullaby.[4]

Katharine's brother, Sam, was graduated from the Milton Academy in
Massachusetts in the spring of 1922. That summer he played semi-professional
baseball. Unfortunately, after the season ended, Sam contracted the mumps
and suffered serious complications that family members say left him with
certain permanent disabilities. Although she adored her brother, there is no
evidence that Katharine ever felt that she could turn to him for advice or
guidance concerning her professional or personal life. Nonetheless, they
were close, and Katharine would always be fiercely protective of him.[5]

Katharine's musical activities continued uninterrupted during this year,
but she also found time for her many friends. One was Honor Leeming,
who, at age twenty-one, had become the guardian of her two younger sisters,
Esther and Lee, after the death of their parents. Esther Leeming Tuttle
would later become an actress on Broadway. She remembered Katharine
and Sam with great fondness. Occasionally Sam would take Esther and Lee
to swim. Esther, then aged ten or eleven, remembered that Sam was "quite

handsome. He looked like Rudolph Valentino . . . and he had a car." She also recalled that Kay had beautiful clothes and gave Honor some of her evening gowns to make over and wear herself. "Kay was darling." She was apparently extremely generous and very kind to Esther, "a young kid who sort of had a crush on her." Another close friend was Mary Woodard Reinhardt, with whom she remained friends her entire life. With Mary she shared her designer clothes and last-year's mink coats.[6]

Life in New York City for the Warburgs was strikingly different from life in Cambridge, which had remained fairly provincial. Noting that the city was not as they had left it three years earlier, James Warburg later recalled that the "postwar revolution in customs, manners, and morals had overtaken New York." He cited the "altered relationship between men and women" that had developed. Women now smoked in public, wore more relaxed clothing, bobbed their hair, and danced the turkey trot. Another noticeable change was the unpopular condition of Prohibition, instituted in 1920 but widely and openly violated. This mild rebellion reached "even such law-abiding citizens as my parents [who] seemed to see nothing wrong about serving wine at dinner," wrote James. New Yorkers were acutely aware of international events and political unrest, as well as of the domestic changes that were occurring. Many of Warburg's friends, disappointed in the lack of a satisfactory resolution to World War I, had lost interest in international affairs. "Some retreated into the Scott Fitzgerald world of wild parties, bathtub gin, and sexual promiscuity." Although James was joining his father's bank, he was not ready to accept his father's conservative routine. With his dashing good looks, brash independence, and intellectual humor, he cultivated a far livelier social circle than Paul and Nina Warburg.[7]

Many of James and Katharine's friends moved in theatrical, literary, and musical circles. Some were writers and critics who lunched daily at the Algonquin Hotel on West Forty-fourth Street. Anchored by the indomitable Alexander Woollcott, drama critic for the *New York Times,* this group's early regulars included Harold Ross, editor of the *Home Sector,* a stateside publication for returned veterans of World War I, and three young writers for *Vanity Fair*—drama critic Dorothy Parker, editor Robert Sherwood, and managing editor Robert Benchley. *Vanity Fair* publisher Frank Crowninshield called the three "those amazing whelps" because of their sarcastic wit and irreverent banter, and when he fired them, they all moved to *Life* magazine. Parker subsequently produced volumes of urbane poetry, and Sherwood, several plays. Benchley later moved to the *New Yorker,* and gained additional recognition in short films, presenting such satirical monologues as *The Treasurer's Report.* Another regular, Franklin P. Adams, was a radio commentator and author of the column "The Conning Tower" in the *New York World.* Other members included budding playwrights Marc Connelly, a reporter for the *New York Morning Telegraph* who would produce his Pulitzer Prize–winning *Green Pastures* in 1930, and George S. Kaufman, who would earn a Pulitzer in 1932 for his book for *Of Thee I Sing,* the political Broadway musical by George and Ira Gershwin. While Connelly and Kaufman collaborated on six plays during the 1920s, the loosely organized group's main purpose was to exchange witticisms and report on each other's activities in their respective columns. Their "barbed and often malevolent wit" exemplified the humor and sarcasm of the decade, and the Algonquin regulars became known as the "Vicious Circle."[8]

Robert Sherwood and Marc Connelly were "old friends" of James Warburg. Franklin P. Adams had been a friend of Katharine's father when he was music critic at the New York *Mail and Express.* It was Adams who introduced the Warburgs to this selective crowd. Although they were not among the lunch regulars, they did sometimes join the group when it reconvened in the evenings. Theatrical events were central to the Algonquin circle. Often after an opening night at the theater, parties took place in various private homes. They usually ended with everyone playing backgammon, poker, or the latest parlor game, which ranged from various forms of imaginary crime and detection to charades. "Most of the men and women in this intellectual group were distinguished in their various fields, but there was almost never any talk of shop," wrote James in his autobiography. "They met after working hours to amuse each other and to play games against each other with often passionate fervor. . . . In all this semi-serious play, the one unforgivable sin was to be found slow or dull-witted."[9]

Warburg recalled being invited to a poker game of the Thanatopsis Pleasure and Inside Straight Club, an offshoot of the Algonquin crowd. "Usually there were three or four regulars and one or two guests, the latter hopefully invited as victims. As one such putative victim, I played one night with

Adams, Woollcott, Connolly [sic], [Bayard] Swope, Harold Ross, and Raoul Fleischmann, the two latter respectively editor and founder of _The New Yorker_." Although he was a novice poker player, Warburg could not lose that evening. He continued,

> The stakes were high and, as the evening progressed, grew higher. . . . As midnight approached, I found myself the big winner. Fleischmann was not doing badly either, and the faces of the regulars become more and more elongated until all four of them looked like ravening wolves. None of these people ever got up in the morning, but I had to be at the bank at nine o'clock. In the circumstances, it was, of course, impossible for me to go home. For the next three hours, I tried my best to lose; and the more I tried to lose, the more I won. Finally, the game broke up in the early hours of dawn. I went home loaded with I.O.U.s and was never invited again.[10]

The Algonquin regulars, though notorious for their scathing humor, seem to have shared a certain insecurity that their daily meetings alleviated. Warburg's uncanny success with poker—although just a game—did not endear him to this competitive crowd.

It was into this atmosphere that the Warburgs brought their young marriage. With the births of daughters Andrea and Kay in 1922 and 1924, the Warburgs' townhouse on East Seventieth Street was becoming crowded. In 1926, Warburg bought the adjacent townhouse and joined the two, creating larger living quarters for his growing family and domestic staff. Unfortunately, although such luxury gave the family more space and opportunities for separation or privacy, it may have prevented Katharine from having as happy and close a relationship with her children as she had enjoyed with her own parents. Their oldest daughter, April, recalls that during much of their childhood they were isolated from their parents' activities. Katharine and James visited them briefly in the nursery while the children ate their dinners. They dined later and did not participate significantly in the girls' everyday routines. April shared some memories of her early years: "We led a very 'nursery' sort of life, very sheltered on East Seventieth Street.

We did not really live with our parents, or at least did not live in the same world as our parents. We lived on a different floor. We had a maid and a cook and a governess. We sometimes only saw them every couple of days, although we usually had Sunday lunch with them." In her essay "The Memory of All That," Swift's granddaughter Katharine Weber reflects, "She was, I guess, a truly terrible mother. The life of many parties, she was mostly absent from the daily lives of her daughters."[11]

The Warburg girls did manage to entertain themselves. Daughter Andrea recalled the time that, when she was nine or ten years old, she persuaded her eight-year-old sister Kay to climb into the dumbwaiter that transported food from the kitchen to the nursery. When the cook opened the door expecting dirty dishes, she and Kay both screamed. Neither had seen the other before.[12]

Katharine and James enjoyed spending time with their many friends, and their newly expanded home gave them more space and elegance in which to entertain. Esther Leeming Tuttle recalled, "The Warburgs' home [on East Seventieth Street], between Park and Lexington, was beautiful. It was Spanish style, with lovely arched windows. There were two grand pianos in the drawing room. Kay played very well. She was very tiny, but had strong hands." In *The Warburgs*, Ron Chernow elaborates on the decor and ambiance of their home: "Jimmy and Kay decorated their East Seventieth Street town house in sleek black and white and threw parties as wild and glamorous as the setting, with lots of heavy drinking and urbane people lounging by two back-to-back grand pianos. They were among the social darlings of the era, with Kay—vain, childish, witty, delightful—the beautiful flapper who reliably taught guests how to do the Charleston." Their parties, both planned and spontaneous, evidently occurred frequently. Wrote Warburg, "Thirty-four East Seventieth Street became one of the places where cafe society, artists, and musicians foregathered, and a sort of pub for young doctors and nurses from the hospital across the street. Coming home from work in the late afternoon, I never knew whom I would find there or what plans were afoot for the evening."[13]

In addition to the Algonquin crowd, the Warburgs' guests frequently included entertainers, writers, composers, and prominent businessmen who had made their marks by 1926. Fred and Adele Astaire were a successful brother-sister tap-dancing team in vaudeville before they danced on Broadway in Sigmund Romberg's musical revue *Over the Top* in 1917. They went on to star in the Gershwins' *Lady, Be Good!* (1924) and *Funny Face* (1927) before Adele married and retired from the stage in 1932. Beatrice Lillie had been a singer and comedienne in Britain since World War I, but her success in French producer Andre Charlot's *Revue of 1924* in New York made her an international celebrity. She split her comedic skills between London and New York for the next decade, starring again on Broadway in *Seven Lively Arts* (1944). Marshall Field III, grandson of the department store founder, began the publication of the *Chicago Sun-Times* and *World Book Encyclopedia*. In addition to managing the Field estate, he later became an early supporter of Franklin Roosevelt's New Deal and pursued philanthropic projects. William Averell Harriman, the son of a banker, inherited an interest in finance as well as railroad holdings. A Yale graduate, he established a private bank, became chairman of the Board of Union Pacific Railway, and developed Sun Valley resort in Idaho. He, too, became a supporter of FDR's New Deal and later served as ambassador to Russia and Great Britain.[14]

Composer Richard Rodgers and lyricist Lorenz Hart were also often present at the Warburgs' parties. Rodgers had spent two years at Columbia University before transferring to the Institute of Musical Art. There he furthered his classical music education but harbored a goal of composing for the stage. He would have been at the institute in 1921–22, when Katharine returned for additional study with Percy Goetschius. Although it is not documented that they knew each other as students, Rodgers's closest friend at the institute was Gerald Warburg, one of Felix Warburg's sons and James's cousin. Gerald was a cellist who pursued music as a passionate avocation while following the routine of the family banking career. It seems logical that Rodgers and Katharine Warburg would have at least met that year. Gerald Warburg was fond of Katharine, one of few family members who supported his desire to pursue a career in music. Lorenz Hart was recommended as a lyricist for Rodgers when his professional objectives became known and had attended Columbia before Rodgers did. The duo began work together in 1919, furnishing satirical scores for two annual Columbia Varsity Shows and two year-end musical revues at the Institute of Musical

Art before finding success on Broadway with the song "Manhattan" in *The Garrick Gaieties* of 1925.[15]

James Warburg also described attending "musical evenings" at the home of maestro Walter Damrosch, distinguished conductor of the New York Symphony Orchestra. Both Walter and his brother Frank Damrosch had known Katharine's father during his days as music critic. These gatherings at the Damrosches' brought together "composers, virtuosi, orchestra leaders, teachers, and mere amateurs," and balanced the Warburgs' interest in Broadway and the theater with the more traditional, formal values that classical music represented. Although these gatherings differed somewhat from the theater parties, classical enthusiasts, too, appreciated the alcohol outlawed by Prohibition. Marc Connelly recalled in *Voices Offstage*, "Dr. Walter Damrosch brewed the best beer in New York in the rear of his big house on East 71st Street, using recipes brought to America by his German ancestors. Every Saturday night at least a score of friends, mostly musicians, would arrive for buffet supper and after a night of music, mirth, and Münchener, go home to the sound of church bells."[16]

Katharine and James, both attractive and outgoing, seemed to thrive on this social life, delighting in the stimulation that new acquaintances presented. "Jimmy faced constant temptation and often submitted to it," writes Chernow. "Women were smitten by him and he had a long list of conquests. Kay was a dazzling, effervescent personality. Encouraged by the prevailing social license, Kay and Jimmy had an open marriage and neither lacked for willing partners." In a sense, Katharine and James adopted the excessive and carefree lifestyle immortalized in Fitzgerald's *Great Gatsby*. The pursuit of glamour, fortune, and personal pleasure directed their lives, with little thought to the consequences. Warburg enjoyed the entertaining at first, though he later claimed to dislike it increasingly. "Neither my wife nor I realized for some time the effect on our marriage of the life we were leading during the twenties, or its influence on our children."[17]

Katharine did oversee her daughters' musical educations. April studied voice with Balthazar Gagliano, and Andrea studied cello with Leo Rosanoff, husband of Marie Romeat Rosanoff. All three girls studied piano at the David Mannes School of Music. Katharine sometimes taught them songs and simple dances. There was little religious instruction in the household, however. James's efforts to downplay his family's heritage were apparently so successful that Andrea did not know of her Jewish heritage until she was twelve, when informed by one of her classmates at the Brearley School.[18]

In 1924 Katharine's mother, Ellen, remarried. Cousin John Dorr had managed to divorce his long-estranged wife and marry his cousin's widow on June 20. A graduate and trustee of Rutgers University, Dorr was a well-known chemical and metallurgical engineer. After a brief honeymoon in Europe, the couple settled in New York City. Although the marriage did not approach the perfect union that Ellen and Samuel Swift had seemed to share, it was a positive match. Kay later recalled, "C. J. adored her, and she had real affection for him. I loved him deeply. . . . There were some stormy times, probably because Mother never felt completely married to anyone except my father, who had been the one real love of her life." Unfortunately, the marriage would only last four years, until Ellen Swift Dorr succumbed to breast cancer on July 4, 1928.[19]

Seeking a weekend retreat from city nightlife, in 1924 the Warburgs purchased Bydale, a twenty-five acre farm in Greenwich, Connecticut. At the time Connecticut was a very conservative and "very Christian" place, and James's purchase of a home there represents another excursion from his parents' Jewish world and heritage. To the colonial house and barn the Warburgs added a tennis court, a swimming pool, and stables. Eventually they increased the farm's size to eighty-two acres, where they and their guests enjoyed horseback riding. The Warburgs were able to spend more time with their children at Bydale in summer.[20]

Life at Bydale was not entirely serene, however. Their daughter April recalls that many boisterous parties were held there.

> Bydale was a mixed blessing because it was noisier. . . . They threw large parties with lots of shouting and drinking, and it was difficult for us to get to sleep. Of course we were not invited to those parties, either. Sometimes we would be dragged out of our beds at night to sing close harmony for the guests. Andrea and I would sing something that my mother had practiced with us. We had very good ears and could sing. ([Young] Kay was cute and had a bright,

lovely smile, but she couldn't carry a tune.) It was not very pleasant having to sing for guests in your pajamas, but we did it. In those days you did as you were told.[21]

Katharine Swift had quickly made the transition from working musician to hostess, graciously charming the elite of the music and literary worlds in the city and in the country. She added the sports of tennis, swimming, and horseback riding to her musical interests and raising children. No longer did she need to rely on her passion for music to earn a living—the Warburg fortune allowed her the freedom to live and entertain in elegance. In fact, as Warburg later acknowledged, their way of life was so excessive that it typified Thorstein Veblen's critique of conspicuous consumption. He elaborated, "Like many of my contemporaries who also 'struck it rich' I lived like an obnoxious parvenu. In place of the one servant, we now had five. A chauffeur drove the children to school."[22]

It was amid that excess in 1925 that George and Ira Gershwin first met the Warburgs. On April 17, Katharine Warburg gave a party for violinist Jascha Heifetz. Pauline Heifetz, his sister, had been seeing George for several months and brought him as her date. Like other Broadway personalities who mingled at the Warburgs' parties, Gershwin was already a celebrity in 1925. His first hit, "Swanee," had been popularized by Al Jolson in 1919. He had written for George White's *Scandals* from 1920 through 1924, and his *Rhapsody in Blue* in 1924 had made his career. Katharine had already identified Gershwin as one of the few composers of popular song who interested her. With her thorough background in classical music, she herself claimed to have been a "terrible snob about musical comedy music and didn't like any at all. I liked blues, spirituals, fast music, but not musical comedy. It never would have occurred to me to write any." After this denunciation of musical comedy, it is rather surprising to know that Swift enthusiastically attended the show *Shuffle Along* six times during its run in 1921–22. With an all-black cast, music by Eubie Blake, and words by Noble Sissle, *Shuffle Along* offered exuberant, syncopated numbers with tap-dancing and soft-shoe routines that white audiences found innovative and irresistible. Soon after *Shuffle Along,* her brother, Sam, played her recordings of Gershwin's "I'll Build a Stairway to Paradise" and "Do It Again," and her attitude toward Broadway changed. Show tunes had been "patently predictable at that time, until George's music. I thought that one had to have this element of surprise in all music, any music. . . . When I heard those records, his music seemed fresh and new, instantly identifiable." The African-American rhythms and energy in the music of Sissle and Blake, and now in the music of Gershwin, caught her attention.[23]

Pauline Heifetz apparently sensed an immediate attraction between George and Katharine. In her biography of Gershwin, Joan Peyser reports that Pauline's diary for April 17, 1925, reads: "Party at Warburgs." Her drawing of a skull and crossbones was accompanied by the caption, "'Finita Really,' Pauline's shorthand for 'La commedia est finita,' which she borrowed from the end of *Pagliacci*."[24]

Swift recalled inviting Gershwin to another of her parties months later in March 1926. There he characteristically spent most of the evening at the piano playing his own compositions—a habit that prompted Oscar Levant's famous barb, "An evening with Gershwin is a Gershwin evening." After several hours, Gershwin jumped up and said, "Well, I've got to go to Europe now," and Katharine thought that was "rather charming." Already intrigued by his music, Katharine evidently became equally intrigued with Gershwin the man. Years later she commented: "He and his music were all of a piece —he was exactly like his music. And he had the face, personality, and the looks, and he moved exactly the way you'd expect from his music. . . . George was somebody I'd rather hear play than anybody else. He went right to the piano and sat down with joy. . . . It was an electric experience."[25]

George Gershwin was a dynamic musician and a handsome and confident young man, but his family life and musical background contrasted sharply with Katharine Warburg's. His parents, as Russian Jewish immigrants, were most concerned with becoming Americanized and making financial ends meet. George's education and cultural experiences had been severely limited, his musical training relatively late and largely self-taught. The Gershwins acquired a piano for their older son, Ira, when George was twelve, but George astounded them when he showed that he could already play with some facility, displaying skills he had developed by experimenting on a friend's player piano. George's lessons began at that point. His creativity and intelligence, coupled with his determination to learn, spurred him to seek knowledge and make discoveries. The success of his popular songs in the early 1920s gave him the confidence to pursue his passion, though they also contributed to his grand ego. With *Rhapsody in Blue* (1924) and the *Concerto in F* (1925), however, Gershwin established himself as much more than another Tin Pan Alley or Broadway songwriter. His drive to excel as a composer was all-consuming, his attentions narrowly focused on his music. This self-centeredness is commented on by all of his biographers. Some who knew him perceived him as rude and even crude. Others, like novelist DuBose Heyward, simply considered him authentic. "His self-appreciations were beyond modesty and beyond conceit. He was incapable of insincerity; he didn't see why he should suppress a virtue or a talent simply because it happened to belong to him. He was just plain dazzled by the spectacle of his own music and his own career; his unaffected delight in it was somewhat astonishing, but it was also amusing and refreshing." Katharine Warburg was immediately attracted to him, and she offered him her social as well as musical expertise.[26]

When Gershwin returned from Europe in May 1926, James Warburg was traveling extensively on business. Katharine had invitations to many social events, and George began escorting her to galleries and concerts. She recalled accompanying Gershwin to many after-theater parties at Jules Glaenzer's. Glaenzer was the New York proprietor of Cartier, the fashionable jewelry store, and a noted host in both Paris and New York. His celebrated guests regularly included entertainers who would perform for each other. Around this time George began calling Swift "Kay" rather than "Katharine," just as he later convinced Russian émigré composer Vladimir Dukelsky to change his name to "Vernon Duke," and composer Annie Rosenblatt to become "Ann Ronell." Gershwin's 1926 show *Oh, Kay!* not so coincidentally featured characters "Kay" and "Jimmy Winter." The two were becoming very close friends.[27]

Gershwin's originality and success with the popular song genre kindled Swift's growing attraction to it as she expanded her musical tastes. He undoubtedly played many of his own songs for her (as he did for everyone). And his enthusiasm was contagious, not just for his own compositions, but also for those of his contemporaries. He told Swift of his great admiration for Irving Berlin, pointing out ingenious devices the veteran songwriter used. (She especially enjoyed hearing him play Berlin's "At the Devil's Ball.") Together they purchased a copy of Hoagy Carmichael's "Washboard Blues" (1926), and Gershwin played it "seven or eight times right then and there. He loved it." Most observers and biographers acknowledge that the common interests of Swift and Gershwin cemented a friendship that quickly surpassed the category of professionalism, even though much of their time together was spent exchanging musical ideas. She coached him on orchestration and counterpoint as well as in horseback riding, fashion, and etiquette. Their fascination with each other became a serious flirtation, and his interests became hers.[28]

When Gershwin traveled to Europe in the summer of 1926, Kay resumed composing and produced two works for piano. How much music she had written since 1922 when she left the institute is not known; there are no scores remaining from these years. Perhaps, given the birth of her third daughter in 1924, the purchase of Bydale, the expansion of the New York townhouse, and the Warburgs' active social life, this was Swift's first chance to concentrate on composition in several years. Or perhaps she was inspired by the friendship she had struck with George Gershwin and wanted to demonstrate to him her musical abilities. Composers often played their works on the piano at parties, so these two pieces, "Mazurka" and "Furlana," would have allowed her to share her talents with others more easily than her compositions for voice or chamber ensemble would have. In this year also Gershwin played his three Piano Preludes at a December recital in which he accompanied singer Marguerite d'Alvarez. He had conceived a larger work, *The Melting Pot,* to consist of twenty-four preludes, but published only three. The last of those, the "Spanish Prelude," was one he had composed in Swift's apartment and that she had helped to notate. Gershwin's work on these short piano pieces may have inspired Swift to work in the same genre.[29]

Swift's pieces are both dance movements. "Mazurka" is modeled after Frédéric Chopin's renditions of the Polish dance, with its reliance on dotted rhythms, triple meter, and accents on beats two and three. She had earlier been exposed to this dance form when she performed Claude Debussy's "Mazurka" (1890) in 1916; her composition is not unlike Debussy's. Swift's "Mazurka," eighty-eight measures long, is in 3/4 meter except for the trio.

Most phrases are four measures long, combining, like Debussy's, to create regular eight-measure sections. Only in the trio does Swift depart significantly from tradition as she introduces an unusual 5/4 section in even eighth notes, a contrasting theme that underscores her desire for a fresh approach to this traditional form. Both Swift's and Debussy's mazurkas feature a three-sharp key signature suggesting F sharp minor, although harmonies wander through unrelated keys and hint at fleeting tonal areas. Both use mostly triadic harmonies and seventh chords yet abandon strict functional harmony. Debussy uses half cadences and plagal cadences to avoid finality until the one authentic cadence at the end. Swift's cadences are even more evasive. They feature traditional linear approaches to tonic in the melody, while the waltz bass confounds convention, moving to the tonic by third or tritone. Her chords often progress by intervals of a third or move in parallel motion by step, featuring planes of dominant seventh chords in an impressionistic style. Fluctuations from major to minor occur in several places. The greatest difference from Debussy's mazurka is offered by Swift's angular melody, although both melodies use triplets. The excerpt illustrates the main theme as it reenters on its initial pitch, the major seventh. An appoggiatura figure emphasizing the second beat is prominent throughout the mazurka and provides repeated dissonance before its resolution up by half step. Whereas the initial statement features a one-voice melody over a simple waltz bass, the reentry embellishes the accompaniment with triplets (ex. 3.1).

"Furlana," a Spanish dance dated September 30, 1926, is a piano piece of 121 measures in rondo form that alternates two basic themes. The piece is in 6/8 meter, and the first theme (A) in D minor features an ostinato dance rhythm (quarter-eighth, quarter-eighth) on the tonic pitch. Swift supports the melody with parallel thirds, triads, and seventh chords moving in chromatic motion. She then states it in B flat major before fragmenting it and returning to D minor. The second theme (B) smoothes out the rhythm and features parallel triads in long, even note values over a sustained accompaniment. It is in F major and repeatedly uses a flat VII chord (E flat–G–B flat), which creates a modal flavor and sets up a return of the A theme in the new key of E flat major. This version of the main theme features an unmistakable blue subdominant (a IV chord with a lowered seventh), as well as blue notes in the melody. The final treatment of the second theme (B) features an

3.1   "Mazurka," measures 30–40

accompaniment in a popular, arpeggiated style before returning to the original theme (A).

This influence of the blues is somewhat unusual, given Swift's classical training, although she had used ragtime and jazz elements in her graduation piece at the Institute of Musical Art. Her continued experimentation with blues elements, however subtle, in an essentially classical piano piece may reflect her emulation of Dvořák's embrace of African-American spirituals during the 1890s and his fascination with combining "the music of the people" with classical European art forms. It may also suggest the influence Gershwin was having on her musical tastes and how compatible her philosophy of composition was with Gershwin's. She was not concerned about maintaining separate genres but felt that contrasting styles could enhance each other, just as he had included jazz elements in his concert works.[30]

Another composer who had embraced this eclecticism was Charles Martin Loeffler, with whom Swift had maintained contact. In April 1927, Loeffler was in New York for a performance of his *Music for Four Stringed Instruments* by the Musical Art Quartet, of which Marie Rosanoff was a member. Swift surprised him with a party at East Seventieth Street after the performance, where she, violist Louis Kauffman, and singer Greta Torpadie performed his *Quatre poèmes*. At the party Loeffler met many of her musician friends, including Jascha Heifetz, his sister Pauline and her husband, music critic Samuel Chotzinoff, and the irrepressible George Gershwin. As usual, Gershwin played, and he and Loeffler developed "an instant rapport." Loeffler "moved up close beside the piano and every time George paused, he'd ask for 'More, please.'" The two composers maintained a friendship and professional relationship for years, and Loeffler even experimented with jazz elements in some of his music. In a letter to Swift he commented on Gershwin's "unusual gifts which often touch on genius, and for that rare something indefinably lovable in the man."[31]

The Warburgs' return to New York City had transformed the proper, private world of Katharine Swift Warburg into the energetic, public world of Kay Swift. Her life was disrupted by circumstances not totally beyond her control—a mischievous spirit, an adventuresome, ambitious husband, enough money to support her discriminating tastes, and the immaturity of youth. The highbrow culture of classical music, ballet, and literature had been tainted with the lowbrow thrills of Broadway, Tin Pan Alley, and Harlem. Where classical music represented disciplined, traditional values, a growing interest in popular music was reflective of a youthful America. Most of all, Kay Swift was dazzled by George Gershwin and his music, confounded by the contradictions between his genius, his naïveté, and his ego. Influenced by his music and his personality, she turned her eyes and ears toward his world of Broadway.

Broadway Beginnings

In an effort to learn more about popular songwriting, Swift joined the Musician's Union, which permitted her to play the piano in a pit orchestra. She and her friend Honor Leeming worked on stage sets with theatrical designer Norman Bel Geddes. And Richard Rodgers offered Swift the position of rehearsal pianist for his Broadway show *A Connecticut Yankee,* which opened November 3, 1927. Gershwin may have recommended Swift for the assignment; he was known to have performed similar favors for other young talents trying to make their way on Broadway. By 1927, though, Swift and Rodgers were friends, attending the same parties, such as those at Jules Glaenzer's home.[32]

Richard Rodgers and Lorenz Hart were producing some of the most innovative music on Broadway, specializing in the witty, urbane fare that typified the 1920s. Rodgers's well-crafted, tuneful melodies featured enough syncopation for Hart to introduce his imaginative interior rhymes and irreverent lyrics in such memorable shows as *The Girl Friend* (1926) and, later, *On Your Toes* (1936) and *Pal Joey* (1940). As rehearsal pianist, Swift's close contact with their music in *A Connecticut Yankee* exposed her to cutting-edge work from one of the most creative songwriting teams ever to work on Broadway, as well as to the world of George Gershwin.

Swift accepted the job, even though her children were only eight, five, and three years old. In an ordinary middle-class family, this action would have been extremely disruptive, but Swift's absence during long hours of rehearsal probably inconvenienced no one. She reported that she regularly worked from 10:00 A.M. until 6:00 P.M. Later the hours shifted to the evening, "from 8:00 P.M. until—during the last month, almost all night. That's how I learned about the fast opening music, the ice-breaker song, and that the big song hit should be introduced towards the latter part of the first act." Swift wanted to learn not only how Broadway songs were written and arranged but also how entire shows were created. "By this time I was writing one popular song after another," she claimed. "Writing them, but I was not selling them. Every time I wasn't working, I spent hours and days waiting around publisher's and producer's offices trying to get a number over."[33]

Swift's song compositions before now had been limited to setting the texts of well-known poets. Her foray into popular music would require witty, not sentimental, lyrics. Fortunately, her husband had dabbled in poetry. The Warburg family had a tradition of composing light verse at the dinner table, and several of James's poems had been published in *Century* magazine. Warburg later admitted that since his days at Harvard, he had harbored a "secret ambition to become a writer," but he did not think he could support a wife and family in that profession, even had his parents considered it a suitable occupation. So, after his banking hours, James Paul Warburg wrote lyrics for his wife under the pseudonym Paul James, and Katharine wrote under the name Kay Swift. Although their relationship was strained by the intrusion of George Gershwin, they managed to work creatively as a team. James enjoyed his banker-by-day and lyricist-by-night double life, though maintaining the demanding schedules that both required was difficult. This arrangement did enable Kay to pursue a growing interest; and it kept James involved in Kay's glamorous world of the theater and popular music. Another year would pass, however, before any of their songs would attract attention.[34]

In 1928, two of their efforts, "Little White Lies" and "When the Lights Turn Green," were finally interpolated into the first new musical of the season, *Say When*. The show, co-produced by Elisabeth Marbury, featured songs by various composers, but the production had many weaknesses. *Say When* closed on July 7, after only fifteen performances, and the first Swift-James compositions to reach the stage disappeared with it. Paul James collaborated with another composer, Michael Cleary, on a song that was heard just months later in Earl Carroll's *Vanities of 1928*. Although the revue lasted two hundred performances, their title song, "Vaniteaser," did not survive.[35]

Sadly Ellen Swift Dorr succumbed to breast cancer on July 4, 1928, at the age of fifty-six. Her last months of suffering would have overlapped with Kay's breakthroughs on Broadway. Although it must have been hard to promote her music at this time, Swift may have gained relief from the stress of her mother's illness by pursuing song publications and working on the show. Kay Swift never discussed her mother's condition or passing in her unfinished memoirs, although she had commented at length on the deaths of her father and Bertha Tapper when she was seventeen. Perhaps she was better able to cope with death as an adult. Or perhaps this most difficult chapter was planned but not yet composed.

Four more Swift-James songs were interpolated into the Broadway revues *The Little Show* (1929), *9:15 Revue* (1930), and *The Garrick Gaieties* (1930). Revues generally featured a string of unrelated musical numbers, often written by a single composer but sometimes contributed by many composers.

The potluck format offered new writers a chance to break into musical theater without the need to conform to a particular style. If a number did not work, it could easily be replaced without affecting the plot or later numbers. If successful, the composer might be offered additional opportunities. The revue provided an opening for many successful composers, including Richard Rodgers, Irving Berlin, George Gershwin, and the team of Arthur Schwartz and Howard Dietz. The Algonquin group had written the sketches for a 1922 production, *The 49ers*. Since several of the Warburgs' friends were involved in the production of musical revues, it seemed a natural and ideal means for Kay Swift and Paul James to enter the world of Broadway.[36]

The most elaborate revues were Florenz Ziegfeld's famous *Follies*. Ziegfeld's concept of the revue has been summarized as being "the girls, spectacular sets and costumes, and vaudeville with nothing but headline acts." But at the outset of the Depression, financing became a major concern, and more modest casts and settings were often a necessity.[37]

Swift and James wrote "Can't We Be Friends?" in 1929 for *The Little Show*. This revue had better-known stars than some of its era—Libby Holman, Fred Allen, and Clifton Webb—and included a sketch by Algonquin associate George S. Kaufman. The show was successful, running for 321 performances. Although the songwriting team Dietz and Schwartz wrote most of the songs, the revue also featured music by twelve other composers. The hits of the show, ironically, were not songs by Dietz and Schwartz, but "Moanin' Low," by Ralph Rainger, and Swift's "Can't We Be Friends?" Both were sung by Libby Holman, a rising young star deemed "torch singer par excellence" by gossip columnist Walter Winchell. Holman was a sultry, well-proportioned young woman with a deep, chesty voice who used all of her physical and emotional assets to sell a song. In *The Little Show*, garbed in a "dark cerise strapless gown" long before strapless gowns were commonplace, Holman stood motionless "in a slit in the curtain . . . perfectly stationary," and sang "Can't We Be Friends?" to Clifton Webb in a mesmerizing largo tempo. Composer Alec Wilder sat entranced in the audience, and considered it one of the most "theatrical moments" he had witnessed.[38]

Holman was controversial both on and off stage, a favorite topic in gossip columns because of her penchant for speakeasies, expletives, and flamboyant lovers both male and female. Married in 1931 to Zachary Smith Reynolds, heir to the tobacco fortune, she was indicted eight months later for his murder, although the case never went to trial. Libby seemed to attract attention and controversy wherever she went. As lyricist Howard Dietz said, "No one in the theatre was more discussable than Libby Holman." She seemed to him "an outrageous woman, who appeared in the nude in her dressing room and, therefore, had a lot of visitors." Regardless of her antics, Holman was a talented entertainer. Kay Swift was a good friend of Libby's and was unruffled by her singular behavior. She said that she had written the melody of "Can't We Be Friends?" before the words and had played it for Holman. "When Libby said she wanted to sing it in the show, my husband wrote the lyric. As soon as I heard her sing it, I knew she was right for the part." Although Holman's dramatic performances undoubtedly enhanced the piece, "Can't We Be Friends?" was an enduring song in its own right. F. Scott Fitzgerald mentioned it in his short story "A New Leaf," which appeared in the *Saturday Evening Post* in 1931. The song has been recorded by Frank Sinatra, Ella Fitzgerald, Bing Crosby, and Linda Ronstadt, among others, over the decades since its composition and is a standard of the repertory.[39]

Many popular songs of the day that originated on Broadway or in Tin Pan Alley featured the harmonic language of tonal music in the European classical tradition. By the 1920s, however, an interest in jazz was sweeping the nation. Black and white performers gathered in such urban centers as New York, Chicago, and Kansas City to hear and play the new sounds. New York City in fact became the center of an explosion in African-American arts and literature as the Harlem Renaissance flourished in the 1920s and 1930s. Argues historian David Levering Lewis, "Harlem's exciting reputation had sparked a white invasion. . . . Sophisticated white fascination with the Afro-American would run wild in the summer of 1925" owing to a plethora of literary, theatrical, and musical works. The 1926 Broadway musical *Lulu Belle*, "a melodrama of Harlem street life, . . . sent whites straight to Harlem in unprecedented numbers for a taste of the real thing." Many white New Yorkers found the African-American culture they found there exciting artistically, emotionally, and intellectually. Although some blacks considered jazz to be the expression of uneducated musicians and would have preferred to omit it from the Renaissance accomplishments, jazz music was what many whites found most intriguing. They visited nightclubs and record shops in Harlem to hear black musicians experimenting with this new style. The blues harmonies, syncopated rhythms, and innovative tone colors were infectious, and audiences began to expect to hear such ebullience in other popular music, including that of the musical theater. Gershwin had experimented with an "all-star jazz band" to accompany the 1930 remake of *Strike Up the Band*. He used the same musicians in *Girl Crazy*, his musical of 1930 featuring the now-legendary song "I Got Rhythm," which needed a livelier accompaniment than the traditional pit orchestra.[40]

Considering Kay Swift's earlier interest in spirituals, it is not surprising that she, too, absorbed some of these jazz traits. "Can't We Be Friends?" shows how quickly she adapted the popular style while infusing creativity into her songs. She patterned her compositions after the current Broadway masters—Jerome Kern, Richard Rodgers, and George Gershwin—borrowing standard practices while adding creative touches. For many of her songs, including this one, she adopted the standard AABA song form, with each section eight measures in length. Her harmonies included "flat VI" chords and chromatic mediants used by many nineteenth-century classical composers, as well as elements of the jazz world—added-tone chords and chords with blue notes, such as the blue subdominant, a chord she would use frequently and one that George Gershwin favored. The melody of "Can't We Be Friends?" places an unusual emphasis on the sixth scale degree, which begins a general three-note chromatic motion downward, a motive that is repeated at the lower octave and becomes the hook of the piece (m. 3–4; ex. 3.2). This sixth scale degree also implies a pentatonic framework that suggests African-American influences and a scale that became increasingly important in popular music. A winding, meandering line, the melody is highlighted by chromatic inflections and several well-placed skips. Though the song is a ballad, the rhythm exhibits moderate syncopation and irregular phrasing to avoid the predictability that Swift so disliked.[41]

Paul James's lyric captures a feeling of dejection, which is set up by using an unusual minor key for the verse and a blues character for the refrain. He composed the lyric to this song as his marriage was slipping away, and it is possible to view this lyric as an expression of his personal situation (in

3.2 "Can't We Be Friends?" measures 1–5

spite of the opposite gender reference). The verse ends with the comment "I should have seen it, / Now it's too late!" The refrain follows:

> I thought I'd found the man of my dreams.
> Now it seems this is how the story ends:
> He's goin' to turn me down and say,
> "Can't We Be Friends?"

> I thought for once it couldn't go wrong,
> Not for long! I can see the way this ends;
> He's goin' to turn me down and say,
> "Can't We Be Friends?"

> Never again! Through with love, Through with men!
> They play their game without shame,
> And who's to blame?

> I thought I'd found a man I could trust,
> What a bust! This is how the story ends:
> He's goin' to turn me down and say,
> "Can't We Be Friends?"

"Can't We Be Friends?" became a hit, not just because of Libby Holman's dramatic rendition, but because it fulfilled the audience's expectations (standard form, text, meter, overall melodic contour) while introducing unique variations in its harmonic language, rhythm, and melodic line, features that later became common in many popular songs of the era. "Can't We Be Friends?" is one of the most enduring of Swift and James's collaborations. At the time of its writing, the Warburgs' union was disintegrating, and Swift and Gershwin were clearly much more than friends.

"Up Among the Chimney Pots" and "How Would a City Gal Know?" were written for *9:15 Revue,* which opened February 11, 1930. "How Would a City Gal Know?" was sung by Ruth Etting, Frances Shelly, and Helen Gray, but despite its intriguing title, the song has been lost. "Up Among the Chimney Pots," however, has survived. It is a lovely ballad (a "very feminine" song, says composer William Bolcom), with attractive and imaginative harmonies (including the blue subdominant again). It displays the same meandering lines as "Can't We Be Friends?" and after a rather chromatic opening gesture, it also emphasizes the pentatonic scale. It is Swift's only song in an ABA form, three eight-bar phrases totaling twenty-four measures rather than the thirty-two bars she adopted for most of her other Broadway compositions. It was introduced by Ruth Etting, who received special mention in the press for her rendition of this number; but it never received the recognition of "Can't We Be Friends?" Swift recalled that Leon Leonidoff, later a producer of stage shows at Radio City Music Hall, danced a pantomime to the song in the show.[42]

The sixth Swift-James song to reach Broadway within two years was "Johnny Wanamaker," one of the most celebrated numbers of *The Garrick Gaieties* of 1930. The song is a spoof about John Wanamaker's department store in New York City and Grover Whalen, a former police commissioner who became general manager of Wanamaker's. As police commissioner, Whalen had maintained law and order with a heavy hand. The lyric has him placing officers in the middle of the store, much to New Yorkers' ridicule. Brooks Atkinson of the *New York Times* wrote, "As the virtues of this emporium pile up in the verses, the chorus swells into a paean of thanksgiving and jubilation, and the audience does as much. For Paul James, who has written the lyric, and Kay Swift, who has written the music, have touched perfection in topical satire." The Swift-James songwriting team was finding its stride with the appropriate combination of wit and romance even as their own romance was ending.[43]

CHAPTER 4

Fine and Dandy

Some couples, when faced with a marital crisis, have a baby. My grand-parents had a Broadway musical.—Katharine Weber

Although the Swift-James songs had enjoyed some success, the New York theater scene was more precarious than usual in 1930. The popularity of film musicals and the stock market crash of 1929 had led to a reduced num-ber of musical productions on Broadway. In spite of these obstacles, the Warburgs now undertook the task of writing music and lyrics for a com-plete show. This was an unusual venture, not simply because of the unfavor-able economic conditions and the strains in the Warburgs' marriage. Their collaboration would produce the first Broadway musical whose score was written entirely by a woman, a fact that apparently did not daunt Kay Swift in the least.[1]

Fine and Dandy opened at Erlanger's Theatre on West Forty-fourth Street (now the St. James Theatre) on September 23, 1930. Featuring a book by Donald Ogden Stewart, orchestrations by Hans Spialek, and performances of the Merriel Abbott Dancers, the show also starred comedians Joe Cook and Dave Chasen and the young tap-dancing sensation Eleanor Powell.[2]

The show was not without its financial problems and had met with some difficulties before it finally opened; James Warburg's connections kept it afloat. "When the producers went broke just before the opening," writes Nicholas Fox Weber, "Paul James simply took up his Jimmy Warburg side and came up with the necessary funds—aided by two of his best friends, Marshall Field and Averell Harriman, who had liked the musical in rehearsal. Although the three investors never saw cash returns on the project, the show was a great success, running for more than 250 performances. . . . Moreover, two Swift and James songs, 'Fine and Dandy' and 'Can This Be Love?,' entered the mainstream." Along with the Gershwins' *Girl Crazy* and *Three's a Crowd* by Dietz and Schwartz, *Fine and Dandy* was one of the few hits of the 1930–31 season.[3]

The Machine Age on Broadway

Although the musical score of *Fine and Dandy* is the first written by a woman, that fact was not acknowledged in the reviews or promotions of the time, and nothing in the score suggests a female rather than a male composer. Most of the songs are similar in form, rhythm, and harmony to works of Swift's contemporaries Richard Rodgers and George Gershwin, both of whom would have had direct input into her writing, and many are similar to the previous Swift-James songs. Hans Spialek, the orchestrator, enjoyed a long career on Broadway and arranged more than 150 musicals for Chappell Music, including shows by Cole Porter and Rodgers and Hart. The style and treatment of the music for *Fine and Dandy* were identical to other musicals of the decade, and eight of the fifteen songs for the show were published. The producers either did not see Swift's gender as significant or chose not to emphasize the unique fact.[4]

Fine and Dandy is set in a factory, the Fordyce Drop Forge and Tool Company, where conflicts between workers and management, men and women, and sense and nonsense abound. Interestingly, this groundbreaking show for female composers is set in a machine shop, where male management, physical strength, and mechanized motions prevail. This was the age of efficiency, of streamlining tasks. Engineering and its achievements were being hailed in such popular magazines as *Literary Digest, Collier's,* and the *Saturday Evening Post,* where "articles emphasized the power and resourcefulness of engineering. . . . All such articles endorsed the ingenuity of those conceiving, building, and using machinery." Such engineers would of course all have been male.[5]

Fine and Dandy's opening number, "The Machine Shop Chant," highlights this mania for efficiency: male and female workers sing, "If you loaf a single second you'll be fired out / When the whistle blows we're all completely tired out." The men and women sing in unison, a simple device that signifies worker solidarity. The song also reflects Kay Swift's writing craft, and uses some techniques she had not had a chance to apply since her days at the Institute of Musical Art. She begins with a pentatonic four-measure theme in half and quarter notes. The theme evokes simple folk tunes and African influences on American popular music. Not only the melody but its use carries folk connotations. This is a work song that "keeps time to the rhythm of the turning machines." Although this reflects a populist sentiment, Swift's treatment of the theme is not simple. The rhythm is immediately reduced to quarter and eighth notes; such diminution is a technique common to eighteenth-century counterpoint. The perpetual motion of the eighth notes, many on repeated pitches, suggests the constant motion of the machinery in the factory.[6]

The first theme, built on a repetitive two-measure pattern, is sixteen bars long, but its blue notes and harmonies recall a twelve-bar blues pattern, another African-American reference. A second theme combines a motive of repeated eighth notes with the same two-measure pattern from the first theme. The repetition of pitches, rhythms, and motives may represent the repetition and monotony that a factory worker experiences. Yet Swift takes the two themes into fresh harmonic areas, juxtaposing unusual key relationships, so that the effect is anything but monotonous. It is an imaginative opening for a score that is far more than a succession of predictable thirty-two-bar songs.

Neither Kay Swift nor Paul James would have spent any time in a factory like the Fordyce Drop Forge and Tool Company. Katharine may have visited her father's plant in New Haven when she was a young girl and remembered the physical labor and mechanized motions. James probably observed factories in the textile industry as he became an expert in textile finance. But this is not a musical about the plight of factory workers during the Depression.

On one level *Fine and Dandy* is simply a three-pronged romantic comedy. On another, it is a satire of management and the upper class. Although Swift and James and writer Donald Ogden Stewart may not have had first-hand experience with factory workers, they would certainly have been exposed to the attitudes toward them that were shared by those in executive positions.

Synopsis and Songs, Act 1

At the outset, Mrs. Cynthia Fordyce (played by Dora Maughan), widow of the former owner of the plant, has assumed control of the company. Unfamiliar with the operation of Fordyce Drop Forge and Tool Company, she arrives with her daughter, Marabelle (Nell O'Day), to inspect her inheritance. Marabelle has become infatuated with George (Joe Wagstaff), a recent Yale graduate and son of the plant manager, Mr. Ellis (George A. Schiller). George is about to begin work at the plant, eager to start with the most menial of positions and work his way up to the top, so that he will be worthy to marry Marabelle. This concern for the difference in their social classes prompts the song "Rich or Poor," a ballad typical of the show. Although it begins with a popular harmonic formula, I–vi–ii–V, it quickly avoids predictability by moving through chromatic harmonies with ease and modulating to an unrelated key in the bridge (G major to B major). Its syncopations allow George and Marabelle to proclaim their intentions in a light-hearted way before they break into dance with the Merriel Abbott Dancers. A later number, "Starting at the Bottom," features George alone, as he remains determined to climb the ladder of success and win Marabelle. This piece is more rhythmic than melodic in nature, with pronounced syncopation. Although the melody is more conjunct than "Rich or Poor," it features two well-placed skips of a sixth in the opening section. The bridge of this song is far more disjunct than the opening eight bars, as it outlines triads and offers a balance to the opening section. It moves to the expected dominant key and features chromatic chords common to the nineteenth-century art song tradition, including secondary dominants and borrowed harmonies. Consistently in her popular songs, Swift experiments with one or more musical parameters, such as melody, harmony, or rhythm, pushing the limits of standard practices to avoid predictability. Yet she is careful to balance the extremes by tempering the remaining parameters and offering audiences something they can recognize as familiar.[7]

Central to the plot is Joe Squibb, the most popular worker in the plant. Squibb was played by star comedian Joe Cook, a former vaudevillian famous for his slapstick humor, juggling abilities, acrobatics, and convoluted mechanical creations. Much of the script simply gives directions to Cook to improvise, with cues such as "Business with cigar," "Business with machines," "Collapsible Chair business," or "Business with ukelele." Audiences in 1930 were enthralled with Cook's talents and charm. His childlike disregard for the Fordyce management further endeared him to audiences. Inevitably, Mr. Ellis's daughter, Nancy (Alice Boulden), becomes attracted to Joe, although she is engaged to the assistant plant manager, Edgar Little (John W. Ehrle). Nancy and Joe spend the show in mutual flirtation.[8]

The well-known title song "Fine and Dandy" first occurs as a duet between Nancy and Joe shortly after she and Edgar have had a spat. It is representative of the many songs during the late 1920s and 1930s that were introduced on the Broadway stage and became popularized by means of radio broadcasts, phonograph recordings, and sheet music sales. The first eight bars of the chorus are often the only measures of the song that are recognized (ex. 4.1).[9]

The rhythm provides the greatest interest in this piece. This is a syncopated number, but regular harmonic changes and bass notes on the downbeats produce a steady drive. Against that regular bass is a syncopated melodic line whose entire rhythm is generated from the motive in measures one and two. This incessant two-bar motive, or one of its variants, occurs fourteen times. The rhythm pervades the song until the last four measures. Matching the irregularity set up by the syncopation, the melody of "Fine and Dandy" features frequent skips that are used in sequential patterns. Balance is achieved through the contour of the phrases and the general progression of the melodic line.[10]

"Fine and Dandy" features an ABAC arrangement in its refrain. Both verse and refrain are in F major, and the song does not modulate. The harmony, however, features some chromatic activity, especially chords that use the lowered seventh and lowered sixth scale degrees. The plagal cadence with the blue subdominant (I–IV flat 7–I) is reminiscent of the blues har-

4.1 "Fine and Dandy," measures 1–8

mony that Swift had used at the end of "Can't We Be Friends?" Additional
dissonances are created by major seventh chords, embellishing diminished
seventh chords, minor ninths, major ninths, and added sixth chords—harmonies typical of popular songs in the 1930s. A summary of "Fine and
Dandy" musical elements shows that the stabilizing factors of the diatonic
melody, recurring melodic and rhythmic motives, and fairly regular harmonic
rhythm balance the extremely active harmonies, syncopated rhythms, and
disjunct melodic line.

The lyric of "Fine and Dandy" avoids unpleasant allusions to the Depression and affirms the positive side of life. The original lyrics from the show
could not have been more carefree, with Nancy's closing line, "Check and
double check," quoting the popular radio show "Amos 'n' Andy," which
first aired nationally in 1929.

Joe: How are you, Sugar Candy?
Nancy: Fine and dandy. And how are you?
Joe: Everything is looking fine to me.
Nancy: All the world seems too divine to me.
Joe: How are tricks, Sugar Candy?
Nancy: Fine and dandy. What's new with you?

Joe: Gee, it's dandy to have you handy,
Nancy: Check and double check to you.[11]

The song returns later with similar lyrics as a reprise involving all the characters, a practice that not only unified the show but gave the song greater exposure and encouraged sheet music sales. The sheet music version, however, is noticeably different; Joe sings the first verse of the refrain alone.

Joe: Gee, it's all fine and dandy,
          Sugar Candy, when I've got you.
          Then I only see the sunny side,
          Even trouble has its funny side.
          When you're gone, Sugar Candy,
          I get lonesome, I get so blue.
          When you're handy it's fine and dandy,
          But when you're gone what can I do?

All the singer needs to "see the sunny side" is the presence of his sweetheart. Although this lyric hints at "trouble" and loneliness, the theater version interestingly disavows any such problems. Possibly the published lyric, acknowledging that there are difficulties in life and in love, may have been seen as more appealing to the public. It also underscores the musical balance of the song, suggesting both positive and negative possibilities before reaching an ambivalent conclusion. Gerald Bordman interpreted the ending as positive, for he reports, "The title song was one of the first public pronouncements of facile optimism that became so prevalent in the depression." Its message provided encouragement for those in distress.[12]

The plot of *Fine and Dandy* develops as Mrs. Fordyce, disgusted with "that old goat" Mr. Ellis, decides the company needs more youthful leadership. Conveniently, Joe has also flirted heavily with Mrs. Fordyce, hoping for a promotion. Although he has no qualifications other than his good nature and personality, Mrs. Fordyce promotes him to general manager, hoping to get a new husband. He seems to have as much free rein in the Fordyce Drop Forge and Tool Company as he has on the stage. The chaos that results produces further humor.[13]

Joe Cook's comic actions dominated the show. All other roles, male and female, were secondary. Even writer Donald Ogden Stewart recalled only the characters played by Eleanor Powell (as Miss Hunter) and Joe Cook (as Joe Squibb). In his autobiography, he remarked, "I can't remember the other names, but in a Joe Cook production it didn't make any difference. Neither did the script." In fact, the pursuit of love propels all the action, and the desire to win a mate is predominant. Four women's roles function as supporting parts, although three of the women—Mrs. Fordyce, Marabelle Fordyce, and Nancy Ellis—show no purpose in life other than getting married. The one woman with real career ambitions, Miss Hunter, is better remembered for her sensational tap-dancing skills.[14]

Nancy sings the romantic ballad "Can This Be Love?" as she contemplates her engagement to Edgar Little. The song is one of the hit standards to emerge from the show. Its balanced ABAC melody opens with a rising half-step followed by a leap of a sixth, then stepwise motion in the reverse direction—typical Swiftian gestures. The opening tonic harmony moves dramatically to a blue subdominant. The tune's even quarter-note rhythms offer a smooth contrast to many of the show's numbers, though gentle syncopation permeates the piece since every phrase begins with a rest on beat one. The song has an interesting history. During a party at Jules Glaenzer's, Richard Rodgers once suggested, "Let's write a little something for George." Many of the composers present obliged and offered their creations for Gershwin at the next party. Swift's piece, scored for piano trio, later became "Can This Be Love?"[15]

A significant subplot in *Fine and Dandy* involves Mr. Ellis, who lost money in the stock market crash, "borrowed" one hundred thousand dollars from the company to cover it, and is now trying to find money to repay the "loan" before being discovered. He convinces Joe to serve as his accomplice and stay in the position as general manager until he can raise the necessary funds—long after Joe realizes he is not suited for his executive job.

Joe Squibb's secretary, Miss Hunter, is the only woman who displays efficiency and career ambition. She coaches Joe in his role as general manager but decides to take "a much higher position" near the end of the first act, singing "I'll Hit a New High." The verse of this song establishes a calm mood for her lyric, "My life was serene till you came upon the scene," with a narrow melodic range and steady quarter and half notes. The harmony shifts between C7 and B7 chords in the opening four measures, avoiding resolution to the tonic chord until measure eight. The chorus, however, brings much more direction and energy. It is in standard song form, with some predictable "pitch painting" on the lyrics "I'll hit a new *high* whenever you're nigh" and "I touch a new *low*." A syncopated rhythmic motive propels the melody. There are several nervous references to the stock market in the play, and Miss Hunter's parting song reminds the boys, "You know the mechanics / Of booms and of panics." The Tommy Atkins Sextet and the Merriel Abbott Dancers complement Eleanor Powell's tap-dancing as she celebrates her independence from Fordyce.[16]

Graduation exercises for the Fordyce Night School take on a festive nature under the direction of CEO Joe Squibb. Precommencement entertainment includes a novelty song that is a purely comedic vehicle for Joe Cook. "Giddiup Back" features three "vaudeville horses" with two people inside and relates the saga of Irish Nell and Jack, two horses whose genders have been misidentified because of their uncharacteristic behavior ("Then I got an awful jolt, / Nellie laughed and Jack had the colt!"). The music of this skit is treated imaginatively. The chorus in C major relates the equine tale in relatively even quarter-note and eighth-note values. The lyric halfway through, "Whoa there!" is set expressively to a chromatic chord, a variant of the blue subdominant. The underlying rhythmic figure stops as these words are sung to longer half-note values. Repetitions of the chorus are separated by eight-bar phrases that alternate between A minor and A major. These short sections offer contrast in rhythm and harmony to the chorus and extend the song's length from the usual thirty-two bars to forty. The humor of "Giddiup Back" establishes a jovial mood, making the commencement scene that follows even more ridiculous. Immediately after "Giddiup Back," the night school graduates enter and sing the school song, "FORDYCE," a satiric tribute to the factory. In a march tempo the students parody their alma mater: "F is for the furnace that forges the iron / O is for the oxide, and R is for the rust." At this point in the plot neither Joe Squibb nor the writers of *Fine and Dandy* were taking themselves too seriously.

When their engagements to Edgar and Marabelle are broken, Nancy and George console each other by singing "Let's Go Eat Worms in the Garden," a novel way to commiserate. Refusing to wallow in despair, they perform one of the most energetic numbers in the show. Combining humorous lyrics, strong syncopations, and bold harmonies, the song is memorable. If the pursuit of love is to be such a central motivation, the characters had better learn to manage rejection.

In the tradition of Gilbert and Sullivan and musical theater, additional verses of text in "Fine and Dandy" refer to cultural events outside the play. Joe tries to persuade Nancy to join him in portraying various argumentative couples. He suggests being "Amos 'n' Andy" from the radio show and enacting the romance between Napoleon and Josephine. Finally he touches an American nerve by suggesting that the two relive the world heavyweight title fight between the German fighter Max Schmeling and American Jack Sharkey, which had taken place in June 1930. In a decision unpopular with many Americans, Schmeling had won the fight on a questionable foul when Sharkey supposedly hit him below the belt.

Joe: Now we're in the Stadium. You be Schmeling.
Nancy: I'll be Schmeling, and who are you?
Joe: I'll be Sharkey and I'll hit you foul.
Nancy: If you do there'll be an awful howl.
Joe: Just the same, You be Schmeling,
Nancy: I'll be Schmeling. What do I do?
Joe: Clutch your vitals and claim six titles,
           And take the boodle home with you.

It is easy to imagine the Warburgs' sophisticated literary friends' and other New York theatergoers' amusement at Paul James's biting lyrics.

Several unpublished verses for "Fine and Dandy" illustrate that lyrics were often adapted to suit specific audiences. The following verse, composed for the Boston opening of the show, exploited the bitter Harvard-Yale rivalry. James Warburg, a Harvard graduate, here could find satisfaction in needling his collaborator, Donald Ogden Stewart, a Yalie:

Joe: Let's be collegiate. You be Harvard.
Nancy: I'll be Harvard. And who are you?

Joe: I'm an Eli, what would you suppose?
Nancy: Might have known it from your fancy clothes.
Joe: Just the same. You be Harvard.
Nancy: I'll be Harvard. What do I do?
Joe: Talk of football and track and baseball
           But make no mention of the crew.

(Harvard had beaten Yale in football, track, and baseball, although the crew team had lost to Yale in both 1929 and 1930.)[17]

Even timelier is the verse that mentions a bitter Boston political rivalry. John Fitzgerald (John F. Kennedy's grandfather "Honey Fitz") had served three terms in the Massachusetts State Senate and two as mayor of Boston in the early years of the century. Well loved by the Irish Catholics of South Boston, Fitzgerald freely bestowed political favors on his friends and supporters. In his final bid for reelection, he was opposed by James Michael Curley, who brashly challenged Honey Fitz's political ethics. Fitzgerald withdrew from the race.

Joe: Let's be political. You be Curley.
Nancy: I'll be Curley, and who are you?
Joe: I'm Fitzgerald, known as Honey Boy.
Nancy: That makes me your little Sonny Boy.
Joe: Just the same. You be Curley.
Nancy: I'll be Curley. What do I do?
Joe: Give me blazes in homely phrases.
Nancy: And what I say will all be true.[18]

Yet another verse involves international politics and is remarkably accurate in its prescience, suggesting an assassination that took place eighteen years later.

Joe: Now we're in India. You be Gandhi.
Nancy: I'll be Gandhi. And who are you?
Joe: I shall have to be the Viceroy.
Nancy: I don't want to be a colored boy.

Joe: Just the same. You be Gandhi.
Nancy: I'll be Gandhi. What's that to you?
Joe: If I'm handy, I'll murder Gandhi.
Nancy: Say, that is fine and dandy, too!

The reference to Gandhi as a "colored boy" was apparently not objectionable to the theater crowds in 1930, nor was the suggestion of his assassination questioned. References like these kept the show fresh, as new lyrics evolved during its run and offered its audiences humorous commentary on current events. This sophistication was common on Broadway though less typical in the emerging Hollywood musicals. And of course the extra verses meant that the title song would be repeated over and over, helping to ensure its "hit" status with the audience.[19]

An additional verse for the New York opening reflects Paul James's personal situation rather than his political views.

Joe: Let's be composers. You be five or six of them.
Nancy: I'll be five or six of them. And who are you?
Joe: I'll be Gershwin as you might have guessed.
Nancy: What do I do if I'm all the rest?
Joe: Use your brains, dear, must you ask me?
Nancy: I must ask you. What do I do?
Joe: Use my themes and my rhythmic schemes and . . .
Nancy: Swipe your *Rhapsody in Blue*.

Gershwin's success was indisputable, and other composers imitated his style, hoping for similar fortune. Though he may have wished to, in view of Katharine's devotion to Gershwin, Paul James could not deny Gershwin's talent or appeal. It is possible to consider the last two lines of that verse a reference to Gershwin's intrusion into the Warburg marriage. Or perhaps Warburg is fantasizing about retaliating and swiping something back from Gershwin, just as Gershwin was stealing his wife.

In an era when women's rights were severely limited, it is characteristic that Joe is directing the skit and assigning the fictitious parts, while Nancy obeys with little resistance. In all of these verses, Joe tells Nancy what to do.

Joe: Sev'n o'clock! You be Andy,
Nancy: I'll be Andy, and who are you?
Joe: I'll be Amos, which you ought to know.
Nancy: I don't listen on the radio.
Joe: Just the same, you be Andy.
Nancy: Fine and dandy. What do I do?
Joe: Just be handy to Amos, Andy.
Nancy: Check and double check to you.

Joe is a fan of the popular "Amos 'n' Andy" show, but Nancy is not interested ("I don't listen on the radio"). In the end, though, Nancy complies with Joe's suggestion. She may protest mildly, but she defers to his wishes. (This song is first performed early in the first act, when Nancy is a bit more cooperative. She becomes more doubtful of Joe's intentions as the show proceeds.)

One final point about the lyric: the later verses, with gender-specific texts, were doubtless enjoyed in the theater, and several were printed in the sheet music. But recorded versions of "Fine and Dandy" and most live performances of it, seldom use more than the first verse. As Philip Furia writes,

> Romantic lyrics aimed at Tin Pan Alley's popular market . . . were designed so that they could be sung by either a male or female performer—an important aspect of "standardization" in an industry increasingly geared, in the 1920s, to phonograph recordings and radio rather than sheet music. Even on Broadway, the songs written with an eye toward independent popularity were usually romantic duets; there might be "male" and "female" verses but the all-important chorus was "unisex"—sung in unison on stage and by either male or female singers on records.[20]

Although "Fine and Dandy" was originally a duet, it has been recorded only as a solo by both men and women. Recordings by Barbra Streisand and Kathy Barr maintain a slow tempo, turning "Fine and Dandy" into a torch song and suggesting the lyric's negative outcome—that their lovers have indeed gone and they wonder, "What shall I do?" They clearly found the melody more effective at a slow pace, which is how Swift originally conceived it—with the opening words, "Here today, gone tomorrow." In contrast, Kate Smith, Lorez Alexandria, and Chris Connor, as well as Louis Armstrong and numerous jazz combos, have chosen a lively tempo to reflect the inherent optimism in the text. In yet another twist, versions by Eydie Gorme, Anita O'Day, Debbie Reynolds, Jack Lemmon, and Flo Handy feature the first verse sung slowly followed by the same lyric in an up tempo, underscoring the ambivalence of the text.[21]

"Fine and Dandy" became a popular song and produced royalties for Swift throughout her life. It has been recorded by many artists over the years. Its memorable rhythm has made it a common introductory song for stage acts and even weather reports, not to mention a comedian, Art Metrano, who sang the song "wordlessly" in his pantomime magic act in the 1970s. Tim Conway used "Fine and Dandy" as the theme song for his television show in 1980 and 1981. Jazz performers have long used the song's chord progression as a standard for improvisation, as they have also improvised on Gershwin's "I Got Rhythm." The comparison with Gershwin's song can be carried even further, since "Fine and Dandy"'s underlying chord pattern has also been borrowed as the basis for new compositions, such as Lennie Tristano's "Sax of a Kind" (1949). Years later James Warburg mused about the song's success. "I concluded that there could be no crazier business than show business; an 'angel' could lose his money in backing a successful play, while a lyric writer could earn more from a single song written in a few hours than a junior bank officer earned in an entire year."[22]

Issues of class come to the foreground of *Fine and Dandy* as we observe the behavior and comments of both workers and management in this machine shop. Brooks Atkinson called *Fine and Dandy* "an amiable satire upon the fierce solemnity of great manufacturing organizations." Considering that the Gershwins' revival of *Strike Up the Band,* a satire lampooning war, government, and big business, had opened just nine months earlier, the political and social overtones in *Fine and Dandy* are no surprise. Like the Gershwin brothers, Kay Swift and Paul James borrowed from the Gilbert and Sullivan tradition of critiquing the powerful elite. The book's writer, Donald Ogden Stewart, was known for his humor in his pieces for *Vanity Fair* and the *Smart Set*. A member of the Algonquin Round Table in the 1920s, Stewart had published *A Parody Outline of History,* in which he mocked the literary styles of Sinclair Lewis and other writers. He had little interest in politics at the time, but in the 1930s he embraced socialism and prolabor issues. After his celebrated screenplay for *The Philadelphia Story* in 1940, he became an outspoken antifascist in World War II. During the Cold War, Stewart was accused of being a front for the communists and was blacklisted as a "subversive" during the McCarthy trials of the 1950s, after which he moved to Europe to continue his career.[23]

From the opening scene of *Fine and Dandy,* tension is evident between the factory workers and the management. George Ellis, son of the plant manager, wants to learn the business from the lowliest job on the factory floor up to the executive offices. Wishing to prove his worth to Marabelle, he insists on being given no advantages. When the assistant general manager, Edgar Little, a "self-made man," gives George the plant tour, he advises him not to pull "any of that college stuff around here." "Boys, this is George," Little says to the shop workers. "He went to Yale but don't hold it against him." Clearly anyone with too much education is suspect. (Stewart's backhand promotion of his alma mater should not be overlooked.)[24]

The management's position about the work ethic is clear. Mr. Ellis, who has been with the plant for thirty-five years, advises his son, "The chances for college men in the Drop Forge and Tool business were never brighter. This is, of course, if you follow the simple, fundamental rules. Work hard . . . work hard . . . work hard . . . and don't watch the clock." Of course, the management is concerned with the clock at the beginning of each shift, and Edgar Little is annoyed when Joe Squibb shows up late. He boasts, "I'm never late myself and I don't expect the employees to be late." An exchange between two workmen underscores the chasm between management and labor: "Don't watch the clock, boys, or you won't ever be an executive." The response: "Who the hell wants to be an executive?"[25]

Even in times of financial strain, the company executives allocate time on the golf course. As Frederick Lewis Allen notes in *Only Yesterday,* his 1931 informal history of the 1920s, "the country club had become the focus of social life in hundreds of communities," and "the ability to play [golf] had become a part of the almost essential equipment of the aspiring business executive." Donald Ogden Stewart was himself an avid golfer, as was Joe Cook. The second and third scenes of *Fine and Dandy* occur at the country club, where two of the three emerging couples, including Mrs. Fordyce and Joe, are developing their relationships along with their swings.[26]

Synopsis and Songs, Act 2

Of all the main characters, Joe Squibb is most likely to understand the workers' positions. When he is promoted to general manager, he has no idea what to do in his office, and routinely—and ineptly—follows the routine offered by his secretary, Miss Hunter. He institutes a series of changes, including frequent picnics and shorter work hours, which ease the employees' workload. He gambles, smokes cigars, and drinks gin on the job, mindless of Prohibition. Joe is of course extremely popular with the workers. He understands their views and the injustices they feel they have suffered at the hands of previous managers. At one of his newly arranged company picnics, he addresses the workers in the song "Etiquette":

Joe: Gentlemen and ladies, all,
       They have made your life a perfect Hades,
       Paying you a wage that was too small.
       You, who are the masses,
       Working lads and lasses, should
       Live like the so-called upper classes,
       You have been too long misunderstood.

       I will raise your standard of living right away.
       Now that I am head of the business, hear me say,
       Murphys and O'Gradys,
       You shall join the smartest set,
       You shall all be gentlemen and ladies,
       I will teach you perfect etiquette.

Men: We would like to learn the proper way to eat and talk.
       We would like to learn the secrets of the knife and fork.
       How are we to know what clothes to wear?
       Tell us how to part our hair.

> We long to break away from all this life of toil;
> We'd like to have the leisure time to study Hoyle.
> We would like to join the smartest set.
> We aspire to acquire proper etiquette.

> Girls: What is the style
> Out on Long Island?
> Take us to the races,
> Point out famous faces,
> So we will know at whom to smile.[27]

Paul James's lyrics suggest that members of the working class are not just anxious for higher wages but wish to appear and act like those in the "smartest set" or the "so-called upper classes." Remember that his is a top-down view of the plant. His lyrics would lead us to believe that the workers are willing to let the upper classes dictate to them what is appropriate in their free time, allowing them to organize their social lives just as they organize their work routines. This could be an indirect jab at George Gershwin, who relied heavily on Katharine for advice about fashion and etiquette ("How are we to know what clothes to wear?"). Or perhaps Warburg is suggesting that the workers merely pretend to emulate the upper class, putting on a show to please their employers while inwardly scoffing at such pretentious behavior. While James Warburg was raised in such style, he did have an irreverent streak.

"Etiquette" underscores this highbrow elegance in several ways. Both lyrics and music evoke Gilbert and Sullivan operettas, loftier productions than Broadway musicals that often featured satirical social commentary. In the 1920s, the Gershwins had evoked the Gilbert and Sullivan style occasionally in their shows, such as *Lady, Be Good!* ("End of a String") and *Oh, Kay!* ("The Moon Is on the Sea"). Edward Jablonski identifies several numbers in *Strike Up the Band* ("Fletcher's American Cheese Choral Society," "Typical Self-Made American," "The Unofficial Spokesman," and "Patriotic Rally") that are "patent tributes to Gilbert and Sullivan." Swift's music mimics this style in her use of men's and women's choral responses on the final phrases, a quasi-patter in the men's part, and the intertwining of two

4.2 "Etiquette," measures 76–84

melodies in counterpoint. She becomes the composer-as-engineer as she provides the score for this machine-shop musical (ex. 4.2). Although *Fine and Dandy* may be set in a working-class milieu and much of the music is patterned after songs from Tin Pan Alley, elements in both the plot and the score reveal their elite sources.[28]

"Etiquette" also suggests issues of gender and ethnicity. The women ask to be told who is important, so they will know "at whom to smile." Their role is both passive, as they wait for the pertinent information, and reactive, as they stage their behavior accordingly. The smile is the behavior expected from young women by "famous faces." Ethnic attitudes are touched as Joe addresses the workers first as "Murphys and O'Gradys," and in a second verse as "Blums and Blaus and Blitzes / Steins and Lipkowitzes." The implication is that most of the factory workers are Irish, German, or Russian. After his crash course in etiquette, Joe promises, "You shall all be Vans and Macs and Fitzes!" suggesting that those of Dutch and Scottish descent have fared better economically and socially. Also appearing at the company picnic are the four Giersdorf Brothers, comic acrobats who perform their routine to a reprise of "Fine and Dandy." A short dialogue maintains that each brother is the son of a different mother, since each is of a different ethnicity —one German, one Austrian, one Italian, and one Irish—and each speaks with an exaggerated accent. The implications about the family make-up of immigrants, in general, and show-business immigrants, in particular, drive the humor in this scene.[29]

After their performance, a small band of "wandering musicians" is announced that includes Joe Cook on saxophone, his straight man, Dave Chasen, on triangle, and a full-size steam shovel. Chasen's inability to remember his part has inspired the mechanized prompt. The synopsis of *Fine and Dandy* written by Kay Swift describes "Joe Cook's mad steam shovel," an elaborate machine that set in motion a chain reaction of complex steps to accomplish a rather simple task:

> This zany contraption . . . set the mood and tempo of the entire
> production. . . . The machine was an enormous affair, painted
> watermelon pink, and it took up the complete width of the stage.
> It worked in sections . . . starting at the right end with Joe. He sat
> in the cab, high up, and pulled the levers that presumably touched
> off each operation of the thing. . . . Each sequence moved majesti-
> cally along . . . building up to the payoff—which was the dumping
> of a load of bricks on the head of Dave Chasen, Joe's straight
> man. Dave sat, dead-panned and holding a little triangle in his
> hand; every time the bricks landed he hit the triangle twice—ping,
> *ping.* The roar that went up from audiences every night during
> the long run of the show was something you could never forget.[30]

Joe's shovel mirrored the elaborate contraptions seen in the contemporaneous cartoons of Rube Goldberg. Goldberg's machines were funny because they were "overdesigned" and "wasteful," clearly not in keeping with the modern mantra of efficiency. Both Goldberg's machines and Joe's steam shovel can be seen as metaphors for the bureaucracy of big business and big government. Neither conserved energy, effort, or money.[31]

During the course of the play, Nancy develops more independence than some of the other female characters. Disgusted by Joe's flirtations with Mrs. Fordyce, she sings the torch song "Nobody Breaks My Heart." The opening lyric is frank and tough. "I've been just a plaything of passion, / Men have loved me after a fashion, / But no one, no one, nobody breaks my heart." The lyrics in the bridge become more graphic, suggesting a masochistic desire: "I'd like to be bruised, / Beaten down and badly used; / I could be a slave, If they behave like cave men." The subsequent verse continues, "I don't care for dainty romances, / I want rough stuff. I'll take my chances." The lyric bears a striking resemblance to that in the Gershwins' "Treat Me Rough" from *Girl Crazy,* the other hit show from 1930, which opened on Broadway just weeks after *Fine and Dandy.* Obviously, Swift and Gershwin would have been familiar with each other's current songs. And there is a distinct similarity between the two. "Treat Me Rough" is sung by a young New York playboy who hopes to prove his manhood by withstanding the mild manhandling of a western cowgirl. "Nobody Breaks My Heart" is sung by a lusty female who harbors surprising sexual fantasies. The graphic scenario described in the lyrics might be considered domestic violence by today's standards. In 1930, however, many women were willing to play the subservient roles that may have been expected of them in order to win and keep a man. On the other hand, contemporary audiences might celebrate this brassy female's obvious enjoyment of unconventional sex. The strength of Paul James's lyric is in the mental victory that results. "No one, no one, nobody breaks my heart." In spite of physical pleasure and/or abuse, this woman will not surrender her emotions. Unapologetic and callous, this captures the same spirit of resistance that an African American spiritual implies, and certainly echoes the sentiments of many of the black blues singers of the decade. It is an expression of female independence that Bessie Smith would have been proud to sing.[32]

"Nobody Breaks My Heart" is one of Swift's most effective musical settings. In standard form, the song is sprinkled with notes from the African-American blues scale (lowered third, sixth, and seventh scale degrees) and blues harmonies. The syncopated melody is complemented by a steady quarter-note accompaniment that mimics a string bass (ex. 4.3). Its bump-and-grind connotations match the brazen lyrics perfectly. A final line must not go unnoticed: "Yes-men, press-men, lawyers and bankers / Don't give me that for which my soul hankers." It is poignant to imagine Paul James penning these words.

As the play draws to an end, the stage is set for a large wedding, a predictable ending to this convoluted spoof. "Wedding Bells" is sung as two couples—Marabelle and Edgar and Mrs. Fordyce and Joe—prepare to

4.3 "Nobody Breaks My Heart," measures 1–8

marry. Like "Etiquette," this is a contrapuntal song, with the ushers singing one part and the bridesmaids the countermelody. At the last minute, however, the plot twists in several unexpected ways. Marabelle admits that she loves George, not Edgar, and cannot go through with the wedding. In another surprise move, concerned shareholders take action and offer Joe a large sum of money as a gift in honor of his upcoming wedding to Mrs. Fordyce, under the condition that he resign his position and promise never to associate with Fordyce Drop Forge and Tool Company again. This means that Joe can cover Mr. Ellis's loss and escape his job with no financial worries. He has lost the social status that would have permitted him to marry Mrs. Fordyce and instead has the freedom to pursue his dream girl, Nancy. Edgar then approaches Mrs. Fordyce and confesses that he has secretly loved her all along. Mrs. Fordyce agrees to marry Edgar, since she has already engaged Sardi's to do the catering—a rationale that assures the audience that she will not let herself become emotionally involved.

The fairy-tale ending eludes the two who have been flirting since act 1, Joe and Nancy. Although he is free from Mrs. Fordyce, Joe remembers: "I can't marry you! . . . I'm already married and I have four kids." This of course did not prevent him from courting two desirable ladies. Only after regaining Nancy's favor does he admit that he is not an eligible bachelor. The moral slip is soon forgiven, however, and the entire cast forgets their troubles with a rousing reprise of "Fine and Dandy."[33]

The play reveals society's expectations for men and women in 1930. Long-term employment with a company is desirable, and advancement is assured if the rules are followed. One can succeed socially and corporately by working hard, graduating from night school, acquiring a college degree, playing the stock market, flattering the boss, and learning the appropriate leisure activities, including bridge and golf. Conforming to mainstream expectations will further one's career—and the marital indiscretions of husbands will be excused.

The early-twentieth-century efficiency movement sheds light on these values. "Efficiency" not only involves scientific management, or maximum results with minimum effort, but also implies moral qualities, such as "character, competence, energy, hard work and success." Fordyce Drop Forge and Tool Company's upper management is most interested in maintaining those values among its workers, although Mr. Ellis has himself fallen off the wagon with his financial missteps. Joe Squibb, by contrast, cares little for these high ideals. He defies the rules as he drinks, smokes, gambles, and overspends at the company's expense. His naive strategies, designed to please the employees, decrease production by 70 percent and nearly bankrupt the company. And his mechanical affinities reflect the complexities of the overdesigned steam shovel. He is, in short, the antithesis of efficiency. Yet his smooth talk carries him to the top of the company and then out the door unscathed. Ultimately, personality has won over character. The audience discovers that the hero is immature and irresponsible but easily forgive his indiscretions because his nonsensical "business" is so entertaining.[34]

On the surface, life for Kay Swift in 1930 appeared "fine and dandy." She and her husband had three beautiful daughters, and their Broadway offerings had met with success, signaling a bright future in the theater for them. Yet Swift's attraction to George Gershwin was romantic as well as professional. Her liaison with Gershwin would ultimately destroy her marriage and her relationship with her children. Because of her love for Gershwin, Swift would concentrate her musical talents in aid of Gershwin's projects rather than create her own. In some ways she resembled the women of *Fine and Dandy*, who perceived their worth through the success of their husbands; and success in 1930 was charted by a man's wealth, company position, and adherence to a social standard set by an elite few. As the composer of *Fine and Dandy*, Kay Swift had no significant part in shaping the musical's plot, whose script and lyrics were written by men of influence; yet she was very much a part of that society.

Swift's status as a woman in the world of musical theater makes her unique. She deserves credit for pursuing her musical interests and writing for the theater at a time when she could have been content to stay home and entertain celebrities. Her music fits squarely into the context of Broadway show music in that era yet is imaginative enough to warrant recognition. Her publications earned her membership in the American Society of Composers, Authors and Publishers in 1931, which required five songs published by an ASCAP member and sponsorship by two other members. By becoming a member, Swift was joining the likes of Irving Berlin, Jerome Kern, Richard Rodgers, and George Gershwin and taking another step toward music as a profession. But in 1930 even women with talent and ambition were expected to find their fulfillment through men, and Kay Swift was very much a woman of the times.[35]

CHAPTER 5

Stagestruck: The Ballet to Radio City

At a time when most of the country was struggling to survive, here were people who had the means and time to poke fun.—Washington Post

In 1930, Kay Swift and Paul James were poised for further success on Broadway. They had written several successful Broadway songs and the engaging score for *Fine and Dandy*. Suddenly, however, the Swift-James collaboration collapsed and Swift's compositional activity ceased. Swift appears to have written nothing for four years, between *Fine and Dandy* and her next major piece in 1934. This silence had several likely causes. First, during the Depression, the number of new musicals mounted on Broadway declined sharply. Unknown shows represented great financial risk for promoters, and by the 1933–34 season, fewer than twenty new musicals appeared. In addition, James Warburg would have had little time or energy for writing song lyrics during these years. After the death of his father in January 1932, he spent six months in Washington, D.C., in 1933 so that he could serve as an adviser to President Franklin Roosevelt. He testified before Senate committees, spoke at economic meetings, and wrote letters of influence to congressmen supporting the gold standard. When Roosevelt made the decision to devalue the dollar, Warburg published two books in 1934 about the financial crisis,

The Money Muddle and *The Monetary Problem;* additional critical volumes followed in 1935 and 1936. He was helping to find a solution to the international financial crisis, as well as attempting to stabilize M. M. Warburg and Company, the family's banking business in Hamburg, which was further threatened by Hitler's edicts against Jewish banks. James Warburg was spending great lengths of time in Europe when his marriage most needed his presence. He had little time for collaborating with his wife on or off Broadway.[1]

During these same years, 1930 to 1934, George Gershwin was busy producing a string of Broadway shows, including *Strike Up the Band* (1930), *Girl Crazy* (1930), the Pulitzer Prize–winning *Of Thee I Sing* (1931), *Pardon My English* (1933), and *Let 'Em Eat Cake* (1933), writing the film score for *Delicious* (1931), and publishing eighteen transcriptions of his popular songs in the *Song Book* (1932). In the same years he was composing concert works that included the *Second Rhapsody* for orchestra with piano (1932), the *Cuban Overture* for orchestra (1932), Variations on "I Got Rhythm" for piano and orchestra (1934), and the opera *Porgy and Bess* (1935). If Swift was indeed Gershwin's musical confidante and assistant, then she, too, was immersed in the production and the performances of these compositions.

It would seem that Kay Swift was neglecting her own career at a crucial time in order to support that of the most important man in her life. Reporter Verna Arvey, the wife of composer William Grant Still, wrote of Swift's dedication to Gershwin: "Despite her own very special accomplishments, Kay Swift has the ability and the inclination to subordinate herself to someone else, provided she feels that person is eminently worthy." Swift had written a successful Broadway show, but instead of capitalizing on its success and writing more music, she chose to help Gershwin behind the scenes. She seemed to have understood her role as one of support for George Gershwin and was comfortable with that responsibility. Undoubtedly she also felt she was gaining enough both personally and professionally, as she closely listened to and studied Gershwin's innovative compositions and absorbed his style.[2]

Kay Swift's musical hiatus lasted four years. In 1934, the cofounders of the American Ballet of New York commissioned her to write a score for its premiere performance. *Alma Mater* was the first ballet that the Russian émigré George Balanchine would choreograph after he arrived in the United States. Balanchine and Edward Warburg (James's cousin and another of Felix's sons) had founded the dance company and had originally invited Gershwin to compose this score. It was Gershwin's own heavy schedule that prompted Swift's involvement. With his refusal, Gershwin suggested that Swift write the music. Edward Warburg had not only admired Swift's music but appreciated her special qualities. "Where most Warburg women spent most of their time planning menus, organizing the servants, and shopping for gifts, Kay was both gay and brilliant."[3]

The attraction of Swift to Gershwin ultimately became too great to deny. In 1934 she and Warburg agreed to separate, acknowledging that their diverging interests had destroyed their marriage. Warburg had become increasingly disturbed by the attention Kay's affair with such a charismatic public figure as Gershwin aroused and was concerned about the effects on the children their empty marriage was having. Torn by her emotions, Swift had sought advice from the Russian-born psychiatrist Dr. Gregory Zilboorg, who had established a practice in New York analyzing well-to-do clients and treated James Warburg and later Gershwin as well. He proved to be no help to any of them and, moreover, was extremely unethical. Not only did Zilboorg discuss Gershwin's sessions with Swift, but during the last eight months of her eighteen-month treatment, he had sexual intercourse with her. In Joan Peyser's biography of Gershwin, her granddaughter emphasized that "this was not a romantic liaison; the sex took place during the sessions at the patient's expense." Such circumstances may have obscured Swift's ability to make wise choices at this stage in her life, but she proceeded with the divorce.[4]

In 1987 Swift spoke about her decision to Joan Peyser: "I had a happy career, was fond of my husband, had three children. Everything seemed all right. But I didn't like being in love with somebody else while I was married." Late in 1934, she traveled to Reno, Nevada, for "the well-known treatment" —to fulfill the six-weeks' residency required to file for divorce. The breakup was hardly discreet: Swift's arrival in Reno was reported in the *New York Times*. The timing of this trip indicates the high level of distress that she and Warburg were experiencing. By leaving the East Coast in November, she missed the gala opening of *Alma Mater* in Hartford, Connecticut— her first premiere in four years.[5]

Alma Mater

Alma Mater was an excellent opportunity for Swift. The public knew her successful Broadway songs, but this ballet allowed her to demonstrate her musical versatility. As Balanchine's first American ballet, this was a piece of immense importance. Edward Warburg had written the book for the twenty-minute piece, which typified a segment of America by satirizing the annual Yale-Harvard football game, a "ludicrous parody of the world dearest to Ivy Leaguers." John Held, Jr., a cartoonist whose drawings helped define the 1920s, designed the costumes, featuring raccoon coats, flapper chemises, and cheerleading sweaters. Swift's music captured the satire with jazz rhythms and harmonies juxtaposed with more traditional harmonies and dance forms. Several early-twentieth-century trends in contemporary classical music are evident in *Alma Mater*. Swift stretches key areas and explores chromaticism and nonfunctional harmonies while maintaining the rhythmic character of the dance movements. Some sections use parallel harmonies associated with Debussy and jagged melodies of Stravinsky and other early modernists, while others draw heavily on jazz. However, *Alma Mater* is clearly grounded in Broadway harmonies and attitudes. The piece was scored for full orchestra by a young Morton Gould, whom George Gershwin had also recommended. Gould idolized Gershwin and was forever grateful for this opportunity.[6]

Alma Mater relates the rise and fall of the football Hero in a series of dance movements. Swift's extensive notes describe the ballet as it unfolds. They reveal her thoughts behind the composition as well as memories of the premiere performance. The "Opening" portrays a football game between Harvard and Yale in progress on stage. A long, loud referee's whistle begins the piece, which is marked by the bass drums and cymbals of a marching band and the "Rah! Rah!" of the crowd. Swift uses familiar college tunes throughout the work, including a stately version of Yale's "Boola-Boola" by the trumpets and trombones in the opening movement (ex. 5.1).

The second scene, "Bicycle," is scored for strings, piano, and celeste, with light percussion. It serves as background music as a young undergraduate invites his girlfriend to ride a bicycle built for two. The third selection "shows a crowd of adoring fans awaiting the entrance of the hero. . . .

5.1 *Alma Mater*, "Opening," measures 50–55

Harp arpeggios show their idolization of this stuffed-shirt character, pompous and dressed in the [Yale] football uniform of the 30's." "Snake Dance" suggests an unruly victory dance and the tearing down of the goalposts, with fragments of "Hail, Hail, the Gang's All Here" intertwined. This lighthearted theme is interrupted by "The Villain," dressed in a coonskin coat, with a blue "Y" feather in his hat. He is angry and jealous of the Hero (ex. 5.2). After a "grumbling fugue" for strings, he mopes about what he considers his unfair treatment by everyone; then he begins his "Angry Dance," accompanied by piano, percussion, and string bass. In contrast to this severe theme is the "Big Waltz" danced by the Hero and his adoring bride-to-be, which closes the first half.[7]

In the second half, the Hero's romance progresses with the "Bride's Dream," the "Pride Theme," and the "Wedding Procession," which are scored for full orchestra. In the dream, the hero and heroine, now married, raise a family of eleven ill-behaved children. The romance is interrupted by the "Offbeat Waltz," which portrays rowdy, "brattish" children, each wearing a nightgown emblazoned with a Yale insignia. Goaded by the Villain, they tussle with the hero and knock him down. He fakes his own death, and in the "Funeral Procession," he is carried out to a doleful march played by brooding strings. The next sequence, "Morning," features the janitor with a broom sweeping up the house to a "polka-type dance." Its dissonant harmonies, jagged melody, sudden changes in range, and animated dance rhythms offer a sharp contrast in mood and musical style. Swift describes the next scene, "Nightmare," the campus's reaction to their Hero's "death." "It somehow seems to the composer a bit like a universal nightmare; however, it turns out well, with 'London Bridge Is Falling Down' being heard,

5.2 *Alma Mater,* "The Villain," measures 8–18

and the Hero coming in again making a sour grimace at the children, showing he's all right." "Comic Strip" features the whole cast "dancing behind
a large colorful comic strip" so that everyone's identity is obscured. In the

end, when the Villain shows his face from behind the newspaper, he is accosted by the angry mob. Disaster is averted when "Salvation Army Sal" arrives in full uniform to rescue the Villain and calm the crowds. For this, Swift fashions "What a Friend We Have in Jesus" into a syncopated hymn-style tune. "After a hymn (on organ, sounding like a street-corner job) Salvation Sal removes her skirt and goes into a rumba-Charleston dance in which all join for the finale." Swift's sense of satire is displayed by her parodies of familiar college tunes, her placement of dissonance, and her creative use of musical styles (such as the hymn-to-rumba combination and the complex fugue section illustrating the low-life Villain). Her humor is enhanced by Gould's orchestration. He juxtaposes elite instruments and styles with incongruous characters (for example, the harp with the football Hero), underscoring her imagination and wit.[8]

The opening night of *Alma Mater,* as of most premieres, was as much a social as an artistic event, especially since this was the first public performance of the American Ballet of New York. Patrons at the sold-out house in Hartford included Nelson Rockefeller's wife, Katharine Hepburn, Archibald MacLeish and his wife, and Salvador Dalí and his wife. Nicholas Fox Weber has recounted the evening of December 6, 1934 in his book, *Patron Saints.* For New Yorkers, the night began with a train ride to Hartford on the "Ballet Special." Aboard the charter a prestigious theater crowd was treated to a buffet supper. According to Lucius Beebe of the *New York Herald,* Gershwin himself "broke out a hamper of chilled champagne." It was a glorious party that Kay Swift would have loved. That she chose to be in Reno rather than in attendance as a guest of honor signifies the urgent need she felt for the divorce. A phone call from Gershwin after the evening had ended, assuring her of *Alma Mater*'s success, was some consolation.[9]

Alma Mater was written during the Depression. Weber observes that although some art of this period served as social protest, other art offered an escape from the decade's troubles. With its wit and satirical attitude, *Alma Mater* clearly fell into the latter category. Its book and music were written by New York insiders who could mock their own elite society—"the ultimate carryings-on of the smart set." After three performances in Hartford, the ballet played on Broadway at the Adelphi Theatre in New York, at the Lewisohn Stadium, and at Robin Hood Dell. Even people who could not attend the performances were captivated by descriptions of the ballet. *Time* reported, "Girls appear in short leopard-skin jackets, decorated with chrysanthemums and blue satin ribbons, while Kay Swift's music blends bits of 'Boola-Boola' with offstage cheers." The *Washington Post* heralded Swift's "'lively music' in which the composer had 'managed to thumb a nose and stick out a tongue at every sacred college melody.' . . . 'Irreverence is the middle name of the entire production.'" As noted, Kay Swift's involvement with this production came at a crucial point for her, after a four-year drought and just before her divorce from James Warburg. Despite their wealth, the Warburgs were not impervious to the Depression. While their International Acceptance Bank had minimized its losses, the family bank in Hamburg, M. M. Warburg, was experiencing serious financial difficulty. And Swift's looming status as a single woman may have been the source of some anxiety. *Alma Mater* was a declaration of independence, demonstrating that Swift had talent and marketable skills as well as continued standing in New York's elite social circles. It embodied the rebellious spirit of the twenties, as well as a refusal to be beaten by the despair of the thirties. Most important, *Alma Mater* represents Swift's determination to succeed as an independent woman.[10]

Porgy and Bess

After *Alma Mater,* Kay Swift's interests returned to the work of George Gershwin, who had begun writing his opera, *Porgy and Bess.* The work was based on a novel by DuBose Heyward about life among the Gullahs of rural South Carolina. Gershwin had read Heyward's novel, *Porgy,* in 1926 and was instantly intrigued by its operatic possibilities. Yet although Heyward was interested in Gershwin's proposal to base an opera on the novel, he was first committed to the stage version that his wife, Dorothy, was creating. Gershwin took Swift to see *Porgy* when it opened at the Theatre Guild in 1927. She recalled in her memoirs, "The play was impressive and moving. The title role was played by Paul Robeson, who brought sensitivity and power to it. . . . George knew, at this time, that a day would come when he could settle down to a year or two of steady work on the opera he'd planned, without being obliged to devote time to Broadway shows, and he felt excited and stimulated by the stirring play the Heywards had created. . . . I felt that this production put the final seal on George's intense desire to start work as soon as possible." Because of prior commitments, however, Gershwin had to postpone work on the project. He and Heyward did not begin collaborating until November 1932, and it would be three more years before he would realize this dream.[11]

George worked seriously on the project, although the Depression made it necessary for him to pursue other activities, such as a tour to celebrate the tenth anniversary of *Rhapsody in Blue,* and his radio show, "Music by Gershwin," in 1934. Gershwin did not actually begin composing *Porgy and Bess* until February 1934. That summer he joined the Heywards in June and July on Folly Island, South Carolina, near Charleston. Here he was surrounded by Gullah culture. Years later, Swift recalled how vital this time in Folly Island was as Gershwin prepared his score:

> A visit paid to Charleston and to the sea islands, where the scene
> of the opera was laid, familiarized George so completely with the
> spirit and musical idiom of the natives that he expressed to perfec-
> tion their characteristics. I, myself, had the unforgettable experience
> of going, with a friend who, like me, was steeped in the atmosphere
> of 'Porgy and Bess,' to Charleston at a later date. We visited the
> Heywards on Folly Island and also insisted on attending a midnight
> service at the Macedonia church one night, where the parishioners
> trooped, barefooted, to the platform where the minister stood,
> singing ad-libbed prayers to music not unlike, in mood, those heard
> in the score of the opera.

This church service would have been similar to one George attended in the summer of 1934 that moved him to join the congregation and begin "shouting" himself. He experienced the emotional intensity of the music and the worship, and was able to capture the effect for his opera.[12]

Porgy and Bess would feature an African-American cast and music that borrowed harmonies, rhythms, and melodies from African-American genres of blues and jazz as well as native Gullah music. It was an innovative project that required much research and feedback. Swift talked to reporter Jean Sharley in 1959 about being a "sounding board" during its composition. "He'd call me and tell me to rush over to play the orchestra part of a song. He couldn't sing. Neither could Ira. But we'd all sing Ira's or DuBose Heyward's lyrics, sounding like a chorus of crows." Swift later described the "unforgettable experience" of being in close touch with Gershwin while he composed and later orchestrated *Porgy and Bess*. "Each day, as the work grew, a few of us—Bill Daly, his close friend and favorite conductor, and myself, Ira, of course, and DuBose Heyward, who wrote the libretto as well as some of the lyrics, were probably present much of the time. It was thrilling to hear the themes develop, the recitatives build into such an inevitable part of the score that they flowed as naturally as spoken words would. The whole sparkled with a fantastic quality of imagination."[13]

As the show went into rehearsal, Swift attended nearly every rehearsal and was present at many of the casting decisions. She also had an even more direct part in the opera's development. In addition to listening, singing, and playing the work in progress, Swift sometimes notated portions of pieces for Gershwin, evidently to expedite his later work on the compositions. He believed that she wrote faster and more neatly than he could. Several items in the Gershwin Collection at the Library of Congress include sections that feature the handwriting of another person. In a sketch of "I Got Plenty o' Nuttin'," the first sixteen measures of the melody are notated in Kay Swift's hand, followed by Gershwin's own notation, which completes the tune. A more extensive example is featured in the leather-bound pencil copy of the piano score of *Porgy and Bess*. At the end of act 1, scene 1, the "Crown-Robbins fight fugue" is written out twice. One version is entirely in Gershwin's hand. It includes only the instrumental fugue in piano reduction and a few sketches of voice parts above the first few measures. The other, which is actually placed first in the bound volume, includes this piano reduction of the fugue carefully copied in ink (the only ink copy in the bound score). The staves above it were left blank, where Gershwin apparently later worked out and added the vocal lines. This inked accompaniment, in what also appears to be Kay Swift's hand, encompasses seventy-two measures and seventeen pages of the score. These documents illustrate her role as an assistant to the composer and signify the trust he must have placed in her and her notational and musical abilities.[14]

The opera rehearsed and opened in Boston a month before its scheduled

New York run. The director, Rouben Mamoulian, felt that the show, four hours in its Carnegie Hall preview, must be shortened. Gershwin, Mamoulian, composer Alexander Steinert, and Kay Swift walked the Boston Common in the early hours of the morning deciding which portions to cut. Again, Swift occupied a central advisory position, sharing her musical expertise and dramatic judgment. The streamlined *Porgy and Bess* opened at the Alvin Theatre in New York on October 10, 1935, and at the premiere Swift was seated between George and Ira. After the show, she and several friends hosted an elegant party for 430 people at Condé Nast's Park Avenue apartment. Condé Nast, publisher of *Vogue* and later of *Vanity Fair* and *House Beautiful,* had an "exquisite, 30-room penthouse on Park Avenue." (Access to Nast's apartment for the party may have been influenced by the fact that his daughter, Natica, was married to Gerald Warburg. As noted earlier, Gerald was fond of Kay.) According to *Time,* "the star of a Broadway opening was as thrilled by an after-theatre party at Condé Nast's as she was by the first-night applause." The *Porgy and Bess* party was financed by ten men, including Jules Glaenzer, Marshall Field, Averell Harriman, and Bill Paley, president of the Columbia Broadcasting System since 1928 and a strong supporter of musical events in New York. Swift recounted, "I remember taking whole days making lists, sending telegrams, and there was almost nothing but acceptances. We hired a Spanish orchestra [as well as Paul Whiteman's orchestra]. All the men were in white tie and tails. It was the dress-up era. . . . [It] was not until seven [in the morning] that we all got to bed." Before the evening ended, Gershwin was presented with a silver tray engraved with facsimile signatures of many of his close friends and supporters. Swift had telegrammed one hundred of them, soliciting signatures and a donation of seven dollars and fifty cents each for the tray. Swift had transferred her hostessing skills from the Warburg household to the Gershwin cause, and she helped him perfect his social graces. Swift played all the roles for Gershwin that a wife would have played, apparently hoping for the final commitment that never came.[15]

The *Porgy and Bess* party represented a major effort by Swift that was complicated by her schedule. As part of the promotion for what Gershwin referred to as his "folk opera," Swift would be traveling and delivering lectures on *Porgy and Bess.* The first post-opening talk took her to the Art

Institute in Philadelphia the day after the opening, and Swift had to catch a train for that city at 11:00 A.M.—four hours after the party had ended. Ira recalled that she had memorized the entire 559-page score and would be illustrating songs from it at the piano. Yet despite *Porgy and Bess*'s extensive promotion and enthusiastic audiences, critics did not react favorably to a work that combined an elite musical form, opera, with the harmonies and rhythms of jazz and blues. Folk opera did not fit into an established category, and they were not convinced of the form's validity. In an article for the Sunday *New York Times*, Gershwin attempted to explain his hybrid form and to validate the use of accessible songs in an operatic context. To his great disappointment, he failed to convince the critics, and *Porgy and Bess* closed after 124 performances. In a Broadway season that spawned only twelve new productions, this in itself was a considerable achievement. The only musical to endure longer than seven months was *On Your Toes*, with music by Rodgers and Hart, which enjoyed a ten-month run. Besides, Gershwin's composition was not a musical but a folk opera. When compared to other contemporaneous operas, the production's success is even clearer. Gershwin, however, had been hoping for an unequivocal hit, not a financial failure.[16]

Radio City Music Hall

In early 1935, after the excitement of *Alma Mater*, Kay Swift was single and seeking employment at the height of the Depression. Although she had married into a wealthy family and might have spent all her time assisting Gershwin on *Porgy and Bess*, neither her divorce settlement nor her ambition would allow her to remain idle. Fortunately, Swift was hired quickly to do exactly what she wanted to do—write music—in what might be considered one of the most glamorous jobs in New York City. Radio City Music Hall, "Showplace of the Nation," had opened on December 27, 1932, and featured "a magnitude and splendor heretofore undreamed of in the theater," according to its designer and first director of production, S. L. "Roxy" Rothafel. Signifying the modernity of his venture, Roxy designed this palace in the art deco style. He created a theater on a monstrous scale featuring a grand foyer, stage, and seating capacity for 6,200, the largest in America. (The staff referred to it as "The Howl.") John D. Rockefeller, Jr., had financed the project, "demonstrating his faith in the American future by opening this first of a number of new buildings in the sprawling Radio City complex."

Motion pictures made in the 1920s had featured lavish sets and costumes and depicted gracious living. Movie theaters, too, were lavish structures, often decorated as elaborate castles, to offer patrons a more tangible escape into a world of glamour. Radio City took the movie theater to another level in size, architecture, and class. Although the opening night had featured a lengthy variety show, the management recognized the growing popularity of motion pictures and settled on a performance format of a first-run motion picture in addition to a fifty-minute stage show, which featured the Radio City Ballet Corps as well as the thirty-six Roxyettes (later the Rockettes) in their famous kick-line. The show also included an overture played on the Wurlitzer theater organ and a presentation by the Music Hall Symphony Orchestra, which rose on an elevated platform from the pit to stage level. These extravaganzas played four and sometimes five times a day, fifty-two weeks a year.[17]

Swift was hired early in 1935 to write songs for the Rockettes' routines. The contract guaranteed Swift two of her greatest wishes, "a chance to write a lot of music, and to hear it played every chance I can." Years later, in 1943, she reminisced about the experience with Margaret McBride on New York radio station WEAF. Swift downplayed her talents, saying, "I wrote a song a week for eighteen months. It didn't have to be a good song, just a song." But Radio City Music Hall was no ordinary theater; it was a grand showplace. And it had a reputation to uphold, so music of a high caliber was expected. Under the music direction of Erno Rapée were three associate conductors, Charles Previn, Joseph Littau, and Macklin Marrow, and three staff organists. In addition to the orchestra and organists were a men's chorus and a mixed choir. Swift was one of five composers and arrangers on the staff, including Ferde Grofé and Earle Moss. Alfred Stern, who in later years became a producer, had been hired as assistant to costume designer Vincent Minelli and producer John Murray Anderson. (Anderson was soon replaced by Leon Leonidoff.) Stern helped to design the sets and would see Swift at weekly production meetings. He admired her work with her new lyricist, Al Stillman. (Originally Al Silverman, he, too, had changed his name at George Gershwin's suggestion.) Swift and Stillman became

close friends and effective collaborators. Swift recalled, "Al proved the easiest imaginable person to work with, for he was brilliantly talented, flexible
and so quick to pick up an idea that one hardly had to finish a sentence."
They shared a small office on the fifth floor with an upright piano, a desk,
and two chairs. In the office next to them were two male singers that they
befriended. Swift and Stillman were always happy when either sang one of
their songs, for the two were fine singers destined to become celebrities at
the Metropolitan Opera House—tenor Jan Peerce and baritone Robert
Weede. Peerce's sixty-year career included stage performances, recordings,
and radio and television appearances. Weede also sang with the San Francisco
Opera and appeared in many Broadway shows, carrying the starring role
in Frank Loesser's *Most Happy Fella* (1956).[18]

Swift prepared this brief biographical blurb for the corporation's publicity:

Composes songs while you wait—a sort of Dorothy Parker at the
piano. Wise-cracking, social and regular. Divorced wife of James P.
Warburg, the banker. Wrote the music for some of the American
Ballet's numbers last winter. Started out by writing the song that
sent Libby Holman soaring to fame, "Can't We Be Friends," and
also did Joe Cook's show, "Fine and Dandy." On short order, she'll
write you a song about anything from Grasshoppers to Galoshes.
Has an apartment on East 52nd Street, with zebra skins all over the
place. Writes stories as well as songs, and has had a number of
things published. Father was a music critic and took her to all the
concerts. She'd sit and watch the serious recitals and funny things
always kept popping into her head. Thought she should do something about it, so she began fiddling around at the piano keyboard,
her long legs dangling from the piano bench. Friend of George
Gershwin, Cole Porter and such. Never still a minute—always has
something doing—works for eighteen hours at a stretch, then gets
all dressed up, goes out someplace to dance to her own music.[19]

This self-description offers us a glimpse of Swift's personality, revealing
her high energy level, irreverent sense of humor, and exotic decorating
tastes. She was gregarious and confident in her musical abilities and in her

social skills. Alfred Stern remembered her at Radio City as a single mother who had an apartment on Eighty-sixth Street, near the East River, and a maid. "Kay Swift was very social, very chic, very funny. She had a marvelous leopard-skin coat. She was the kind of lady who would be in *Vogue* or *Vanity Fair*." A talented writer, she was also generating scripts for radio shows for both CBS and NBC—the first time her literary skills were used professionally. She produced shows and wrote copy for all varieties of music, including André Kostelanetz's program and "other more serious music."[20]

Although Swift's sketch suggests a degree of confidence and independence, it also reveals a sense of insecurity. She apparently believed it advantageous to mention that she was divorced from "James P. Warburg, the banker," as well as to advertise her friendships with Gershwin and Porter—relationships that would identify her social and musical positions. Further confusion about her priorities and her roles must have arisen, since this position at Radio City created a serious conflict with her family. Although the job gave her career a boost, the work schedule and the level of professional commitment it required left Swift little time for her daughters. After the divorce, April was attending Miss Madeira's School in Washington, D.C., and had decided to live with her father on vacation breaks. The plan had been for the two younger girls to live with their mother in New York during the school year and spend summers with their father at Bydale. James Warburg remarried within three months of the divorce, however, making his the more regular schedule and home life. Swift recognized that "her work in the theater made it difficult for her to spend evenings at home and that the two girls were being left too much alone." For this reason, they went to live with their father and his new wife, the former Phyllis Baldwin. April and Phyllis did not get along, but Andrea and Kay embraced their stepmother. For the next twelve years Phyllis Warburg created a stable and happy home life for them. The Radio City contract was thus a mixed blessing for Kay Swift. Although it gave her the freedom of a single professional woman working in a position that she loved, the loss of custody and daily contact with her children undoubtedly compounded the guilt she must have felt in divorcing Warburg. She had made herself available for a commitment from George Gershwin, yet he remained elusive.[21]

Music that Swift and Stillman wrote in 1935 and 1936 has been found in the Radio City Music Hall's archives. Nearly thirty songs are extant. Generally they are typical Broadway show-stoppers, with interludes for dances by the Rockettes or the Ballet troupe. Many are highly rhythmic and syncopated, and the lyrics are witty while remaining acceptable family fare, one of the Music Hall's requirements. ("Little Church Around the Corner," with a more conservative theme, was danced by the Ballet troupe.) Some of Swift's numbers include "Blond or Brunette," "Coney by the Sea," "Graduating Gibson Girls," "Physical Culture," and "Professor, How Could You?" These titles and others easily suggest choreography for a bevy of beautiful dancers. The Rockettes moved in a synchronized chorus line, uniformly clad in imaginative costumes that usually revealed lots of leg and facilitated their famous "eye-high" kicks.[22]

Less typical is a number whose theme was suggested by Leon Leonidoff, the producer of the stage shows. "We have an old cat head fifteen feet high in the basement and out of it the Rockettes should stroll." The Swift-Stillman response to his challenge was the novelty song, "I'm All Washed Up on Love." Stillman's lyric is not a typical love lament. Presented from the point of view of a mother cat that has just delivered a new litter, it is a humorous rejection of further advances by "Tom, Tom, Thomas Cat." Typical of many stage works of the day that cited current events, one of the verses refers to the birth of the Dionne quintuplets. The Dionnes had been born in June 1934 in Ontario and had quickly become world news. Mother Cat sees no reason to make such a fuss over five babies, when she routinely delivers six or more.[23]

The song illustrates Swift's tendency to incorporate large skips into her melodic writing, resulting in a disjunct and expressive melody (ex. 5.3). These wide leaps in the melody underscore the mother cat's agitation. Accompanying seventh-chord harmonies and added sixth chords soften the effect of these skips. Although the song remains in the key of F major, the chromatic harmonies are very active.

Swift and Stillman were always delighted when the theme of the weekly show did not require a routine romantic ballad. One of their most popular songs for the Radio City stage, published in 1935, was "Sawing a Woman in Half." It was a tribute to the popularity of magic shows, reflecting how this favorite trick had become a parlor game.

When you talk of love's young dream, I just think of fish and cream. Give

up the mew - ing, there's noth - ing do - ing. I'm all washed up on___ love.

5.3 "I'm All Washed Up on Love," measures 1–8

When you're sitting around in the parlor
And you've posed for the group photograph
If you're through playing Nola upon the victrola,
Try Sawing a Woman in Half.

It's an interesting game, kinda rough on the dame,
She seldom enjoys it, but then
She can hardly object if she'll only reflect
There are many more women than men.[24]

Al Stillman's lyrics might raise some eyebrows today. The humor is understatement ("It's an interesting game / kinda rough on the dame") followed by the satiric suggestion that the woman's pain is unimportant since the greater supply of women makes them a less valuable commodity.

Subsequent phrases and verses focus more graphically on various body parts and their dismemberment. The phrase, "A beginner may start at the bottom / And work his way down to the calf," is followed by lines that scold the complaining woman for being so selfish.

If the lady complains of abdominal pains
Just tell her she's spoiling the fun.
Great relief she will find if she'll just bear in mind
Half a body is better than none.

Furthermore, she should experience "great relief" to know she has even "half a body" left, probably enough to service the small brain and soul of a female! The final verse includes a bit of sexual innuendo.

If she starts in to moan that she don't like the tone
Protesting it grates on her nerves
And she'd simply adore a more musical saw
That sings as it's rounding the curves.

In the end, the poor woman has no recourse but to excuse her misfortune, for the magician is not only deceptive, but also irresponsible.

If she begs you to put her together
Just tell her, "You must stand the gaff.
Madam, I'm no physician, I'm just a magician
Sawing a Woman in Half."[25]

Ironically, Swift's music is a waltz, a romantic dance setting to complement the pleasures of the "old meanie" magician. It suggests an elegant atmosphere, capturing the carefree attitudes of those who amuse themselves and others with such sleights of hand. Swift later described the Radio City production.

[Baritone Robert] Weede, as a magician, sang it, while sawing
the whole line of Rockettes in half. The use of Strobel light made
the upper half of them light, while the lower halves were invisible
in a dark light. Then ballet corps entered, wearing costumes painted
in exactly the opposite way—invisible upper halves, lowers in
Strobel light. Weede sawed the ballet girls in half, too. The number
was effective. It has been repeated numerous times at Radio City

and has figured in the repertoires of such night-club singers as Joan Morris and William Bolcom, Ronny White and long ago, the great Jimmy Savo.

In spite of its questionable appropriateness, the song continues to be sung at annual magicians' conventions.[26]

Radio City Music Hall symbolized how popular culture reflected wide-ranging values of the public. Its mammoth size and art deco design looked ahead to the future, as did the technical wizardry of its stage equipment. And Hollywood's newest offerings were presented each week to eager audiences. Yet, the conservative management maintained respect for tradition. The variety show had its roots in vaudeville, a proven and popular format. Ballet and classical music were also included in the stage shows, in part as a nod to members of elite society who still had doubts about the propriety of movie theaters, and in part as a mission to educate the masses in the joys of classical repertoire. The corporation showed only films that were appropriate for family viewing. And the Rockettes could be seen as a modified burlesque, catering to male desires and perpetuating the image of the ideal American woman presented in the Ziegfeld Follies of earlier decades.

Kay Swift presented many of these opposing values in her own compositions for Radio City Music Hall. Vin Lindhe, director of the Glee Club at Radio City, summarized the tension in an article for the program magazine in June 1935. He maintained that the "yawning chasm between popular and classical music" seemed to be diminishing. While "symphonic jazz, and the blasphemy of dressing up a classical composition (hitherto clothed in majestic ermine) in a sport outfit" had been shocking to purists in the audience, the trend to blend the styles was growing. "Songs began to be born which did not fall into either of the two categories, popular or classic. Ballads which fell easily into a rhythmic tempo, and which were too highbrow to be termed mere jazz, were termed semipopular. Melodies which were definitely written along idyllic lines, but which became immediate favorites with the parlor tenors, were dubbed semi-classics." Kay Swift would continually obscure the boundaries between the two styles, with her classical training and her Broadway experience informing both. Her tenure at Radio City Music Hall was fitting.[27]

5.4 "A Song for String Quartet," measures 13–24

Near the end of her Radio City work, Swift received a commission from the Musical Art Quartet, of which her friend Marie Rosanoff was a member. The result was *A Song for String Quartet,* a five-minute, one-movement piece based on an original pentatonic theme in the style of a folk tune. Typifying the "semi-classic" category, this accessible piece features a simple, memorable melody. It can be viewed as an extended song with an introductory "verse." The wordless verse of twelve measures employs three phrases (aa'b), followed by a simple songlike melody that constantly shifts between A major and A minor (ex. 5.4). The main theme features five statements of a four-measure phrase with slightly different endings, followed by two statements of a contrasting phrase, a derivative of A. The rather lengthy development section transforms the thematic material through the use of imitation, fragmentation, and syncopation. The main theme in its various forms closes the movement. Swift wrote this piece in the years after Gershwin's study with Joseph Schillinger, and she may have been applying some of his composition theory, which emphasized economy of material through fragmentation and reordering.

Swift's folklike theme is remarkably similar to the second theme in the first movement of Dvořák's "American" String Quartet in F, from 1893. In this work and in his *New World Symphony,* also from 1893, Dvořák employed themes inspired by African-American and Native American tunes. Swift very likely knew the Dvořák quartet, because the Kneisel Quartet premiered it and repeated it in many of their concerts. The Kneisel Quartet had taken up residence at the Institute of Musical Art while Swift was there and had played at Blue Hill, Maine. The blend of classical form with folklike content recalls Gershwin's more recent *Porgy and Bess* and his belief that musical styles should not be compartmentalized. *Song for String Quartet* was Swift's first excursion back into classical music since *Alma Mater* and was probably a welcome project after the pressure of writing for the Rockettes week after week. The piece bridges the classical and popular worlds just as Radio City Music Hall did.[28]

CHAPTER 6

Gershwin Obsession

George was somebody I'd rather hear play than anybody else. He went right to the piano and sat down with joy. . . . It was an electric experience.
—*Kay Swift*

One of Kay Swift's granddaughters, the writer Katharine Weber, had a special bond with her grandmother. With Nicholas Fox Weber, her husband, she is the co-trustee of the Kay Swift Memorial Trust, dedicated to preserving and promoting Swift's memory and music. One of her earliest childhood memories is of a time when she was still small enough to fit into the mesh seat of a grocery cart in the local supermarket. The music on the store intercom had stopped and a new melody had begun. Weber writes in an essay, "The Memory of All That,"

> My mother, whose shopping list and pocketbook I hold, cocks her
> head in a particularly focused way and leans down, murmuring
> to me, "That's George." Inevitably, I developed a precocious abil-
> ity to recognize Gershwin tunes everywhere. . . . It occurs to
> me now that the skill I had acquired was not, in fact, the ability to
> recognize Gershwin music, though that certainly came with time.

My primary expertise was a highly attuned ability to recognize the look on my mother's face and take it as a cue to pipe up, "That's George!" In this way I could join my mother in her pleasure.[1]

Knowing George Gershwin and his music was a source of pride for Kay Swift's middle daughter, Andrea, and she shared in the reverence her mother had accorded him. The ritual of listening for George created a secret bond among three generations of Swift women.

In 1930 Kay Swift was balancing her private and public lives, her domestic and professional roles, and her relationship with two powerful, talented, and captivating males. Both were handsome, aggressive, and driven to success. However, George Gershwin and James Warburg were very different men.[2]

Warburg's training for his profession was highly scripted, with his father as his sage mentor. It had begun in a prestigious prep school, followed with a Harvard education and graduation with honors, and was capped by apprenticeships at respected banking firms. Gershwin's preparation for his profession had been rather haphazard. A tough street kid, he had preferred athletics to school or music. His musical interest was aroused relatively late, and formal lessons had not occurred before his teenage years, a delay that put him at a distinct disadvantage with other classical composers. He had dropped out of high school to become a song plugger at Jerome H. Remick and Company. His lack of formal education did not dull his burning intellectual curiosity, and he later pursued advanced study in art and music with intense passion. He developed his songwriting skills while plugging songs in Tin Pan Alley, yet his determination to be remembered as an "American composer" ultimately led to the performance of his concert works at Carnegie Hall.

Both Warburg's and Gershwin's parents had immigrated to New York City within the same decade. Warburg's parents were wealthy German Jewish immigrants who lived on the fashionable Upper East Side of New York City, relying comfortably on their family financial operations, M. M. Warburg in Hamburg and Kuhn, Loeb in New York. They were highly respected in the community, gracious, and supportive of a variety of artistic and Jewish social causes. Gershwin's parents were Russian Jewish immigrants who settled on the crowded Lower East Side. His father, Morris, was involved in many small businesses, some more successful than others, and his mother, Rose, was always intent on improving her station in life. Gershwin's songs and Broadway shows brought him fortune and fame, yet he lacked the culture and social graces that were second nature to the Warburg family.

Although both families were Jewish, neither family attended temple regularly. The Warburgs observed tradition enough to satisfy Felix's father-in-law, Jacob Schiff. But Paul and Nina did not hold strong religious views, and they downplayed their heritage to encourage their children's assimilation into American society. The Gershwins were concerned less about their religion than about their economic situation. Ira was the only one of the three Gershwin brothers to be bar mitzvahed.[3]

James Warburg was a relatively mature adult who had made calculated career decisions so that he could maintain the family fortune and way of life. Although he deeply respected his father, he could not wait to leave the smothering influence of his family, and he did so at age twenty-two. George Gershwin had no career plan, but when he followed his passions in a series of jobs that intrigued him, he found tremendous success and popularity. His family was not demonstrative with their affection, but his mother exerted strong influence over them all and he continued to share living space with the family. Although he was the sole occupant of the fifth floor in the home to which they moved in 1925, he did not rent an apartment independently until age thirty. Whereas Warburg needed to prove his abilities and independence in a family that expected him to be successful, Gershwin far exceeded his parents' expectations with his talent and good fortune.[4]

Warburg and Gershwin, both handsome and gregarious, exuded confidence and ambition, and were highly successful at very young ages. Warburg's talents and accomplishments in finance, as well as his family and political connections, contributed to his business acumen and his willingness to take risks. Gershwin's success with his popular songs and concert works in the early 1920s had given him the confidence to pursue his passion yet also contributed to his grand ego. His pleasure in his own pieces and his desire to share them usually led to his quick dominance of the piano at parties, prompting George S. Kaufman's remark, "I'd bet on George any time —in a hundred yard dash to the piano." Katharine clearly found both men not only attractive but irresistible, at first.[5]

Gershwin's energy, his pianistic talent, and "his joyous delight in whatever he was doing" immediately captivated Katharine. His influence on her musical tastes and his guidance in her Broadway development have been noted. Although some criticized his self-absorbed interest in his music, Swift later spoke of his support for the music of others: "An encourager, an enthusiast, he not only was caught up in his own work but in the creations of so many others—so much so that he behaved like a fan. I know first hand of his great love for Irving Berlin and Jerome Kern, for early Harold Arlen music and the playing of jazz pianist Fats Waller."[6]

While Gershwin had a tremendous impact on Swift's acceptance of popular music, she also had an influence on his musical development. With her solid musical training, Swift was able to help Gershwin as he wrote his music. In 1948, reporter Verna Arvey interviewed Swift and wrote of her work with Gershwin: "So it happened that after George Gershwin discovered that she was capable of taking fast musical dictation, they very often worked together. When he was writing a piano piece, he used to work at the piano and let her write down what he played. She would notate, usually the melody, although she could and often did take down the harmonies too. The 'Spanish Prelude' was one she notated for him." The third prelude (the "Spanish Prelude") was composed in 1926 in Swift's townhouse.[7]

Framed and displayed in the George and Ira Gershwin Room at the Library of Congress is a page of the manuscript "In a Mandarin's Orchid Garden," featuring both Swift's and Gershwin's handwriting. It was a song written in 1929 for a Ziegfeld production, *East Is West*, that never materialized. Swift acted as a sounding board for many of Gershwin's musical ideas and offered her piano skills when he needed to hear two-piano versions of his compositions in progress. Gershwin offered Swift advice on her songs, while she provided suggestions about counterpoint and orchestration. She later modestly admitted, "I knew just enough that I could help him."[8]

But Swift's attraction to Gershwin went far beyond his music. Handsome and brash, George Gershwin had a reputation as a ladies' man. Many biographers and friends have commented on his numerous affairs, most of which he never took seriously, and none seriously enough to marry. An amused Kitty Carlisle Hart remembered his "enormous charm," as well as "a little waltz, which he played for every young lady, that had a blank space for the name of the lady. . . . I considered it his mating call." Mabel Pleshette Schirmer, a family friend since childhood, suggests, "Maybe he had too many women. . . . He would come home with about two or three women from a party. They just followed him home." Gershwin was notorious for escorting other men's wives, perhaps in part for the continued freedom it guaranteed him. His sister Frances agreed that "he never could give himself entirely somehow. Because we led such lives of our own as children, it was very difficult to make a relationship." Mabel Schirmer mused, "I don't remember any real attachment that he had . . . except for Kay. And he loved her because they had horses and they went horseback riding."[9]

Yet there was clearly more to their friendship than horses, or even their strong musical and artistic interests. By the time James Warburg was aware how dangerously close Gershwin and his wife had grown, it was too late to sever the relationship. He seemed to prefer remaining open-minded, since, in the spirit of the twenties, he had had affairs with other women. In "The Memory of All That," Katharine Weber writes about the difficult situation in the Warburg household.

> Kay and George were a glamorous couple when they were together
> at parties or the theater. They wafted through those years, flouting
> convention, having a good time, breaking all the rules. But no mat-
> ter how much "fun" everyone was having, their romance caused
> tremendous pain for my grandfather and my mother and her sisters.
> (For years I have wondered if Kay and George were an inspiration
> for Thorne Smith—a frequent houseguest in Greenwich in those
> years—when he conjured up George and Marian, the ghostly mad-
> cap couple in his novel *Topper,* who blithely cause trouble but never
> have to pay the consequences.)[10]

Warburg, aware of Gershwin's fickle nature, probably felt fairly sure that the interest would dissipate, that Gershwin would become enamored with someone new, and that the marital crisis would be over. Warburg was "remarkably obliging" about the affair at the time. The night before Gershwin's departure for his last European trip in March 1928, the Warburgs threw a bon voyage party that lasted until five in the morning. When Gershwin returned from Europe on June 18, 1928, Warburg agreed to let Gershwin stay in the guest cottage at Bydale, and Gershwin probably occupied the cottage from then until the end of the summer. Gershwin composed parts of *An American in Paris* there, reporting to Walter Damrosch on August 1 that the solo piano version of the work was complete and that the two-piano version was nearly finished. Kay Swift was very likely assisting with the two-piano version, if Gershwin was composing at her country home. Gershwin's stay at Bydale probably overlapped with the illness and death of Swift's mother, who had died on July 4. His presence during a family crisis may have been consolation to Swift and further annoyance to James Warburg.[11]

In his autobiography, Warburg noted that Gershwin visited their house in Connecticut frequently and, in addition to *An American in Paris,* composed most of his Second Rhapsody and much of *Porgy and Bess* in the guest cottage.

> George was a fascinating but disturbing element at Bydale. His exuberant vitality and many-sided zest for life knew no bounds. He wanted to learn and experience literally everything that he had not known in a childhood on Manhattan's Lower East Side. He wanted to learn to ride a horse, to buy and wear the right country clothes, to play with young children, and, most of all, to acquire from Kay the techniques of orchestration. He would sit for hours at the piano, experimenting in contagious excitement with a new melody or rhythm while Kay suggested harmonic treatment. Day turned into night and night into day when George was in the throes of creation.[12]

There was further evidence that the relationship between Swift and Gershwin had become serious. Significant was the set of gold bracelets Gershwin purchased as a gift for her late in 1928, since he did not often present gifts to women. Walter Damrosch had premiered *An American in Paris* with the New York Symphony Orchestra on December 13, a concert attended by the entire Gershwin family and many friends, including Rosamond Walling and Kay Swift. Reviews of the performance were mixed, due in part to conductor Damrosch's difficulty in grasping the piece's "complex rhythms and breezy tempos." Gershwin invited Swift to attend the afternoon performance again the following day. He was disappointed at the slow tempo Damrosch chose for the piece, and he and Swift left immediately after the performance ended. Swift later recalled, "The composer, anxious to forget the occasion, hurried out to go Christmas shopping with me. Antique gold bracelets, seen in the window of a Madison Avenue jeweler, had attracted his attention, and he had bought them for me forthwith." Swift treasured the bracelets until her death.[13]

Other events they shared have been documented. On January 14, 1930, the re-make of *Strike Up the Band* opened, with Gershwin conducting the premiere. One of the songs featured was "I've Got a Crush on You," a song that Swift's daughters, April and Andrea (Andy), ages ten and eight, had evidently learned and to which they had danced a soft-shoe routine. On opening night in New York, Kay sat immediately behind the podium. As that song began, Gershwin turned to her and whispered, "April and Andy!" an action which she found quite touching. Swift also remembered the opening night of *Of Thee I Sing* on December 26, 1931: "[It] had a wonderful opening night. Beatrice Kaufman and I gave a party. The critics came and read their reviews. I'd never heard of such a thing before. I was running everywhere, and [columnist] Alice Duer Miller said, 'Stop running. It will be all right.'"[14]

On November 2, 1930, Kay was one of a few guests in attendance at the impromptu wedding of George's sister Frances to Leopold Godowsky, scheduled just hours before Rose and Morris Gershwin left for a Florida vacation. The corsage Kay had sent to Rose Gershwin as a bon voyage gift was fashioned into a bouquet for Frankie. Gershwin dedicated the manuscripts of his 1932 *Song Book* to her, not an insignificant gesture since he rarely dedicated his scores to anyone. The same year, James Warburg published a small volume of poetry under his pseudonym, *Shoes and Ships and Sealing Wax*, in which he addressed the topics of love, success, and death. In a poignant gesture, Paul James dedicated his poetry volume "To K.S. (if you can stand another one)."[15]

Ira Gershwin recollected that George and Kay frequently played a waltz on two pianos based on the song "Tonight," from *Pardon My English,* a show that flopped in 1933. First they played the song "Tonight"; then they played a countermelody; and finally they played the two songs together in counterpoint. "Ira referred to the piece as 'Her Waltz, His Waltz, Their Waltz.'"[16]

Gershwin studied with theorist Joseph Schillinger from 1932 to 1936, sometimes three sessions per week, and Swift remembered attending all his lessons with him. "It was stimulating. . . . I was muscling in on it—two for the price of one! I really got the benefit. . . . I would just go to George's and he would say, 'I'm going to Schillinger's, would you like to go along?'" Schillinger did not offer comments on Swift's music, but she listened attentively to his methods and his critiques of Gershwin's, which often involved economizing material and "shortening up one's work." She was present when Gershwin wrote the *Cuban Overture*, the first piece in which he applied Schillinger's suggestions.[17]

Another project on which they both participated in 1934 was Gershwin's radio show, "Music by Gershwin," which aired twice a week from February through May and once a week from September through December. Kay Swift attended all the rehearsals and broadcasts. The script from the April 6 program indicates that the orchestra played two of her songs, "Can't We Be Friends?" and "Fine and Dandy." Later Gershwin featured a guest composer every week but never devoted an entire program to Swift's music. He felt that to feature her in a greater capacity would be perceived as partiality based on their friendship rather than on her talent.[18]

Swift accompanied Gershwin many times as he went to Harlem clubs to hear African-American jazz. Said Verna Arvey of her interview with Swift in 1948, "She remembers going with him at 3, 4, 5 A.M., after their respective shows were over, to little places in Harlem where there were recordings by Negro artists that couldn't be gotten downtown. There the composer would listen intently, making mental notes and absorbing the style."[19]

Kay gave George a wire-haired fox terrier named Tinker, and George later presented Kay with a black poodle, which she named Porgy. Swift saw that Gershwin's boutonnieres arrived on time before concerts (his favorite flower was the blue cornflower, which she ordered for him), and she waited for him backstage when the performances were over. After her yeoman's effort during *Porgy and Bess*, he presented her with a leather-bound autographed score that reads simply, "To Kay. Best. George." "Best," their code word for "love," allowed them to be discreet. Entertainer Michael Feinstein, who worked as Ira's assistant during his last six years, reported that Gershwin wore a pocket watch when he played concerts and that Swift had given him a gold fob with a small good luck charm. It was a gold dove with a diamond in one eye and a sapphire in the other—their birthstones. "She knew that it would be concealed under his jacket and would be a secret token of their love." In his 1956 biography of Gershwin, David Ewen wrote,

> If there was one woman whom Gershwin esteemed most highly and who filled a major role in his life, she was Kay Swift. . . . Kay had an impressive training in serious music to which she brought a trenchant intellect, a retentive memory and a rare critical discernment. Gershwin admired all these things in her; but he also admired her wit, culture, refinement, social position, savoir-faire and personal charm. . . . [She brought to Gershwin a] sensitive appreciation for the subtle refinements of gracious living and for cultural interests outside of music. She looked after him with a solicitude born out of tenderness. Gershwin, in turn, came as close to being completely in love with her as he did with any woman.[20]

As close as their relationship was, it was not without its difficulties. Esther Leeming Tuttle remembers visiting Kay's apartment on East Eighty-sixth Street after her divorce. "She was going with George Gershwin then. Gershwin said to her, 'You would have to get an apartment way over here on East 86th Street. This little Jewish boy has a hard time walking through the German section!' It was in the midst of an area where lots of Germans lived, dined, drank beer, and sang Heidelberg songs." Yet Gershwin evidently endured the discomfort in order to visit his best girl.[21]

Of greater consequence was Swift's recognition that Gershwin admired beautiful women; she was aware that "he had several affairs and flirtations." Since meeting Rosamund Walling in 1928 he had corresponded with her and seen her when possible, but Walling was twelve years younger than he and studying at Swarthmore College. Some claim that he had an affair with a showgirl, Molly Charleston, and that in 1926 she bore him a son, Alan (also known as Albert Schneider)—whom no Gershwin or Kay ever publicly acknowledged. Swift maintained that she was the only one of his love interests with such extensive musical knowledge. She claimed that she did not mind his seeing other women, "because I always felt I held a unique position. I was not jealous. I would have been if I'd thought he cared terribly much for somebody else, but he didn't."[22]

Gershwin often spoke of wanting to marry, particularly in the last years of his life, but he could not seem to make the final decision, valuing his bachelor existence. Some acquaintances claimed that Gershwin was too self-centered to give enough of himself to any woman and would never have married. (On seeing Swift and Gershwin enter a nightclub together, pianist and friend Oscar Levant quipped, "Ah, look! Here comes George Gershwin with the future Miss Kay Swift!") Feinstein reports that Ira's assessment of their relationship was "very simple. Kay had everything that George wanted but she also had something he didn't want—children. He loved her three daughters but he didn't want to be responsible for them." Even Kay sensed that he was uncomfortable around children. She recalled, "He was very fond of my children, but he made a mistake with them some-times because he was very direct, moreso than he was with grown-ups. He would say, 'Don't you like me?' That embarrassed them." More important, Swift admitted to Robert Kimball that "removing the obstacle created a big-ger obstacle." His lack of commitment became a source of immense frustra-tion for her.[23]

While her eldest daughter April had a difficult time accepting her relation-ship with Gershwin, middle daughter Andrea loved his attentions. George also became quite friendly with Kay's brother, Sam. In 1931, Sam had married an intensely devout Catholic named Claire. Gershwin's presence at family occasions posed an awkward situation for Sam's in-laws, all deeply religious Catholics who did not accept divorce. Although Sam's wife later cautioned her son, Shippen, about nonbelievers, she and her mother seemed to manage George's visits with the family. Years later Shippen, Kay's nephew, explained:

He [Gershwin] was *talent* and talent throws its own reflective aura. Besides, he was an 'old friend of the family' and even was permit-ted to visit the Hall Of The Holy Grail—the g'mother's place in coastal Allenhurst, New Jersey. . . . He came, he saw, and he drank. I of course was a lapling at the time but I remember the furor when George and Sam and probably the maternal uncle lapped up some 90 Proof while they were eating grapes. The grapes were not of the seedless variety, and one of the trio thought it might be fun to hold a contest—see who could spit the seeds from a designated point [in the living room] onto the screen covering the living room window. I do not know who won, but the g'mother awarded no trophy.[24]

Gershwin struggled with his indecision about marriage. He often spent time at Emil Mosbacher's Westchester home to finish his compositions in the early 1930s, and Kay would come up to visit him when he was working. In *The Gershwins,* Mosbacher noted, "I don't know if you realize the class of this girl or the home that Kay left, the home where she gave the parties after the openings. Oh, she had the place loaded with class. George had such great admiration for her, and they both talked to me about marriage —separately mind you. . . . From George, I'd get it every day. He was nuts about her. You know, she used to work night and day to help George with his orchestrations."[25]

In spite of her misgivings and understanding of Gershwin's weaknesses, Swift seems to have been firmly committed to their relationship. She was evidently at peace with her decision to divorce Warburg, apparently hoping that she and Gershwin might someday marry, even though they had not discussed that possibility and he continued to see other women. In an unpublished and unfinished short story that tells of two women, Mary and Kay, as they journey to Reno to seek divorces, Swift identifies Kay, "a chic, twenty-seven-year-old in a dream of a tailored suit," and her beau, "none other than George Gregor, world-famous composer of Broadway songs and symphonic music." George Gregor has sent a bottle of champagne to the train, and the women sip it from paper cups as they travel. Swift writes,

Both girls are on their way to Reno to divorce their respective husbands; whether or not they will eventually marry their beaux is problematic, but each believes such will be the case. Kay, whose life with her husband . . . has been a series of storms, worries maternally about him, and hopes her successor, whom he has already selected, will take care of him. . . .

The train wheels form a musical pattern accompanied by a monotonously reiterated phrase, "Make-it-work"; Kay, herself a composer, whips out a pencil and a bit of manuscript paper, [and] jots it down. "I hope we can," Mary remarks sadly, and raises her paper cup in a silent toast to their doing so.[26]

The manuscript details their arrival in Reno. The portion quoted is significant for several reasons, assuming that it is essentially autobiographical. (In 1934 Swift was actually thirty-seven rather than twenty-seven, a purposeful error she would make regularly. She did travel to Reno with her close friend, Mary Woodard Reinhardt, who was also getting her first divorce. And Swift later wrote several stories and articles in the form of a diary or journal, and even published a book about a portion of her life.) First, Swift recognizes the repetitive sounds made by the train as a "musical pattern" in the same way that Gershwin had detailed the perception to his first biographer, Isaac Goldberg, in 1931: "It was on the train, with its steely rhythms, its rattle-ty-bang that is often so stimulating to a composer . . . I frequently hear music in the very heart of Noise." Swift undoubtedly read Goldberg's book—he had presented her with an autographed copy. She may have been reminded of the train anecdote as she rode. Second, she confirms that Warburg must also have found someone better suited to his marital ideal. And last, she suggests that she was, indeed, contemplating marriage to Gershwin. Years later, however, she would deny that she obtained a divorce in order to marry George. She claimed that she just wanted it to be easier for them to be together.[27]

Swift returned to New York before Christmas, and she and Gershwin spent Christmas Eve 1934 together, a fact confirmed by composer Richard Rodgers in Robert Kimball and Alfred Simon's book *The Gershwins*. His wife, bedridden as she awaited the birth of their second daughter, was low in spirits, so George and Kay "burst in on us like irrepressible magi, bearing a present that only George Gershwin could have given." Gershwin proceeded to play and sing for her the entire score of *Porgy and Bess* months before it opened. Kay must have been euphoric at this time in her life. She had rejected the dishonesty of a loveless marriage by securing a divorce, which was final on December 20; she had resumed composing and received accolades for her ballet; and she was back in New York spending the holidays with the man she loved. Her efforts to assist Gershwin in any way were unselfish favors for a close friend, and after *Alma Mater*, in 1935, she turned her efforts to his *Porgy and Bess*.[28]

Swift and Gershwin continued to see each other through the first half of 1936. She recalls attending a performance of Richard Wagner's opera *Die Meistersinger* with him before the winter's snow had melted.

> We had splendid seats in the orchestra, and, like most people at the time, which was nineteen thirty-six, we dressed up for the occasion. Gershwin and I were rather proud of the fact that, although we always stayed for the final curtain, we were wizards at reaching the street afterwards, ahead of most of the audience. We invariably caught the first available taxi outside. When we loped up the aisle, after this performance, . . . we ended up in step, rather like Astaire and Ginger when they went into their famous stride, with which they used to circle the stage before their final exit.
>
> This time, we worked up such speed that on leaving the building we were unable to slow down before loping into a heap of dirty snow that had been shoveled onto the edge of the sidewalk. Sitting waist-deep, George in his white tie, tails and top hat, and I in a long white fur cape, . . . burst into a loud laugh, in which we were joined by a few fans who had recognized Gershwin. Scrambling out of this mess, we leapt into the first taxi in sight. I remember that George muttered, "Always leave them laughing when you say Goodbye."[29]

And "Goodbye" came soon for Gershwin and Swift. After what Edward Jablonksi terms a "postpartum letdown" prompted by the closing of *Porgy and Bess*, George and Ira Gershwin made plans to go to Hollywood to write a film score for a musical starring Fred Astaire and Ginger Rogers, *Shall We Dance*. Apparently the relationship between Swift and Gershwin had begun to wane by this time, perhaps in part because Swift was now available and therefore less attractive to Gershwin. Years later Swift, responding to the question, "Did he ever propose?" answered, "'Once he said, "I think it should be tried." I said, "I don't know." I think I had an instinct that it would kill the romance and it would become "Toothbrush time."' . . . [This was] her favorite way of describing a glamorous relationship spoiled by marriage." *Philadelphia Evening Bulletin* reporter Doris B. Wiley had apparently sanitized Swift's definition of "toothbrush time." Friends William Bolcom and Joan Morris recall that by the late 1970s Swift more explicitly described her relationship with Gershwin as including "the best sex I ever had, but he never stayed over till 'toothbrush time.'" Intrigued by the phrase, Bolcom shared it with his poet-lyricist, Arnold Weinstein, who immediately acknowledged, "That's a song!" The two wrote their tribute to "Toothbrush Time" in New York in 1979.[30]

Gershwin and Swift had mutually agreed that they would not see each other during the year George was in Hollywood, although they did correspond. They were each free to see others and planned to assess their relationship upon his return. On August 10, 1936, a large crowd of friends gathered at the airport to bid George and Ira farewell. That was the last time most of them ever saw George Gershwin. After three film scores, he was suddenly stricken with a brain tumor and died in California on July 11, 1937. Kay Swift remembered their parting at the airport:

> I never saw him after that photograph of him standing on the step
> of the ramp at the airport. And he had a mark around his head,
> which was a deep groove from a straw hat that was too small for
> him. . . . He and Ira went to the airport separately. George and I
> went in a taxi. We had decided we were not going to see each other
> or write and see how it went and if it would be a happy arrange-
> ment. We kept everything cheery and bright. He laughed and talked
> about the picture. We said good by, and he walked up the ramp.
> And I knew for sure I'd never see him again. I didn't know why, but
> I knew that was all; that was it. And he stood at the top of the ramp,
> and he waved the hat, and all I could see was the groove that went
> around his head like an Indian headband.[31]

Gershwin's death was a tragedy to the music world and a personal tragedy for Kay Swift. They had exchanged letters, and he had repeatedly asked friends about her and demonstrated concern for her happiness. At the same time, he was supposedly very attracted to a French film actress, Simone Simon, as well as to Paulette Goddard, Charlie Chaplin's wife. Goddard apparently even inspired thoughts of marriage in him, however fleeting. Alfred Stern recalls consoling Swift during "weeping cocktail time," when she was particularly upset with Gershwin's intense interests in Simon and Goddard. Nevertheless, Swift reports that she contacted him when she discovered he was ill. In her 1976 interview with Doris B. Wiley, she recalled, "When I knew he was in the hospital, I sent him a telegram. He answered it just before he died, wiring me, 'I'm going to get well for both of us and will come back.'" But it was not to be. Swift recalls being at a concert with her daughter April at the moment Gershwin died. She abruptly stood at the end of one of the pieces, and in response to her daughter's query answered, "We're going home. George is gone." Later that afternoon Lee Gershwin, Ira's wife, called Kay confirming her suspicions. In an effort to keep their relationship private, she burned all the correspondence from George that she had and asked Ira to destroy her letters to him.[32]

Swift's association with George Gershwin permanently changed the course of her life. She had spent her early years involved with classical music, from attending operas at the Met with her father to playing in a classical piano trio. As Katharine Warburg, she had no financial need to work either as a pianist or a composer, and her musical activities could have become an avocation as she juggled her time among her husband, her three daughters, and her social obligations. Gershwin awakened her to the possibilities of popular music and Broadway and led her to career opportunities she otherwise may not have explored. More important, George Gershwin dazzled Kay Swift, and the two enjoyed a friendship known to few. They shared their music, the theater, friends, and love. Their relationship was one of musical understanding and diligence; of mutual admiration and respect; and one that they both must have ultimately sensed as having its limitations. He permeated every aspect of her world as long as she lived. In "The Memory of All That," her granddaughter wrote, "Ganz [her nickname for 'Grandma'] had loved George, and then he had died all of a sudden. . . . She seemed so much like his widow, despite the two subsequent husbands. . . . I have never really understood how she came to make that dangerous leap, but her having done so was always an essential part of her, and a central aspect of my family's sensibility." Swift spoke of Gershwin's approach to life: "George approached life as if it was an extraordinary adventure. He extracted a great deal out of the meanings of every day. By translating them beautifully into music, making each experience and feeling personal and meaningful to all of us, he gave so much more back."[33]

In retrospect, we can only wonder what Kay Swift might have done had she continued composing during those critical years between 1930 and 1934. Gershwin was clearly not interested in collaborating with her or in crediting her with her part in his work. Her roles as a musical secretary, social director, and loyal supporter were extremely valuable to Gershwin as he created one major work after another. To suggest that he purposely manipulated her into helping him would be less than fair, because he truly cared for her. Swift certainly put Gershwin at the center of her life, sacrificing her career to enhance his. Her affair with him destroyed her marriage and damaged her relationship with her daughters. It interrupted her budding Broadway career. It became an overriding obsession. Yet through it all she never regretted her years with Gershwin. She always felt fortunate to have been a central component in his life, contributing to his "extraordinary adventure." Her respect and love for him remained forever a part of her world. It was a part that some in her family would never understand but that one daughter would pass on to her own child, ever aware that "That's George."

CHAPTER 7

New Frontiers

I'll close this Gate to Nowhere.—Kay Swift

After two years, Swift left "The Showplace of the Nation" to help prepare for the 1939 New York World's Fair. The World's Fair organization seems to have relied upon the reputation of Radio City, seeking fine, young talent seasoned by the rigor of the Music Hall's expectations. Swift joined her colleague Alfred Stern and moved to the World's Fair offices in the Empire State Building. Stern was assistant to the director of exhibits and concessions, and Swift was appointed director of music. As Stern said, "The general assumption was that anyone who came from Radio City Music Hall knew a lot about spectacle shows." Both now gained positions of increased responsibility for the purpose of welcoming a wider audience to New York City.[1]

New York World's Fair

After a decade of financial trauma, the New York World's Fair of 1939 promoted hope and prosperity for the future. Franklin D. Roosevelt's New Deal had succeeded in restoring work and dignity, if not yet prosperity, to millions of Americans. In an era of populist politics, "the people" had emerged as a familiar concept, and this fair was conceived as "everyman's fair." Grover A. Whalen, former general manager of Wanamaker's department store, New York police commissioner, and now the fair's president, noted that the purpose of the fair was "to delight and instruct" the people. It was hoped that each visitor might be reminded of "the interdependence of man on man, class on class, nation on nation." However ideological the stated purpose may have been, Whalen was also a showman, having orchestrated the 1927 New York reception for Charles Lindbergh as well as the National Recovery Act parade in New York City in 1933. He understood festival and spectacle and sensed that the educational aspect of the fair should not overshadow the celebration.[2]

Music was extremely important to this "festival of sight and sound." As the scope of the position of director of music unfolded, the duties of that job were divided between two professionals, now housed in offices at Flushing Meadows, site of the fair. Olin Downes, music critic for the *New York Times*, was appointed director and was responsible for the classical artists and events. The Hall of Music, an air-conditioned auditorium that seated 2,500, was the site for an ambitious schedule of classical music that included symphonic programs and solo recitals by world-class artists, as well as a Russian ballet, the Paris Opera, and a performance of Beethoven's Ninth Symphony. In response to criticisms that the admission fees and tickets for classical entertainment were too high, the fair management sought to emphasize "entertainment for the masses" by hiring "bands of strolling players —singers, dancers, musicians, clowns, acrobats, minstrels and the like" to appear free of charge in the amusement zone, exhibit area, and rest spots. Cultural historian Warren Susman reports, "The colorful tractor trains that toured the Fairgrounds played a few bars of 'The Sidewalks of New York,' and there were always bands, orchestras, and even, from some exhibits, the allure of interior sound floating out onto the general grounds." Kay Swift's appointment to the position of director of light music gave her the responsibility for the popular music and less formal performances by groups that abounded throughout the fair. This was a testament not only to her well-respected musical skills, honed most recently at Radio City Music Hall, but also to her fine organizational skills and a sense of drama, first awakened through her love of opera.[3]

One of her initial tasks was to oversee the creation of a popular fair theme song. The fair president, Grover Whalen, wanted a Gershwin song, if possible, both to commemorate the fair and to honor the recently deceased American composer. Swift was probably very pleased to acknowledge her closest friend and colleague in this manner. Ira Gershwin was perfectly comfortable collaborating with Kay on his brother's music. He recalled that Kay "knew almost everything George had ever written, had frequently taken down sketches as he composed in his New York apartment, and had total musical recall." Together in 1938 they pieced together unused phrases from George's sketchbooks to create a "new" Gershwin tune as a theme song, "Dawn of a New Day," for the World's Fair. Philip Furia describes their collaboration: "Ira found that she even worked much as George did, rummaging around in the tunebooks, pulling out strands from several different melodic fragments, then piecing them together. For the New York World's Fair anthem, she wove several melodies, including a 1930s song called 'Come, Come, Come to Jesus,' into 'Dawn of a New Day.'" Ira remembered that they began with the sketch, "Revolution in Blue," one of the unused marches the composer wrote for the first act finale of *Let 'Em Eat Cake*. For the verse he used a portion of "Come, Come, Come to Jesus," a hymn-style song from a previously proposed show. A 1939 recording of "Dawn of a New Day" features the march and its martial rhythms played by a spirited dance band. Between the punctuations of a snare drum, it anticipates a decade of hope after the long depression.[4]

The organization and physical plant of the World's Fair were impressive as plans unfolded for its opening. The Theme Center included the imposing Trylon (a seven-hundred-foot-high triangular pylon) and the Perisphere (a two-hundred-foot-wide sphere), both massive structures painted pure white. Inside the Perisphere was a display, "a vast diorama of Democracity, a planned urban and exurban complex of the future." Swift had commissioned African-American composer William Grant Still to write the orchestral music for the theme show, something for which Alfred Stern commended her. Although a committee selected Still from a group of finalists after hearing samples of the unidentified candidates' music, it was Swift who had included Still as one of that group. She appreciated his talent without thought to his color, and her method for selecting the winner prevented race from becoming an issue for the committee. Stern commented, "There were few in 1939 who would think that the theme music for the Fair should be done by a black, but Kay persevered." After all, this was "everyman's fair," according to Grover Whalen, one that touted "the immediate necessity of enlightened and harmonious cooperation." Swift, who was never known to bear prejudice against anyone, offered Still a chance to compete on an equal footing with other composers. He was pleased to have received the commission and, in a letter to Alain Locke, explained his pride: "It seems to me that this must be the first time, musically speaking, that a colored man has ever been asked to write something extremely important that does not necessarily have to be Negroid." Still had been charged with writing music to represent all Americans, not just African Americans. His piece also provided what Swift described as "one of the choicest lyric assignments of the Fair—the writing of verses to be sung by a hundred voices, pre-recorded and heard in the perisphere." Swift recommended her former lyricist, Al Stillman, for the assignment, "which he carried out with style."[5]

Swift's position as director of light music increased in stature at the end of May 1939, when the World's Fair management assessed disappointing attendance at the Hall of Music concerts and canceled all the remaining classical music programs on the schedule. Olin Downes resigned as director of music as contracts with the Hungarian Opera, Lawrence Tibbett, and Josef Hoffmann were broken. The planning committee for the fair, trying to balance the education versus entertainment objectives, had miscalculated the public's interest in classical music and was now forced to alter the schedule to avoid devastating financial losses. Evaluation after the first month's receipts suggested that a change in programming might attract greater crowds with selections from Broadway musicals, light opera, and swing bands.[6]

The New York World's Fair, like Radio City Music Hall, embodied the tension between traditional values and progress. On one hand, it tried "to preserve and save the best of modern civilization as it was then known." On the other, it attempted to visualize the "city of the future." Its stated purpose was both to educate and to entertain. Kay Swift's task was to use her skills to orchestrate the desired effects. She was in a position of responsibility and independence, earning a living in a profession she loved. She was also acquiring a wide range of experiences in the entertainment industry that she drew on for subsequent projects.[7]

At the same time, she indulged herself in the World's Fair's many attractions, visiting it regularly after it opened. Alfred Stern remembers Swift often taking the boat up the East River from her Manhattan apartment to the fair in Queens in the late afternoon. He frequently met her for cocktails, after which they would ride the "Parachute Jump" and then enjoy dinner at one of the fair's many fine foreign restaurants. *Life* named the Parachute Jump the "most sensational ride" on July 3, 1939. "Tied into chairs, customers are hoisted up to the top of a 250-ft. tower in 58 sec. and dropped down in 15 sec. Squeals of Fair parachute jumpers almost drown the joyous uproar of nearby barkers, bus horns, bands and Frank Buck's monkeys." The Parachute Jump had been designed in 1934 by Commander James H. Strong to train army and navy fliers. It eventually became a permanent attraction at Coney Island Amusement Park. Another attraction, the American Jubilee, would capitalize on the western fascination that had seemed to reach all areas of the country. Produced by the general manager of the Ringling Brothers circus, this entertainment featured three hundred performers, including bona fide cowboys, and forty trained horses. With her interest in horseback riding, Swift visited the Jubilee regularly. Forty bulls were assembled for the bull-dogging contests. Championship bull-dogger Faye Hubbard described the show years later in a newspaper article. "It was rodeo and wild west. We had nineteen Lady Godivas who rode out side-saddle, and we walked out beside them with a big spear and dressed like a knight." The article continued, "The Godivas, who wore a scant more than the original and probably accounted for more of the New York gate receipts than Hubbard's bulls, called the rodeo competitor 'Mother Hubbard.'"[8]

Swift was instantly intrigued with this rodeo star. (Alfred Stern never understood her attraction to him. In his opinion, "He wasn't a very good cowboy. He fell off his horse quite often.") As Swift told it, one day Hubbard got hurt while bull-dogging and gave the hospital her name as his next of kin. Shortly thereafter Swift made decisions that would change her life in countless ways. Swift and Hubbard eloped within weeks. By the fall, she had moved with her new husband to a ranch in Bend, Oregon, which they affectionately dubbed "The Faye-and-Kay."

Western Fever

The cowboy hero had been riding his way into the hearts of Americans since the 1880s. Buffalo Bill Cody's Wild West show had delighted crowds from 1883 to 1916, and Owen Wister's novel *The Virginian* had been published in 1902. After Frederick Jackson Turner had announced the "closing of the American frontier" in 1890, the nation was swept with nostalgia for the independence, ingenuity, and determination needed to survive in the wild, open country of the Old West. The romance of the western was quickly transferred to silent movies, such as Edwin S. Porter's *Great Train Robbery* in 1903, and it contributed to a vastly popular genre comprising art, novels, movies, and music. F. Scott Fitzgerald may have been the most sophisticated and urbane novelist of the 1920s, but Zane Grey and W. S. Hart were among America's best-selling authors, producing such classics as *Riders of the Purple Sage* and *Hell's Hinges.* The consummate adult movie western, John Ford's *Stagecoach,* was released in 1939, perpetuating an interest in all things western that did not peak until the late 1950s. Buffalo Bill's Wild West show had made its first appearance in New York in 1897, and Madison Square Garden now hosted a fall rodeo annually.[9]

The cowboy image invaded the music industry as well, and the romantic myth of the West was explored in song. In the late 1920s and early 1930s Jimmie Rodgers, with his western-style dress and "blue yodel," was one of the first singers who brought the "singing cowboy" image to country music, blending southern hillbilly sounds with western references and symbols. He inspired several generations of singing cowboys, with Gene Autry among the most successful.[10]

Through national radio, the influence of the singing cowboys reached not only Hollywood in the 1930s but New York City, where it found the Broadway stage, the college lecture circuit, and the world of classical music. Many cowboy songs were written by Broadway composers, among them Johnny Mercer's "I'm an Old Cowhand," which was heard in the film *Rhythm on the Range* (1936), and Cole Porter's "Don't Fence Me In" (written for the 1935 film *Adios Argentina* that was never produced; it became popular after it was heard in 1944's *Hollywood Canteen*). Billy Hill was a native Bostonian who had spent fifteen years traveling and living in the West. He returned to New York City in the late 1920s and wrote songs about his western experiences. His greatest hit, "The Last Roundup," was one of the most popular tunes in the country in 1933. Another direct link between the West and the East is Tex Ritter. Although he was born and raised in Texas, Ritter was not a cowboy. He was highly educated and after a year of law school moved to New York City to pursue acting. His contact with western and mountain songs was as an interested collector. While starring in Lynn Riggs's *Green Grow the Lilacs,* the play on which *Oklahoma!* was later based, Ritter built his image as a cowboy with a Texas drawl and was soon in demand in eastern colleges as a lecturer on the cowboy and his songs. Even the world of classical music was susceptible to cowboy fever, as Aaron Copland used cowboy songs in his ballets *Billy the Kid* (1938) and *Rodeo* (1942). The cowboy image had permeated all aspects of American art, music, film, theater, and literature.[11]

Kay Swift's fascination with Faye Hubbard, then, may not have been so startling as it had first appeared. The nation's keen interest in western novels and movies may have reminded Swift of the regenerative powers a less developed, less congested region might hold for her. She had enjoyed horseback riding since her childhood visits to her grandfather's home in Wilmington. As a young man, Joseph Swift had actually traveled to Montana via train and steamboat to recover from tuberculosis. Two years of rugged outdoor living and driving steers across the Rocky Mountains restored Swift to health. (Family legends that he drove the Deadwood Gulch stagecoach are unfounded.) He may have shared his appreciation for the fresh air and fascination with the West with his granddaughter. After her divorce Kay Swift would have had no access to Bydale or to the horses and the escape they offered. The wide, open spaces of the mythical West may have been a powerful attraction.[12]

The Faye-and-Kay

By the fall of 1939 Swift had left her job, her New York apartment, and her daughters for the Wild West. On the modest ranch that they purchased in central Oregon, she helped raise horses and Faye's two daughters—far from her own three children, whom she had left in the care of their father.

Her marriage to Hubbard (to whom she later referred simply as "the cowboy") was a shock to her friends, since she was a native New Yorker who always reveled in the social and cultural advantages of the city. She herself admitted, "Up until the time [the cowboy] galloped into my life, trampling down all my plans for the future—including a two-year lease on my Beekman Place apartment—I was . . . a confirmed New Yorker who thought that to leave my native city for any period longer than a week end would be to miss some vital happening that would put me hopelessly Out of Touch." Swift did recognize the humor in her situation and in 1943 published an autobiographical novel that described life on the ranch for this city slicker. It was entitled *Who Could Ask for Anything More?* a less-than-subtle reference to the final phrase of the Gershwin tune, "I Got Rhythm," which suggests that in spite of Kay's newfound happiness, George Gershwin was not far from her heart. In the introduction, she explains her decision to leave her New York life:

> Eighteen months spent in Radio City Music Hall as staff composer had been one of my favorite assignments. I had friends, a charming apartment, beaux, and delicious clothes. In short, a fast-moving life that held about everything I wanted, save one. Only that corny old wish common to most women, of being vitally necessary to someone you love, seemed unlikely to be granted. My daughters were nearly grown up and had gone away, two to school and a third to study music. Though they were fond of me, they had outgrown any active need for me; regardless of what I did, their lives went on much the same.

She continued, "I cannot recall making up my mind, at any given moment, to marry Chris [her fictional name for Faye Hubbard]. It just seemed inevitable and entirely natural to step off with him, leaving the place where I had always lived, the people I loved best on earth, and every single thing I had most enjoyed doing up to that time."[13]

The marriage did not appear to be a well-considered decision but rather an impulsive move to change the direction of her life. Swift viewed her move west as an opportunity to experience something different and as a second chance at happiness that many people never receive. "Out here I have the thing everybody in the world wishes for at one time or another—a second chance. Instead of running in the same groove as I'd be doing back home under the best conditions, here I am with a brand-new life, in a marvelous country, with a million Things I Never Knew Till Now." She appears to have reconsidered her values as a result of her age, Gershwin's death, and her loneliness and to have used this move as a means of rectifying her past. She could no longer save her relationships with Warburg or her own children, but perhaps she could prove herself an able wife and mother in a new situation.[14]

Swift certainly downplayed the need her daughters had for her. When she left the World's Fair, her teen-aged girls were hardly "grown up." It seems likely that they were more than "fond" of her, and needed her far more than she was willing to admit. Perhaps she deemphasized their needs in order to justify her own. She may have come to realize that her attention to her children had been deeply impaired by her interest in Gershwin. Interviewed on the documentary film *George Gershwin Remembered*, Swift revealed that April "did not like Gershwin at all because she thought he was a threat to my marriage—which, of course, he was." After the divorce, the girls' move to their father's home had undoubtedly left her somewhat guilt-ridden, and her sudden relocation to Oregon probably alienated them further. Once *Who Could Ask for Anything More?* was published, the girls' resentment must have increased. Aside from the opening disclaimer, Swift had not mentioned her own children, focusing on Hubbard's two daughters for the sake of the story, an omission that was hurtful to April, Andrea, and Kay.[15]

Andrea did visit Oregon several times, once with her sister, Kay, probably in the summer of 1940. They took the train west and found themselves "surrounded by aggressive, drunken cowboys." Andrea recalled being folded into a rumble seat at one point and that Kay had nearly been raped. She was amazed that further harm had not come to them in such wild territory. In a recent interview, April was philosophical about the marriage and her mother's choices. "My mother was very immature when she married my father. She did not know how to cook or keep a house or be a parent. . . . When she married Faye, she was more mature, and ready to raise children." Katharine Weber suggests that Swift was a much better grandmother than she was a mother, affirming April's assessment.[16]

Swift offered another explanation to a reporter in 1943: "A woman with any given ability can do one of two things in marriage: marry a man in her own line who beats her at it, or find a husband in a different line. You just flounder around in his: he looks casually at yours." Although she had not been married to Gershwin, she clearly thought of their relationship as equivalent to marriage. The statement makes no allowance for the variable degree of a man's talent, whether genius or mediocre, but implies that any man "in her own line" would emerge as being more successful than the woman. It suggests that Swift felt inferior in Gershwin's domain, doubting her skills and abilities in light of his. This may also have contributed to her reluctance to continue composing during that four-year period after 1930, in which Gershwin was so prolific. Her marriage to Faye Hubbard would have avoided such musical competition or comparison.[17]

It seems unusual that so little of Kay's rationale for this marriage focuses on her husband. Nine years younger than she, he was an imposing figure, well over six and a half feet tall and solidly built. He used to brag that he had broken every bone in his body at least once. April remembered him years later as "big, good natured, . . . Not exactly a Gary Cooper. . . . But he loved kids and he was nice." By his own admittance, he drank too much, and was unable to control his habit until he joined Alcoholics Anonymous in 1959. Kay's nephew Shippen Swift was just eight when the World's Fair opened, and he met Faye in the fall, after Kay and Faye were married. He has very vivid memories of the cowboy being kind, generous, and ever a child at heart—thus sometimes exercising poor judgment. On Faye's first visit to meet Shippen's grandmother (Sam's formidable mother-in-law), he unwisely demonstrated an Indian dance on the living room carpet. Shippen recounted, "He did the Chippewa Two-Step after about four or five Dr. Peppers. He opened a Coca-Cola bottle with his teeth! And you know what happens when you shake the Coke! [It sprayed all over] the Oriental carpet. And then he did a war dance and he had me [pounding] on an inverted scrap basket. He was leaping around the living room." Such exuberance would have been foreign to this grandmother, but the evening was just beginning. Shippen continued, "And then we went into dinner. Kay gave him the sign to hold the [grandmother's] chair. He sprang at her and she reacted like he was [attacking her]." When Faye finally sat down at the table, he straddled the chair, "put his bucket this high, and he split the back of the chair from the seat [upward]." The introduction was one the grandmother did not soon forget.[18]

Despite his recklessness and a strong temper, Faye was kind-hearted. On the ranch they kept eleven dogs, many of them greyhounds that Faye had adopted after they were retired from the racetrack. He and Kay both were friendly with the local Native American population, and employed Indians on their ranch. Indians could not purchase alcohol in Oregon, and since the Hubbards believed that the government should not be depriving people of their rights, Kay was occasionally known to buy a bottle or two for her Native American friends.[19]

Faye and Kay sold their horses to Hollywood production companies for use in the movies. They found it was easier to sell a horse already fitted with a saddle and bridle, so they returned to New York annually to buy tack at Miller's or Kauffman's Saddlery. During these visits to the city, Shippen got to know his aunt and new uncle better. They regularly took him along to shop, to lunch, to the rodeo, or to the theater. Once just Faye and Shippen went to lunch ("Do you want I-talian food or Mexican food?"). Shippen recalled that on their way to the restaurant, they stopped by a café where Faye slipped a substantial handout to an old friend, a lion tamer who had been mauled by a lion and had been unable to work since. The simple, generous gesture made a lasting impression. Kay's brother, Sam, was also very friendly with Faye and even went out west to visit them at the ranch. Shippen's mother did not allow him to accompany his father because they would have been too far from a Catholic church.[20]

Swift observed in her book that "Chris . . . gave the immediate impression of being resolved, like a number reduced to its lowest terms. He had that something which numberless people I know—myself included—have raised heaven and earth to acquire, a simple, happy adjustment to living. To be with him was, from the beginning, a refreshing, tonic sensation." The description "tonic sensation" suggests that Swift's attraction to Hubbard was more emotional than intellectual. She focused on his physical strength, his direct honesty and simplicity, his concern for his children, and his need for her, qualities that George Gershwin had not altogether possessed.[21]

Swift received a great deal of satisfaction from having someone else depend upon her. She comments in her book, "Three people out here, Chris and his two girls, really count on me and wouldn't get along as well without me." Faye Hubbard was a symbol of physical strength who offered her some direction at a time when she had none. At the same time he exhibited a need that she felt she could meet. In a maternal way, she administered to Hubbard, which may have brought her a sense of fulfillment.[22]

Perhaps the realization that Gershwin would never marry her had shaken her confidence far more than she realized. In 1939 Swift may have reasoned that the first season with the World's Fair was about to end, that she was now forty-two years of age and unmarried, and that she had lived most of her life in New York City. Her mother had died, and her brother was married to a woman whose family's intense devotion to Catholicism alienated Kay and the Warburg girls. With her daughter April away studying music and the other two daughters living with their father and his wife, Phyllis, Swift was very much alone. A ranch in Oregon would certainly offer her an escape from her loneliness and a change from the metropolitan culture and social life she knew.

Although Hubbard seemed to be the antithesis of James Warburg, he did share some traits with Gershwin. His family had been poor as he grew up on a farm near Spokane, and his social graces were limited. Swift may have thrilled at the prospect of experiencing a new way of life, as well as at the possibility of bringing an appreciation of the finer things in life to yet another beau. Of course, Gershwin's genius and celebrity balanced his lack of polish somewhat better than Hubbard's ranching skills offset his.

Remote as Bend, Oregon, was, Swift managed to continue musical activities there. They had a piano, so she could practice and compose. She recalled that her husband's favorite piece was Fauré's Impromptu in F, which evoked memories of Bertha Tapper. She gave piano lessons to Faye's daughters, Jo and Pat, and wrote a set of finger exercises for them to practice. She was also able to follow popular musical trends and publications. In her papers is a copy of George Gershwin's *Song Album*, published in 1938 by Harms and stamped with the address of "Bend Music Company, Bend, Oregon." Their annual trips to New York to buy saddlery kept Kay and Faye in contact with friends and the latest Broadway shows and fashion, so she had not altogether lost touch with her old life.[23]

Nephew Shippen recalled that during one such visit they came to see him when he was in the hospital with polio. Rather than the kind expressions of sympathy most visitors displayed, Faye strode in and bellowed, "Get up out of that ———— bed!" Shippen healed thoroughly, never forgetting Faye's persuasive cure. In contrast to Faye's bluntness was Kay's ever-present sense of propriety. In 1945, as Shippen was recovering from the polio, "she and I went to see [the revival of] *The Red Mill* and we sat up in the very first row behind the orchestra. Kay was greeting the orchestra members, 'Hello Ed, Bill.' . . . So I was thirteen. I said, 'I've got a cramp in my leg,' during some very poignant moment. 'I gotta stretch it!' Kay, who was supple, put both of her feet up on her seat and allowed me to stretch my leg into her space, all the while shushing me to be quiet."[24]

Swift did continue to compose a bit in Oregon, although little was published. Some of her creative energies were spent writing songs for her daughters, still in New York. A setting of the poem, "Velvet Shoes" by Elinor Wylie, for voice and piano, was written in 1940 for her daughter Kay and dated November 26, 1940, Kay's sixteenth birthday. Swift made a recording of the song in a studio in Bend for Kay. Swift did not sew or make handcrafted items, and money on the Oregon ranch was scarce. Compositions were gifts from the heart for her children.

Swift also wrote and recorded a song for her daughter Andrea's nineteenth birthday on September 29, 1941. She made a demonstration record in the Bend studio and sent it to Andrea. This recording features a three-part dedication in which Swift sings and accompanies herself on the piano. The first segment is an adaptation of "Happy Birthday" with a boogie-woogie bass. ("'Happy Birthday, dear Andy!' / How I wish it wasn't so unhandy / To say on your day / From three thousand miles away.") The second features a tuneful Broadway-style melody that Swift has modeled after the masters. ("If I could write you a melody like Rodgers or Kern.") It introduces a western bass during the piano interlude. The third, "When Are You Comin' Out West?" invites Andy to come back to the ranch.

> When are you comin' out west,
> When are you comin' to Oregon,
> To the state the sun's always shinin' on?
> When are you takin' that train?

Your mare is getting' lonesome for you.
You haven't seen her colt—it's true.
You'll stare at all the hounds that are new,
The twelve runnin' rascals and the puppies, too.

When are you comin' to stay?
Lordy, how we miss you at the Faye-and-Kay
Tell us by the state of that happy day,
When are you comin' out west?

On the final number, she loosens up during the piano interlude and comments, "Oh, how I wish I had an ocarina!" a small handheld wind instrument commonly known as a sweet potato. In theory the instrument would have allowed her to improvise on the melody more effectively, but its absence did not prevent her from adding scat singing to the interlude. The result is Kay Swift with a wish for her daughter's happy birthday and a heartfelt invitation to return to "The Faye-and-Kay."[25]

The flip side of the recording is equally unique. It features local cowboy Fritz Hoppe, who yodels and sings in two vocals, "Sweet Baby" and "The Tenderfoot," with Kay Swift on the piano. Apparently Faye and several cowboys had been drinking, mourning the death of Learack, a favorite old racehorse. After singing "Empty Saddles" several times and toasting the steed, they had ridden to the recording studio in Bend on their horses to help Kay send her birthday greetings. These two cowboy songs offer explicit evidence of the kind of music Swift encountered during her western retreat. Swift's vocal improvisations on "When Are You Comin' Out West" are not exactly yodels, but they do represent her spontaneity and carefree singing style. Both birthday greetings remained unpublished, but their existence in 1940 and 1941 indicates that Swift was continuing to compose in Oregon, if at a slow pace.[26]

Although Swift maintained contact with her daughters while she was on the West Coast and honored their birthdays with her songs, it was hard to remain closely connected to their lives at such a distance. By the spring of 1941, Andrea was married to Justin Feldman, whom she had met that year as a freshman at Barnard College. The wedding was held at the Warburgs' townhouse on East Seventieth Street in New York, hosted by James and Phyllis. Swift's birthday greeting, recorded the following September, does not mention Andrea's new husband.

Swift was a woman of great compassion and fortitude. When the nation entered World War II, she was very sympathetic to the cause, the dedication of soldiers sent overseas, the sacrifices of those who were injured or killed, and the importance of the supporting roles played by the women who were left at home. Like many of her colleagues who published songs in support of the war effort, such as Irving Berlin, Harold Arlen, Cole Porter, and Ann Ronell, Swift penned melody and lyrics for a song, "Fighting on the Home Front Wins," which urges women to save and sacrifice for the armed forces.

> We're not the Army. We're not the Navy.
> We got the work without the gravy.
> We're the dust pan crew standing back of you.
> Fighting on the home front wins!
>
> In every kitchen, we've got to pitch in
> If we're to save the food we're rich in.
> There's a job to do, but we'll all come through.
> Fighting on the home front wins!

The song expresses Swift's beliefs that women's support and cooperation were vital for morale. She herself visited the veterans' hospitals near Los Angeles during and after the war, very likely entertaining recovering soldiers with her music. "Fighting on the Home Front Wins," published in 1943, was among the many sheet music titles that cheered the war effort. Swift was offering her own support for the war while maintaining her professional activity and contacts with songwriters in the East.[27]

Who Could Ask for Anything More?

Kay Swift's decision to write her memoir while married to the cowboy was not unusual. Many women, including her grandmother, kept extensive journals for years. Not exactly a memoir, *Who Could Ask for Anything More?* was an exaggerated, fictional account of her life on the ranch, and it offered her impressions of carnival men, butchering, and the Fourth of July in Juniper Junction. What was unusual was its publication, an extremely important step for Swift. She had left New York and was not in close contact with her former career associates. This marriage removed Swift from the New York musical scene, including Broadway and Radio City Music Hall, which had so kindly nurtured her promising career. The book, released by Simon and Schuster four years after she left New York, put her name back in front of the public and gave her a reason to be celebrated when she did return to the city. She gave radio and newspaper interviews in conjunction with the book, and almost all referred to her accomplishments as a composer. That the book was published is probably a testament to her reputation as a composer rather than as a writer, although the novel was relatively well received. Writing was a talent she had inherited from her grandmother and father, and this professional endeavor followed the scriptwriting she had done at NBC and CBS. Swift must have found satisfaction in writing, for she produced articles, scripts, lyrics, and memoirs until the end of her life.

Many reviewers found the prose in her book "amiable and beguiling," and one exclaimed, "At last, a cowboy-meets-sophisticated-city-girl yarn that doesn't gag the reader!" In a radio interview with both Faye and Kay in August 1943, Margaret McBride, of New York station WEAF, told her listeners that she remembered Kay Swift as a "super-sophisticated New Yorker seen on opening nights." Other writers focused on different topics. An article by Helen Harrison in *New York Journal America* quotes Swift at length as she shares her opinions about western men. "Western men make Eastern men look like sissies! . . . Easterners have a phony quality. That is . . . the great majority of them. They're so fatally understanding even when a triangle turns up. It's talk, talk, talk. The guy from the cactus country is straight from the shoulder, wonderfully direct. He simply hauls off and socks his rival. In a word, he's masterful." Harrison observes, "This out of doorsy directness seems 'more advanced' to tiny, brunette Kay. . . . She thinks the pseudo-sophistication of the effete East is a hangover from the flaming '20s and is post-the-other-War stuff. 'What was very "Let Us Be Gay" of that period is just smartypants today,' she maintains." The rest of the article continues with Swift extolling the virtues of the West and criticizing aspects of her former life.

> "Western men," she asserts, "have attained that exhilarating quality for which people in the East pay psychiatrists huge sums of money. Perhaps it comes from the way of life out there, which is one of emergency, not only mental, but physical. Like stepping out of the path of the bull, for instance, and you can take that both ways! At home (. . . the ranch), one is apt to say exactly what one thinks— and take the consequences. Men there are enormously jealous and extremely possessive. And, more often than not, words lead to physical combat. Many a time I've watched my man fight it out with his fists. You learn to respect him. This War is perhaps the one hope for the Easterner who is bound to return not so introverted. He'll get back to fundamentals. . . . And what those larrupin' lads, those woo-men, know about romancing the opposite sex," says Kay, "would make ample material for a Mae West scenario."

These passages are filled with comments that demonstrate her confusion. Swift's admission that "men there are enormously jealous and extremely possessive" may be an indication of Faye Hubbard's behavior. His efforts to contain any flirtations by or toward his attractive wife may have resulted in "physical combat," although her reaction here affirms rather than criticizes such behavior. Her criticism of those who seek psychiatric help was undoubtedly fueled by her own disastrous experience with psychoanalysis under Dr. Gregory Zilboorg in 1934. Although the treatment probably created more problems than it solved, it is doubtful that Swift really believed that physical violence was a preferable alternative. Finally, such scorn toward a life that she admittedly had loved is suspect. She seems to be trying to convince herself of the benefits of westerners' base means of solving problems. To cite participation in the war as therapy for the easterner's "introverted" manner is as outrageous as it is senseless. She was either making a concerted effort to adjust to western ways or employing an effective publicity tactic.[28]

Regardless of the flaws in her book or in her thinking, Swift sold the rights to RKO Pictures, following the pattern of many playwrights and musicians who had left Broadway for Hollywood during the Depression. The book's sale placed Swift in an elite category of authors and garnered her additional recognition from her colleagues and the public. The movie, released in 1950, was entitled *Never a Dull Moment,* with Irene Dunne playing Kay's character, Kay Kingsley, and Fred MacMurray as the cowboy, renamed Chris Heyward. (Katharine Weber insists that John Wayne would have been more appropriate but that he was unavailable.) *Never a Dull Moment* is a romantic comedy, though it shares features common to many westerns, including the desolate landscape and its influence on the hero, as well as the confrontation between "civilization and wilderness, East and West." Kay Kingsley's sophisticated, urban background naturally conflicts with the life she now shares with Chris Heyward on the struggling Cougar Rock Ranch (the fictional name for the "Faye-and-Kay"). The movie reflects the tone and humor of Swift's book and illustrates some of the incidents she had related. Chris, the hero-cowboy, needs a wife to help him manage the distressed ranch and raise his two daughters. His choice of Kay sets up the East-West dichotomy as Kay struggles with Chris and with her eastern habits. Her manicured poodle, designer gowns, and lack of domestic skills provide immediate, comic contrast to the reality of life on the ranch.[29]

It was from the book and the proposed movie that Swift's next popular songs arose. She wrote nine songs for the film, although just three were used. She had hoped for greater exposure of her music in a musical, rather than in a film with several songs, and for a more positive response to the movie. Although western themes were popular in film and other genres, few musicals had featured western settings during the 1930s or 1940s. *Girl of the Golden West* (1938) emerged from Hollywood featuring Jeanette Mac-Donald and Nelson Eddy. Broadway focused on the West with Gershwin's *Girl Crazy* (1930) and Irving Berlin's *Annie Get Your Gun* (1946), the hit musical that was also made into a movie in 1950. Swift's western featured the same kind of wholesome, hard-working folks that had characterized Rodgers and Hammerstein's *Oklahoma!* in 1943. Unfortunately it did not have the magic of its predecessors.

Most of the songs Swift wrote for the musical invoke western images. Many feature the clip-clop dotted rhythms frequently associated with cowboy music, either in the accompaniment or in the melody. They are similar to her rhythmic Radio City pieces with a western drawl. Swift continues to use syncopated rhythms through nearly all the songs, with or without the dotted figures, and the melodies often feature large skips, as did her songs from the mid-1930s. In many cases the opening phrases are very tuneful, but the bridge or contrasting phrases are so chromatic and filled with awkward skips that they are hard to sing—perhaps too hard, from the point of view of the producer.

The western-style pieces include "Sagebrush Lullaby," "Gate to Nowhere," "Down Crooked River Way," "Me and My Jam-Up Friend," "Some of the Time I'll Miss You," "Nightmare in the Desert (Dance Pantomime)," and "He's a Pretty Fair Hand." Only a fragment of one of these songs, "Sagebrush Lullaby," was used in the film. It is a particularly attractive piece. The melody is typical of Swift, featuring chordal outlines, leaps of sevenths and octaves, and blue notes (ex. 7.1). Its unusual chromatic opening is reminiscent of blues influences, moving through chords on the lowered seventh and lowered sixth scale degrees, and contributes to the relaxed pace.

Even so, only the first eight bars are used in the film, in a scene in which composer Kay Kingsley is frustrated by writer's block and cannot seem to get past those opening measures. The two other songs that were used in the film are different in character. They include "The Man with the Big Felt Hat," a rousing number, and "Once You Find Your Guy," the romantic ballad of the film. "The Man with the Big Felt Hat" is a pseudo-folk tune that serves as the basis for a square dance welcoming Kay to Cougar Rock Ranch. Swift had obviously attended her share of western square dances and mimicked the simplicity of melody and rhythms in this lively tune. The song has a simple, singable melody accompanied by an equally simple harmony. Yet it avoids predictability because of its irregular phrase groups. Swift's deep understanding of her craft prevents her from settling for the ordinary, even when a mundane song would have sufficed.

The only song to be published, "Once You Find Your Guy," sounds more like Hollywood film music than any of the others. It occurs at the opening of the movie, while Kay Kingsley is still in New York, so it makes dramatic sense that this piece is more polished and urbane than the others set at the Cougar Rock Ranch. "Once You Find Your Guy" features a static opening

7.1 "Sagebrush Lullaby," measures 5–12

melody that seems to have difficulty in gaining momentum (the first twelve pitches alternate between C and B). The inert tune does meet with some contrast in the bass line, which moves upward and then downward by step and changes harmonies with each beat. The song uses fairly regular rhythms, avoiding the dotted rhythms that permeate the other western songs.

A significant difference between these and earlier songs is that Kay Swift is her own lyricist for these pieces. In each of them she communicates a very traditional ethic, forsaking the loose morals and sexual experimentation of the 1920s and adopting a fierce devotion to her man. This may be a personal statement, indicating that she has abandoned her former social life and chosen to dedicate herself to her home on the range with her cowboy. More likely it is a reflection of larger changes in society, which after a decade of decadence in the 1920s, grew more sober in the Depression, and matured through World War II. A Hollywood film would reach a far greater audience than a Broadway play and had to embody the values of mainstream America. With its strict production code, Hollywood in 1950 was far more conservative than Broadway in 1930. The lyrics of the opening ballad, "Once You Find Your Guy," emphasizes the importance of a long-lasting, monogamous relationship—hence, perhaps, the constancy of the repetitive opening pitches.

Once you find your guy you'll know the words to all the love songs
are true,
And once you find your guy it wouldn't matter if the earth split in
two.
Those lonely days you dreaded will vanish from your sight,
The future that was dark looks bright.

So once you find your guy, the one and only who looks right from
the start,
Don't wait till it's too late, but let him know that he is first in your
heart.
Don't miss the magic moment, don't let it pass you by.
Don't lose him once you find your guy.[30]

To the accompaniment of Hollywood strings, this mellow love song radiates the message that "your guy" will bring joy and that no time should be wasted in finding him. Memories of the marriages and engagements shattered by World War II, as well as the looming conflict in Korea, may certainly have contributed to the urgency imparted by the song.

Some lyrics in the songs written for *Never a Dull Moment* underscore the value of a couple's strong partnership. "Me and My Jam-Up Friend" attests, "Always with it, through thick and thin, / He works outside and I work in." "Down Crooked River Way" begs, "Don't keep me waitin' all year. I'll make you happy, honey, never fear! / Got to have you close to me. Come what may. / Down Crooked River Way." And "Gate to Nowhere" shares the desolation of a lost love. "Nothin' ahead that I can see, / Just like the life I'm livin' now, / My only love's forgotten me / Nothin' to do except to vow / I'll close this gate to nowhere." All imply the notion that one can only find happiness by sharing love with someone.

One piece that retains a bit of 1920s humor and sarcasm is "Some of the Time I'll Miss You": "Some of the time I'll miss you and wish you could be where I'm, / But shed no tear if, throughout the year, I miss you just half the time." (It is impossible to know whether Swift deliberately borrowed the rhyme "I'm/time" from Ira Gershwin's lyric to "I'm Bidin' My Time," from *Girl Crazy*.) The humorous thought continues until the last line, when concern for the relationship emerges more strongly: "Some of the time I'll miss you. I'm hoping you'll miss me too, / Yet, leave us face it, time does erase it, till we're as good as new, / But not where the guy/gal is you!" The harmony, like that in "Sagebrush Lullaby," begins with parallel motion downward by whole steps. The rhythm is syncopated but lacks the regular dotted rhythm of a "Western bass." Like so many other Swift melodies, this one features many leaps, some outlining triads, both diatonic and chromatic. The number and size of the leaps call for a slower tempo, making this a true ballad. Perhaps the colloquial "leave us face it" has been included in an otherwise standard lyric in order to remind the audience of the characters—simple, hard-working cowboys with little education or concern for grammar. This is one of the few pieces from *Never a Dull Moment* without a clear western theme or language, one that might have had a universal popularity—if RKO had used it in the movie.

Swift was fascinated with the western "lingo," although the cowboy slang often seems somewhat forced. ("It's no soap for this dope out here.") Several songs are so heavily laden with slang that someone without insider knowledge might easily not understand the text. Consider the final verse from "Me and My Jam-Up Friend":

Whenever a mark comes by, jerk,
Larry gives me the eye,
Wheel or tip—down, it's all the same,
Duke 'em in, and we know the game,
Weed 'em a fin, and we're not to blame,
Me and my jam-up friend.

Lyrics like these show how integral Swift thought her book would be to both the film and the music. For in *Who Could Ask for Anything More?* these colloquialisms are explained as "carnie talk," the expressions of carnival workers. Unfortunately the movie omits such explanations as well as the song.[31]

Always intrigued by language, Swift would typically adopt idiomatic expressions or the slang of the moment. For instance, she might change her order in a coffee shop by telling the waitress to "eighty-six the whole wheat toast." She was proud of her access to and knowledge of people from a variety of backgrounds, and was genuinely fascinated by cultural differences. Her eldest daughter, April, recalled her use of abbreviations in a slightly different light. She remembered her reassuring quip, "Well, it's not L and D" (life and death), and found her abbreviations unique, if "somewhat maddening." "She had her own little language that sometimes was humorous, and sometimes annoying." Katharine Weber also discussed her speech patterns: "Perhaps because of her English mother, Ganz abbreviated in a Bertie Wooster-ish way, toasting at celebrations with several glasses of 'champers,' telling taxi drivers to go to 'Mad Ave' or greeting friends on the phone with 'How are things in gen?' Once, walking down the street with me, she spotted the open shirt of a hirsute construction worker and then asked if I agreed with her that 'H.C.' (hairy chests) were unattractive." Swift's tendency to speak in a slang that only she and sometimes those close to her could understand is another indication of her creativity and humor, as well as the slight eccentricity that endeared her to friends and family.[32]

Other lyrics in the songs for *Never a Dull Moment* are dated or limited to specific situations by colloquial expressions: "Can't forget a tune that sounds so blue / Can't forget the wacky guy. / Got to love the buckaroo / And the Sagebrush Lullaby." Even in 1950, this song, a lovely ballad, would have had little chance of eliciting universal appeal with expressions like "wacky" and "buckaroo." Another ballad seems to try too hard to re-create the rural *Oklahoma!* formula. It begins: "Down Crooked River Way / Down where the feed is good for man and beast" and continues in the second verse: "Hills look as high as the sky, / Fat herds of cattle stare as we ride by, / Stacks o' good alfalfa an' fields o' rye. / Down Crooked River Way." Too many details about cattle feed and crops apparently provide more realism than the romance can support. The musical setting for this song, a recycling of Andrea's birthday invitation, was very effective, with its dotted rhythms and octave skips. Like George Gershwin and Irving Berlin, among others, Swift was not opposed to reusing a good tune if it had not been widely circulated in its original form. Swift's songs for *Never a Dull Moment* had very tuneful themes and imaginative harmonies. Although RKO may have found weaknesses in the lyrics, more than likely the producers simply cut the music for the sake of time.

Swift's book appeared in 1943 and was sold to RKO a year later, so she probably wrote the songs for *Never a Dull Moment* soon afterward, even though there is no documentation of them until the movie appeared seven years later. Although only one song from the movie was published, these songs kept Swift active in the profession. The movie placed her at the center of artistic activity, for Hollywood was now as prestigious as Broadway had been. Her ability to use her music in a film was a critical accomplishment. It may, however, have given her a false sense of success, as she later admitted. "Thanks to a first-rate publisher and an intrepid agent, the book was duly sold to a movie studio, which caused me to write a lot of music for the film (most of which was cut out of the final version) and to over-extend myself rashly, buying a house in California and going through several of the corny motions of being a successful screen writer, which in fact I was not." Most significant, though, was that Kay Swift was continuing to compose, positioning herself for opportunities in Hollywood.[33]

Hollywood

At the prospect of success on the silver screen, the Hubbards sold their Oregon ranch and moved to Hollywood. Many of Kay's New York friends and associates had come west to work in the booming motion picture industry in the 1930s. Besides George and Ira Gershwin, other veteran songwriters of Broadway, such as Harold Arlen, Richard Rodgers, Yip Harburg, Irving Berlin, and Cole Porter, had found their way to California for a while, and Ira Gershwin and Harold Arlen remained there still. Donald Ogden Stewart, who had written the book for *Fine and Dandy* in 1930, became a successful screenwriter, winning an Academy Award in 1940 for his screenplay for *The Philadelphia Story* and was still in California in the 1940s. Dave Chasen, who had been comedian Joe Cook's straight man in *Fine and Dandy*, had opened his legendary restaurant in Hollywood, the Brown Derby, an establishment frequented by many displaced New Yorkers. To some extent, Swift was able to recapture the old theatrical life on the West Coast.[34]

While in Hollywood, Swift began working with Ira Gershwin on another project. In 1945 the producers of Twentieth Century Fox had approached Ira about supplying lyrics for a film musical, *The Shocking Miss Pilgrim*, starring Betty Grable. When Ira suggested crafting new songs from George's unused music, the producers agreed and Swift was consulted. As critic Mark Steyn has observed, "For many years she was the only one to whom Ira would entrust his brother's unpublished manuscripts." Together they perused George's sketchbooks. Entertainer Michael Feinstein, who spent six years as Ira's secretary, relates the process as Ira had described it to him: "When she found a fragment that looked familiar to her, she wrote it down. If she remembered how he played it at the piano, she wrote out a full piano part for it. She and Ira very carefully went through almost every scrap of George's music that existed and organized and numbered the unpublished melodies." Together they "arranged" more than fifty complete songs, selecting the most appropriate to create a posthumous film score in George's name—the first since *The Goldwyn Follies*. Ira recalled the process: "We spent ten weeks going carefully through all my brother's notebooks and manuscripts; from them she played and then copied for me well over a hundred possibilities —forty or fifty complete tunes (several of which, such as 'Aren't You Kind of Glad We Did?,' I had started setting lyrics to in George's lifetime), plus verses, plus themes for arias, openings, & etc. . . . The music, outside of a few grace notes which I had to add for extra syllables, was all my brother's."[35]

The collaboration for *The Shocking Miss Pilgrim* encouraged Ira to continue sorting through George's papers, notebooks, and scrapbooks, assembling the artifacts for what would later become the Gershwin Archive at the Library of Congress. The "Gershwin Melody Collection," now a part of that archive, begins with the famous Melody Number 17, a piano prelude written in 1925 that Swift recalled in its entirety and reworked from sketches into a song entitled "Sleepless Night." Ira never got around to adding the lyric he intended, so it was finally published without one, as a piano piece in 1987. Lawrence Stewart believes that the numbering begins after the sixteen songs used in the Gershwins' films, *Shall We Dance*, *A Damsel in Distress*, and *The Goldwyn Follies*. The re-creations—some complete songs, some complete melodies with no harmony, and some fragments—end with Number 125.[36]

One of their most effective creations arose from a sketch that Ira had labeled "Gold Mine," Swift's name for this memorable tune. It became "For You, for Me, for Evermore." Steyn writes, "The latter produced a couple of lasting additions to the Gershwin oeuvre—'For You, For Me, For Evermore' and 'Aren't You Kind Of Glad We Did?'—but, over the years, more than a few of us wondered how much of the music was Gershwin and how much Swift." In preparing a Swift-Gershwin program for their cabaret act in the 1990s, Ben Sears and Brad Conner struggled with the style of "For You, for Me, for Evermore." Conner, the pianist, finally realized that if he approached it as a Kay Swift song rather than a George Gershwin song, the results were much more successful. Another song for the film, "Back Bay Polka (But Not in Boston)," lacks the typical Gershwinian syncopations and harmonies, and its authorship has also been questioned. Yet the song's function is to satirize the propriety of Bostonian society. To that end it employs a polka rhythm—not indigenous to that city—and several musical gestures more in keeping with a Gilbert and Sullivan chorus, such as a coda that echoes the closing phrase, and an eight-bar instrumental interlude between each of the four humorous verses. Both Swift and Gershwin had referenced the British duo in a number of situations, so it is difficult to isolate whose influence on this piece was greater. Swift later denied composing any of the music. "'Some of it was unfinished, but then we'd find a wonderful theme for a verse, so we'd make a verse out of it, and then Ira would write a lyric. But the music,' insists Miss Swift modestly, 'is all Gershwin.'" Her loyalty to the composer never wavered.[37]

Although the Hubbards' trip to Hollywood was to have been for a visit, Faye "became infatuated with California because he sold so many of his horses for use in the movies." By 1946 the couple had purchased a home in Van Nuys. Hubbard became a member of the Screen Actors and Wranglers union. He purchased a horse that later did the jumping scenes in *National Velvet*. After Kay sold her script to RKO Pictures, she gained employment in the RKO studios. She and Faye socialized with friends in Hollywood. She recalls two such occasions in her memoirs: "Faye . . . was with me at several Hollywood parties, one given in honor of Clark Gable. Every glamorous woman in the room, including several movie stars, fluttered up to Gable, trying their best to attract his attention, but Clark would have nothing to do with any of them, and spent the entire evening talking with Faye about fishing and hunting." Faye, never shy, would not have been inhibited by a screen star of Gable's status. The second incident shows Faye's less sophisticated side. "Extreme frankness characterized Faye's speech. He always got down, fast, to the nitty-gritty. Once, at a Thanksgiving dinner at the home of Ira Gershwin, Faye sat next to Dorothy Parker. Beaming, he turned to her and said, 'Well, now, little lady, what do you do?' Dorothy liked it fine, and replied that she was a writer."[38]

In spite of Swift's initial optimism and enthusiasm about beginning a new life in the West, her marriage to Faye Hubbard did not last. In her early years on the ranch, she had enjoyed the outdoors, the horses, and the simplicity of being a wife and mother. She was finding strength in the rural culture. Her enthusiasm for the Wild West apparently waned as the honeymoon years ended, however, and she and Hubbard divorced in June 1946, just months after they had purchased their home. Kay later explained that the marriage broke up "when she went to Hollywood and found fame, fortune and her own friends and . . . Hubbard found that he didn't like sharing his wife." She also thought that he might have been overwhelmed by her celebrity status and success with the book, an unusual situation for a cowboy. For his part, Hubbard attributed the breakup to his love of alcohol. "I got to drinking too much," he told a reporter. "She should have killed me." After their divorce Kay sold the Van Nuys house and boarded with a friend in Hollywood before purchasing a home in Benedict Canyon.[39]

Within eleven months of her divorce, Swift, nearly fifty, married for the final time on May 19, 1947, in the garden of her California home. Each successive husband was progressively younger than she, for Hunter Galloway was twelve years her junior. Also a New York City native, he had been born Hunter Galloway Kaufman but had legally changed his name to Hunter Galloway, effective March 12, 1942. During World War II, he spent two and a half years in the Signal Corps. While serving in the Persian Gulf command, he had taken charge of the local radio station. Galloway listed his work experience as an actor, director, and radio broadcaster and producer. Like Kay, he volunteered at a veterans' hospital near Los Angeles during and after the war. Although he did have some experience in radio broadcasting and the theater, after their marriage he seemed to spend most of his time corresponding for Swift (they kept carbon copies of nearly everything), helping her write several unsuccessful theatrical projects and managing her affairs. He sought work from various sources but never found steady employment in Hollywood. One project the couple worked on together was

Then Welcome Each Rebuff, a ninety-eight-page script that relates the story of paraplegics in the California Veterans' Hospital after World War II.[40]

Her compassion for war veterans was accompanied by her growing love for children. Decades later, a man who had lived in Benedict Canyon when Swift was there told her daughter Andrea that he had been a child actor in Hollywood. One summer, he contracted an extended illness, and Swift spent time each day reading aloud to him. He never forgot her kindness.[41]

It was during this period that two of Swift's loveliest ballads seem to have been written. The tune for "Now and Always" can be found in a sketch-book dated 1947, although it was not completed until 1962. A notation in the margin, "G.T.," designates it a "good tune," shorthand that George Gershwin had used to identify exceptional melodies in his own sketchbooks. It is indeed a good tune, featuring dramatic, wide leaps and chromatic motion, two Swiftian traits. Another song, entitled "One Last Look," is among her most melodic and poignant. Although this composition is not dated, the parallel triads in the accompaniment and the triplet figures are both features that she used in songs from the late 1940s. Swift wrote both the music and lyrics, which suggest an unfulfilled relationship and deep disappointment.

> Let's take one last look at what might have been.
> Dream just one more dream that we know can't win.
> If fate had willed our dream fulfilled,
> We two could weather any storm together.
>
> Though we met too late to be more than friends,
> What we've got is something that never ends.
> And so good-by to my good guy,
> We'll say no more but we'll close the book
> With one last look.

The ballad features an attractive melody distinguished by a triplet figure as well as a characteristic leap of a seventh (ex. 7.2). The chromatic harmonies, melodic sequences, and dramatic lyric propel this torch song, which was never published. The song seems to have been a vehicle for Swift to grieve and "close the book" on a particularly significant portion of her life. Although

7.2 "One Last Look," measures 1–8

it is romantic to think that this song may have been yet another farewell to George Gershwin, she apparently wrote it in memory of a serviceman with whom she had become acquainted.[42]

Another piece for voice and piano, "Poems in Praise of Practically Nothing," seems also to date from this period. An art song rather than a popular song, the extended piece is a series of short, whimsical settings of excerpts from five poems by Samuel Hoffenstein. A native New Yorker, Hoffenstein had spent years in Hollywood writing many screenplays and had befriended Swift during her days working for RKO. His death in 1947 may have prompted this tribute.

Aside from these shorter works, Swift and Galloway worked on a number of promising projects while in Hollywood, but nothing ever materialized. Swift worked with Robert Lewis Taylor on *Hark, Hark, the Clark! The Bobby Clark Story*, a musical version of the entertainer Clark's life. Galloway "acted as coordinator," and Cheryl Crawford, who had directed the revival of *Porgy and Bess* in 1942, was planning to produce it. The project fell through in 1948 after Clark expressed reluctance to commit to it a year in advance and the producer reconsidered.[43]

Swift and Galloway also worked with writer George Oppenheimer on a potential Broadway show and television series entitled *Sarah Was There*, based on a character by Frank Sullivan. This project featured a ghost named Aunt Sarah who finds herself in a variety of scenarios. This was to be a musical revue with songs by Swift and a loose plot. Each week Aunt Sarah's adventures would place her in danger of being committed to a sanitarium. The theme song, "Sarah Was There," hints at the ghost's numerous and wide-ranging experiences. "Sarah was there, no matter when, no matter where. / Just look at hist'ry's pages, through the ages Sarah was there. / You swear Sarah was there." Another song, "Donna Sarah's Recitative," conveys the ghost's overbearing presence. "But as I seem to drive men off their rockers, let's agree, / When all is said and done, that I'm the end!" Her self-absorption continues in the second verse: "But women seem to loathe me, so, you see. / We've got to realize, though I have malice toward none. / There's nothing—simply nothing—like me!" This dialogue was to be spoken with the accompaniment of a celeste, whose bell-like tones both contrasted with her strength and represented the celestial existence she now enjoyed. The accompaniment is written in the classical style, with arpeggiated chords and trills, another ironic counter to the brashness of Sarah's claims. Among potential casting choices the writers discussed was Ethel Merman in the starring role.[44]

Several songs for the project bear lyrics by Ralph Freed. Freed had worked with many composers in Hollywood and would collaborate on hundreds of songs, such as "(I Like New York in June) How About You" and "Babes on Broadway," which he wrote with Burton Lane. One of his most effective collaborations with Swift for *Sarah Was There*, "When You Hear This Music (Remember Me)," employs a rumba beat. Written in a minor key, it has a Cole Porter–like melody yet still bears the Swift imprint, featuring wide intervals and sudden chromatic harmonies. The interesting musical arrangement features a detailed and very pianistic accompaniment. Two choruses for piano and voice are followed by a lush nineteen-bar piano interlude before the third chorus. This arrangement was undoubtedly intended to be orchestrated yet works well as a piano accompaniment with its rumba rhythms, Spanish guitarlike riffs, and syncopated countermelodies. It indicates Swift's keyboard conception of music and suggests her excellent performance skills.

"Vienna" is a song intended for an episode or sequence set in that romantic city. It used the waltz meter that Swift so frequently relied on for particular effects; but more pointedly, it parodied the Viennese waltzes of the "Waltz King," Johann Strauss, employing exaggerated dissonances and large leaps in sequential passages. *Sarah Was There* was a speculative venture, and its writers were prepared to work either in Hollywood or on Broadway, wherever they received the first commitment. Although they made a demonstration film as a pilot for the series, apparently no studio on either coast was interested, and the project was dropped.[45]

After working on *The Shocking Miss Pilgrim* and *Never a Dull Moment*, Swift was no doubt hoping for further success in Hollywood. She had contacts there and had proven her versatility. Yet although her work in this period exhibited much musical wit and imagination, it had failed to win financial backing by producers. Since her marriage in 1947, Hunter Galloway had become involved in all of Swift's undertakings. Never employed elsewhere and never a strong entrepreneur or even a reliable businessman, Galloway clearly did not enhance his wife's career. He may indeed have been a detriment to her advancement.

Their prospects in California depleted, Swift and Galloway returned to New York in 1948 to be near her family. Swift's daughters were now all married. April had married her voice teacher, Balthasar Gagliano, in 1943. Swift's youngest daughter, Kay, had wed Robert Levin in October 1947, and Andrea, divorced from her first husband, had married Sidney Kaufman later that year. April was about to have her first baby, Kay's first grandchild. By December, Kay and Hunter were settled in an apartment at 400 East Fifty-ninth Street, adjacent to the Queensborough Bridge. She would live in this building for the next forty-five years. Swift received a substantial advance on her third-quarter royalty check from ASCAP, indicating that the couple was suffering budget problems. Straitened finances probably continued the next year, too, for Swift requested and received advances on her royalty checks for three quarters in 1949.

Kay Swift may have left Hollywood somewhat discouraged about her professional luck, but she had not given up. On the contrary, her western retreat seems to have convinced Swift to become more productive. She soon won the opportunity to write for an assured Broadway production, a show written by and starring her friend Cornelia Otis Skinner.

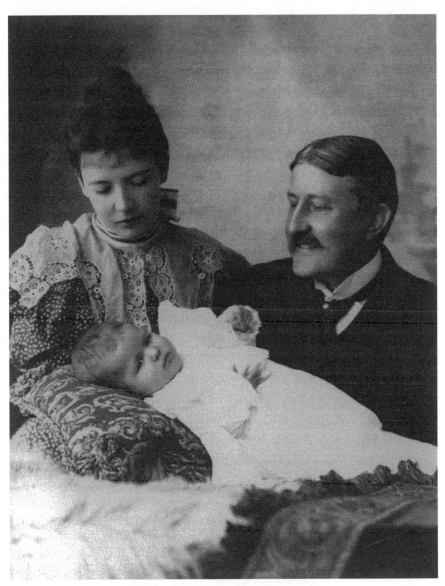

Infant Katharine Swift with her mother, Ellen Faulkner Swift, and her grandfather Joseph Swift, 1897 (Courtesy of Shippen and Eleanor Swift)

Katharine Swift with her parents, Samuel and Ellen Swift, c. 1899 (The Kay Swift Papers, Courtesy of Katharine and Nicholas Weber, Trustees, The Kay Swift Memorial Trust)

Katharine Swift and her brother, Samuel, Jr., Wilmington, Delaware, June 1912
(The Kay Swift Papers, Courtesy of Katharine and Nicholas Weber, Trustees,
The Kay Swift Memorial Trust)

Katharine Swift and James Warburg, wedding photo, 1918 (Bachrach photo, The Kay Swift Papers, Courtesy of Katharine and Nicholas Weber, Trustees, The Kay Swift Memorial Trust)

April, Andrea, and Kay Warburg, 1928 (G. W. Kissling photo, The Kay Swift
Papers, Courtesy of Katharine and Nicholas Weber, Trustees, The Kay Swift
Memorial Trust)

Katharine Swift Warburg and her daughters at Bydale, 1928 (The Kay Swift Papers, Courtesy of Katharine and Nicholas Weber, Trustees, The Kay Swift Memorial Trust)

Kay Swift and George Gershwin riding horses at Bydale, 1928 (Courtesy of Katharine and Nicholas Weber, Trustees, The Kay Swift Memorial Trust)

Rehearsal for *Fine and Dandy,* 1930. *From left,* Joe Cook, Dave Chasen, Kay Swift, James Warburg (Billy Rose Theatre Collection, The New York Public Library for the Performing Arts, Astor, Lenox and Tilden Foundations)

Kay Swift wearing gold bracelets from George Gershwin, c. 1934 (Courtesy of Katharine and Nicholas Weber, Trustees, The Kay Swift Memorial Trust)

Kay Swift in leopard coat, c. 1934 (Courtesy of Katharine and Nicholas Weber, Trustees, The Kay Swift Memorial Trust)

Kay Swift and Faye Hubbard, 1939 (Frank Northap photo, The Kay Swift Papers, Courtesy of Katharine and Nicholas Weber, Trustees, The Kay Swift Memorial Trust)

Kay Swift and Faye Hubbard with trophy deer, 1941 (Courtesy of Shippen and Eleanor Swift)

Kay Swift and Hunter Galloway, wedding photo, 1947 (Courtesy of Katharine and Nicholas Weber, Trustees, The Kay Swift Memorial Trust)

Kay Swift seated, c. 1975 (Edwin Gann Snyder photo, The Kay Swift Papers, Courtesy of Edwinn Gann Snyder Trust)

Kay Swift in front of apartment building, 1980 (Judy Cimaglia photo, The Kay Swift Papers, Courtesy of Katharine and Nicholas Weber, Trustees, The Kay Swift Memorial Trust)

Kay Swift with daughters (*from left*, Kay, Kay, Andrea, April) at Merkin Hall concert, 1986 (The Kay Swift Papers, Courtesy of Katharine and Nicholas Weber, Trustees, The Kay Swift Memorial Trust)

CHAPTER 8

She'll Have Manhattan

Home is a wagtail place, you know.—Kay Swift, "Smiling Betsy"

Initial Efforts

When Kay Swift returned to New York in 1948, she must have felt the thrill of coming home to the city she loved. Having faced a number of disappointments in California, she was, no doubt, eagerly anticipating many professional opportunities for both herself and her new husband. They first tried to capitalize on music she had already written. She promoted a recording of the ballad, "Once You Find Your Guy," before the release of *Never a Dull Moment* in 1950. Singer Louise Carlyle made a demonstration disk of the song, and Swift was hopeful for its future. She recalled that the publisher, Larry Spier, "was keen about Louise, the song, and the lyric." He convinced a recording company on the coast to feature Margaret Whiting, and she made an "excellent" recording. The eternal optimist, Swift was certain that "Once You Find Your Guy" would be in "that enviable group, the Top Ten. . . . I couldn't have been more wrong. Nobody else heard of the song, until a television show called 'The American Theater of the Air' included it in an hour's show devoted to my music." A fortunate outcome of the session was the meeting between Kay Swift and Louise Carlyle. They formed a fast friendship that lasted until Kay's death in 1993.[1]

Kay also resumed her friendship with Mary Reinhardt, now married to Albert D. Lasker, a pioneering advertising executive who would become one of the nation's foremost philanthropists. The Lasker Foundation, established in 1942, continues to present prestigious awards for medical research. Mary and Kay lunched together nearly every week. It was now Mary who gave Kay her hand-me-down mink coats every year or two.[2]

Swift and Galloway made a more extensive demonstration record of Kay's music, which they sent off to the Disney studios. The two of them sang "a flock of songs; I played some instrumental music. Just as I always feel sure I shall win a lottery, I waited confidently for a letter suggesting that we fly back to California to work for Disney. But no such letter came, only the record with its routine 'very sorry, but' note."[3]

A unique collaboration with Deems Taylor in 1950 led to a proposed stage show entitled *Spring Again*. Taylor was an American composer and critic, as well as the opera commentator for NBC radio. While Taylor selected and arranged ten operatic arias by Giacomo Puccini as popular songs, Swift updated the lyrics. This was a common practice that gave beautiful arias renewed life and exposure to the general public, in the manner that the middle section of Chopin's Fantaisie-Impromptu became "I'm Always Chasing Rainbows." *Spring Again* featured music from *Tosca, Manon Lescaut, Madame Butterfly,* and *Girl of the Golden West* with such titles as "You're Impossible to Please," "I'd Forgotten," "Twilight Is Falling," and "Call It Love." Nothing in the subsequent publicity indicates that the show was ever produced, nor is it listed in Taylor's works, but the drafts in Swift's papers indicated that she was again making contacts and working with New York musicians. It is interesting that she was doing so as a lyricist rather than composer, another example of her abilities with text. Also among her collaborations of this time is a song by Roger Machado, "The Dark Wind Plays a Lonely Tune," published by Ricordi in 1953. Originally a Spanish song, Swift wrote English lyrics for it. She was clearly using all of her talents to open doors, receptive to any type of creative work that resulted. She opened an office furnished with an upright piano at 400 East Fifty-seventh

Street, two blocks from her apartment, so that she would have fewer distractions and more privacy to compose.[4]

Return to Broadway

Soon a significant project materialized for Swift and brought her back to the Broadway stage with a friend from childhood. *Paris '90* was a one-woman revue written and performed by Cornelia Otis Skinner. The show played on Broadway for nearly three months in 1952, a record for a solo production, before touring in the United States and Europe. *Paris '90* featured sketches of diverse female characters who might have occupied Parisian cafés, museums, universities, entertainment venues, and streets in the 1890s and was inspired in part by the work of Henri de Toulouse-Lautrec, who depicted scenes and faces of high and low society in late-nineteenth-century Paris. Legend has it that Lautrec was born of nobility during France's Third Republic. His father, Count Alphonse de Toulouse-Lautrec-Monfa, spent his time riding, hunting, and sketching such sporting scenes. Drawing was an acceptable pastime for aristocrats, and even though the Toulouse-Lautrec lineage might not have been as esteemed as others, the family assumed the noble mantle and practices. Although Henri was always small and weak owing to a congenital condition, two broken legs during his adolescent years not only crippled him permanently but stunted the growth of his legs, so that he never reached the height of five feet. When Lautrec decided to pursue art as a profession, his father neither understood nor approved, believing that for nobility, art should be an avocation, not a source of income. Perhaps because of his disability, Lautrec developed an affinity for society's unfortunates. Rather than depict the landed gentry at leisure, he found his themes in Montmartre. He was fascinated with the theater and with the daily activities of the working class and the nightlife, particularly bars, nightclubs, and brothels, and he made these the subjects of his paintings and posters. Lautrec also experimented with light, color, and the broadly applied brush strokes of some of the early impressionists, departing from tradition in style as well as in subject matter.[5]

The daughter of actor Otis Skinner, Cornelia Otis Skinner had been friends with Kay Swift since childhood. Her portrayal of fourteen female characters, some comic and some tragic, comprised the action of *Paris '90*. A series of tableaux included women from all classes and walks of life in Paris in the 1890s. They ranged from "A Lady of Fashion, . . . a worldly, candybox blonde whose major preoccupations are with her luncheons, shopping, social calls and romantic rendezvous," to "A Boston School Teacher," an aging scholar working on her doctorate in Paris who suddenly sees herself as a "dowdy, ridiculous frump." The last four characters—"La Goulue (The Glutton)," "Lion Tamer of the Medrano Circus," "Berthe La Sourde (Deaf Bertha)," and "Yvette Guilbert"—were Lautrec's friends, immortalized in his distinctive posters. Swift offered vocal and instrumental music to accompany each vignette, with orchestrations done by Robert Russell Bennett. This was her first association with Bennett since 1927, when he had orchestrated Richard Rodgers's *Connecticut Yankee* and she had been the rehearsal pianist. (Bennett, who arranged more than three hundred Broadway shows in his long career, later orchestrated four more of her works.) *Paris '90* was the first music for large ensemble that Swift had written since *Alma Mater* in 1934, and its array of eclectic characters offered her the opportunity to juxtapose a variety of musical styles as she portrayed each of them. Skinner sang five of Swift's songs, a first for the actress.[6]

Paris '90 premiered in Northampton, Massachusetts, in January 1952. The preview tour traveled to Wichita, Kansas, and Saint Louis, Missouri, among other cities, before its Broadway opening at the Booth Theatre in March. Swift played piano in the pit orchestra on the tour. She enjoyed traveling, but she also accompanied the show to oversee any changes in the music that might have been made. "One has to protect one's own music, because as the show gets cut, who knows what key the music will go into. I didn't want to go into Q-flat suddenly," she quipped.[7]

This was not musical theater in the traditional sense, since the dramatic action of Miss Skinner was the central focus, and only half of the pieces had lyrics. Swift's score reflects Lautrec's combination of high and low society through the use of light operatic, impressionistic, and popular musical styles. Besides the Overture, which is a joyous can-can, "Calliope" is the main theme music, and it was promoted as the identifying song. Swift's opening lyric assumes the air of a classical ode and features the triple meter of a traditional ballroom waltz, both symbols of American highbrow culture in 1952.

> Calliope, Calliope,
> The sound of your voice means the springtime to me.
> From all of my troubles you set me free,
> My beautiful circus Calliope!

The waltz form, which a century earlier had been considered a vulgar intrusion from Germany requiring far too much speed and body contact for refined society, was now a conservative form, following the wild jitterbugs and jazz dances of the 1940s. In contrast to such dignity, the music's circus connotations set the mood and scene of a carefree Paris in the gay nineties. The second verse, too, tempers the proper lyrics with a boast, "Calliope, Calliope / All other bands can go jump in the sea." Featuring interludes that mimic a carousel organ, "Calliope" embodies the optimism and naïveté of a past era while recalling the elegance of the waltz. Unfortunately, the melody, rhythm, and harmony in this song are rather repetitious and predictable, the one quality Swift loathed.[8]

Another operetta-style piece, "The Waltz I Heard in a Dream," is scored for chorus and is reminiscent of such gay nineties tunes as "After the Ball," by Charles K. Harris. The song is typical of late-nineteenth-century fare, with lyrics equating love and nature. The melody frequently outlines basic chords and uses sequences to shape the well-balanced arch form. The harmony introduces several embellishing chords common to that period. As in "Calliope," the rhythm relies on two regular waltz patterns that permeate the piece and that become somewhat repetitive. Although the song does evoke a picture of a waltzing couple whirling in circles, it is not a tune that would have broken out of the show as a hit in 1952.

Representing a lowbrow style is the number sung by a British con artist operating on the streets of Paris. "Lend Me a Bob Till Monday" provides humor and a shift in focus from the Parisian upper class. Although members of high society certainly enjoyed horse-racing and equestrian activities, there is no doubt that this experience at the race track represents that of the have-nots ("Lend me a bob till Monday, 'erbert, me boy, / I've got an 'orse, winner, of course"). Once again, Kay Swift demonstrates her affinity for dialect and speech patterns. The absence of initial "h" sounds on "'orse" and "'erbert" are a typical cockney touch. This shift in dialect and class is accompanied by a shift in musical style. Swift's wit is evident throughout "Lend Me a Bob Till Monday." She abandons the waltz and returns to the duple meter and syncopation more common to Broadway and popular song. Although the song is only twenty measures long, it includes several chromatic harmonies that lend interest and direction to the syncopated melody. Swift employs a couple of conventional gestures to enhance her setting and to emphasize how routine the gambling effort is. A grace note in the accompaniment on the after-beat punctuates the phrase, "I've got an 'orse, winner, of course," almost like a wink.

"A Woman of Virtue" accompanies the tale of a woman, "a coquettish blonde," who narrowly resists the temptation to have an affair. In spite of her flirtations, "she is determined to remain a faithful wife" while her husband is out of town. Swift's humor surfaces in this instrumental piece as she ironically depicts this woman's virtue and near-fall-from-grace. She uses a seductive rumba rhythm followed by lush romantic harmonies and ends with a hint of the blues, music from the African-American tradition whose performance by classic female blues singers would have covered the topics of loneliness, anger, violence, or self-sufficiency—but probably not virtue.[9]

"A Boston Schoolteacher" is accompanied by an instrumental piece that illustrates Swift's subtle sense of humor to an even greater degree. The aging scholar has had years of proper education yet is dissatisfied with her life. Swift has filled her music with impressionist seventh chords, dissonance, use of pedal, augmented triads, and parallel triads, invoking the musical language of Debussy. The Boston schoolteacher has come to appreciate Debussy's philosophy—that the approach to art and music should be more a sensuous experience than an intellectual exercise. She sees that her pursuit of knowledge has been at the expense of pleasure and now considers abandoning the classical rules and enjoying life more. Swift's musical reference to Debussy's style in *Paris '90* was most appropriate, since the composer had actually frequented Reynold's, the same Irish and American tavern in Paris whose colorful clientele inspired so many of Lautrec's posters.[10]

The music for "A Boston Schoolteacher" begins in E flat minor; although the tonality is not clear from the opening measures, which alternate between A flat 7 and E flat 7 chords and end in measure eight on a deceptive cadence.

8.1 *Paris '90*, "A Boston Schoolteacher," measures 16–23

This may represent the schoolteacher's indecision, her wavering between her former studies and rigid lifestyle and the possibilities that lie before her. The second theme also avoids clear confirmation of E flat, with the use of secondary dominants and chords in third relationships. Swift has not abandoned functional harmonies but has colored them with chromatic pitches and used them in unconventional ways (ex. 8.1).

Unusual in its simplicity and its poignancy is a serene ballad, "The House Where I Was Born (Peaceful Theme)," which describes a pastoral setting in contrast to the bustling streets of Paris. This was performed by character Berthe la Sourde (deaf Bertha), who recalls her childhood home.

> Down by the house where I was born
> There's a brook where the deer came at sundown.
> I used to watch while birds would warn,
> Warn the deer that a stranger was near.
>
> Time went slowly in that peaceful place.
> How I used to want a swifter pace!
> Who can hold you? What can make you stay?
> You know you'll go, you're on your way.

Now there's no house where I was born.
Nothing's left but the brook and the wild deer.
If I return, will new birds warn,
Warn the deer that a pilgrim is near?

The music is a simple ballad with an even rhythm and is consistent with contemporary Broadway trends. It is fairly diatonic, with one well-placed chromatic chord in the opening phrase (on "sundown") that becomes the "hook" of the song (ex. 8.2). (Measure four of this melody is similar to a portion of the first phrase of "Oh, What a Beautiful Mornin'!" which opened *Oklahoma!* in 1943. The fragment of melody that fits Swift's lyric, "the deer came at sundown," corresponds to Rodgers and Hammerstein's "a beautiful mornin'," although the rhythm is altered.) Swift thought that this piece merited recording, and Cornelia Otis Skinner approached Bing Crosby about singing it. Crosby forwarded the request to conductor John Scott Trotter for his opinion, since Crosby did not read music. Trotter was intrigued by "The House Where I Was Born," mesmerized by the music but concerned that the imagery was "too poetic." Although Crosby seemed willing to record a "prestige platter," no recording was ever made.[11]

The final song of *Paris '90* is a French tune popularized by the Paris cabaret singer Yvette Guilbert, the subject of one of the tableaux. Not a beautiful woman, Guilbert was the engaging entertainer who represented the joie de vivre of Paris in the 1890s. "She was a tall, thin young woman, with a skinny neck and skinny arms, made to look even thinner by elbow-length black gloves. Flat-chested, of course; and her face consisted of an immense mouth, a bulbous nose and a pair of black, hollow eyes. . . . love songs were not in her line. So from ten till eleven o'clock in the evening, she delivered her *Pièces acides*." "Madame Arthur," a song Yvette Guilbert actually performed, is sung first in French and then in a "free translation" by Swift. The French version essentially complains that Madame Arthur talks too much but has "that certain thing" that men find attractive. They are always disappointed, for she needs a new lover each day. Swift took more than a few liberties with this theme. Several of her verses suggest (in diminishing degrees of subtlety) that Madame Arthur has a hidden appeal

8.2 *Paris '90,* "The House Where I Was Born," measures 1–4

that seems to be related to her high kicks and the fact that "she wears no pants."[12]

In his posters and paintings, Henri de Toulouse-Lautrec portrayed women in high society as well as in brothels, juxtaposing contrasting classes. In the music for *Paris '90,* Kay Swift employed a variety of musical styles to illustrate class differences—from the sophistication of "The Waltz I Heard in a Dream" to the simplicity of "The House Where I Was Born" to the bawdiness of "Madame Arthur" and "Lend Me a Bob Till Monday."

Following the Broadway run, *Paris '90* traveled throughout the United States and then had engagements in Paris, London, and Dublin. Road engagements lasted more than seven months, from September 1952 through April 1953. Swift felt it was the best work she had written to date, and she sent copies of the *Paris '90* recording to her friends for Christmas in 1952. The *New Yorker* commented on "some really excellent incidental music by Kay Swift" and noted George Gershwin's influences on her musical style. The *New York Times* magazine applauded Swift's score and Nathaniel Shilkret's conducting. "Miss Swift's sentiment is dry and brisk, her style is sophisticated and skimming and she has caught the mood of the show in a portfolio of salty music." Brooks Atkinson enthusiastically noted, "Miss Swift's dry and mettlesome score . . . is a work of delight. Perhaps 'inspiration' would be the better word. For Miss Swift has provided the period and a modern point of view in the music."[13]

Throughout the late 1940s and 1950s, Swift wrote charming music. Putting her great knowledge of classical music to use, she wrote in a more popular vein. Her sense of humor is a delightful but subtle enhancement of the score. *Paris '90* was Kay Swift's last Broadway effort. Songs she wrote after this production were never widely known, and none became as popular as her songs for *Fine and Dandy*. Of course, by 1952 Swift was a grandmother in her fifties. In a few short years, Elvis Presley would steer the course of mainstream popular music away from the swing era and into rock and roll.

Reaching for the Brass Ring

Swift's first grandchild inspired one of her most meaningful works, a blend of elegance, simplicity, and love. Guido Gagliano was born in 1949 to her oldest daughter, April, and as he grew Swift penned a commemorative song for the child, remembering some of his favorite things. April's daughter, Francesca (1951), prompted another, as did Kay's three children, David (1950), Betsy (1951), and Rachel (1954), and Andrea's John (1951) and Katharine (1955). Reminiscent of the nursery songs written for her own daughter in 1921, *Reaching for the Brass Ring* is a cycle of songs, each composed as a gift honoring the youngest child. "I wanted to make something for my grandchildren with my own hands, so to speak—and I can neither sew, knit nor paint anything whatsoever. Each grandchild has his or her own song." In his notes to a 1975 recording of Kay Swift's music, Edward Jablonksi points out that these are "songs for and about children that are not childish. They are musically incisive, making a memorable point, then going on to the next one—like folksong." Titled "Reaching for the Brass Ring," "Bath Time," "I've Got a Horse," "Ridin' His Bike," "The Sleepy Song," "Smiling Betsy," and "My Teeny Restaurant," each song captures an identifying trait or favorite activity of each of Swift's grandchildren.[14]

These are art songs, less formulaic than her Broadway pieces, and they feature fewer jazz rhythms. "Smiling Betsy" is typical, set in a lilting 6/8 meter (ex. 8.3). Each verse is twelve measures long, a four-measure phrase followed by an eight-measure phrase, with piano interludes between each verse—a departure from the regular four-measure phrases of Swift's popular songs. The melody is characteristically a mix of conjunct motion and some very unusual larger skips. Swift extends the second phrase with a motive that could easily have been an ordinary sequence ("Cloudy and grey?

8.3 *Reaching for the Brass Ring,* "Smiling Betsy," measures 8–16

Warmer or cold?"), yet she avoids the predictable and alters the last pitch of the pattern. The piece begins in C major, then modulates up a half-step, to D flat for the final verse. Harmonies are triadic and functional, with sevenths and added tones creating mild dissonances. A favorite chord from her popular songs, the blue subdominant, is used in measure 10; yet this is more sophisticated than a popular song.

Seven of the nine songs from *Reaching for the Brass Ring* were completed by 1952. They were orchestrated by Robert Russell Bennett and performed three times in 1953 by the Philadelphia Symphony Orchestra, with Swift's friend Louise Carlyle as the soloist. They were also performed by the Cleveland Orchestra and New Orleans Symphony, as well as by several orchestras in Western Europe in 1957. Two subsequent additions to the family prompted the final songs of the set, "Rachel Is the Singing One" and "Three Balloons." For a grandmother who did not knit, crochet, or sew, these songs represent personalized gifts from the heart to her children's children.[15]

The 1950s yielded some successes for Kay Swift, but the decade was also shadowed by a series of professional disappointments. After her limited victories in Hollywood (*The Shocking Miss Pilgrim* and *Never a Dull Moment*), a return to Broadway might have triggered a comeback for her, had she been able to follow it with another successful production. Her music for *Paris '90* was extremely attractive and well written. Yet the show was first and foremost a dramatic work with background music and several songs. Since Cornelia Otis Skinner herself was not a singer, she could not very successfully issue a recording. The failure to persuade a big name to record "The House Where I Was Born" in order to appeal to the radio market sealed the song's fate.

Other Efforts

Paris '90 was one of only two stage works by Swift from the 1950s that made it to production. Swift and Galloway tried again to launch a situation comedy for television, this one with a baseball theme, entitled *Here's the Pitch*. Written by Hunter Galloway with Alfred Stern, this was to be a television series that dealt with every facet of the game. No dates are indicated on the material, but the collaboration with Stern and lyricist Ralph Freed places it in New York in the 1950s or 1960s. Swift wrote a theme song, "Baseball, Baseball." Swift and Freed had earlier worked together in California on several songs for the proposed television show *Sarah Was There*. When the opportunity emerged for the two of them to break into television with another series, Freed moved his family to New York. Unfortunately, this project never materialized, either, and Freed returned to California. Three complete songs and a sketch for a fourth remain of their joint efforts.

The refrain of "Baseball, Baseball" ("Baseball, baseball, / Nothing can ever replace ball") sums up a love for the game that Swift had held since the age of eleven. Various episodes in the television series would focus on the minor characters of professional baseball rather than the players—bat boys, mascots, players' wives, and concessionaires. Freed's verses rely on double entendre, so the song is not just a tribute to the game but a humorous novelty song. Her friend Celeste Holm later used it in a nightclub act.

I come from a ball-playing family,
We've played in it year after year.

But Father liked highballs,
And missed all the fly balls
And loused up his baseball career. . . .

Last week I was out with a sore arm.
I gave it a terrible wrench.
But we'd just signed a cute and most pleasant recruit
And the two of us warmed up the bench. . . .

One night the Washington team had me floored,
I was hit harder than I could afford.
But eventually, only one Senator scored!
How I love baseball!

Swift's music reflects this not-so-subtle humor. She has chosen a dignified waltz setting to contrast with the athletic theme and the sexual innuendo. She also has ingeniously hinted at portions of songs traditionally used for sports occasions. The introduction adapts the marchlike opening phrase of "California, Here I Come" (words and music by Al Jolson, Buddy de Sylva, and Joseph Meyer) to her waltz meter. Perhaps this was a jab at the Brooklyn Dodgers and the New York Giants, anticipating or reacting to their move to the West Coast in 1957 and 1958. The change in rhythm gives it a very different feeling, but its reference is undeniable. In addition, the accompaniment at the end of the first chorus quotes a phrase of the familiar "Take Me Out to the Ballgame" (words and music by Jack Norworth and Albert von Tilzer). Although the rhythm has been altered, the pitches of the tune are exact and they project clearly over the harmony.[16]

Swift collaborated once again with Freed on several effective tunes. "Wonderful Day for a Picnic" is a delightful celebration of summer. It was written during the recording of *Reaching for the Brass Ring*, when Swift anticipated extra time on the disk might be available and dashed this off to fill the space. The song features a soprano and a baritone voice in canon, parts which were sung by Louise Carlyle and Stuart Foster. Robert Russell Bennett orchestrated the accompaniment. Two other songs with lyrics by Freed, "Happy New Year" and "Three Cheers for the Next Fifty Years," appear to have been written for specific occasions. They include only melody and lyrics. "Three Cheers" celebrates the editor of a magazine that has been in business for fifty years, a preview for the commercial work Swift would do in later years. Swift and Freed worked well together, but there are no more collaborations after these few.

Swift wrote a piano piece, "Nevermore," dated August 1956, one of the few she wrote (or at least notated) for her own instrument. It is similar in style to her standard popular songs, an extended AABA form, with more elaborate piano figurations and a greater range. It is a most attractive piece and could have been an effective ballad had she added lyrics.

In 1957, Swift and Galloway wrote an entire nightclub act for Celeste Holm to use at the Cotillion Room of the Hotel Pierrant, a fashionable supper club. The first of seven songs was a new one by Swift and Galloway, "Twenty-Six Hours," which became Holm's theme song. Other songs designated for the act included Swift's "Can't We Be Friends?" as well as "Some Enchanted Evening" by Richard Rodgers, "I've Got the World on a String" by Harold Arlen, "I Love to Rhyme" by the Gershwins, and "I Guess I'll Have to Change My Plan" by Arthur Schwartz, which had been sung in *The First Little Show*, along with "Can't We Be Friends?"

Kay Swift's return to New York was exciting for her in many ways. The arrival of her first grandchild was an important event, as were the six additional births that followed. In this decade she would love reading aloud and singing to her grandchildren, and they would all adore "Ganz." The return allowed her to re-energize relationships with her three daughters that had been weakened by distance after her divorce from their father and her move west. April and Balthasar lived in Hastings-on-Hudson. Shortly after Guido and Francesca were born, however, they moved first to Tampa and then to Colombia and Rome, so later contact between Kay and their children was minimal. Kay and Robert lived in Chicago, close enough that Kay and Hunter could visit relatively frequently and enjoy David, Betsy, and Rachel. Andrea and Sidney remained in New York, and Kay became particularly close to their children, Katharine and John. Kay's nephew, Shippen, married in 1951. He was involved in the book and magazine publishing business, and he and his wife, Lee (Eleanor), would remain in New York until 1955, when they moved to Redding, Connecticut. They became close to Kay and maintained a cordial relationship with Hunter. Kay remained very devoted to her brother, Sam, although since she was now twice-divorced, her relationship with his wife's family was further strained. Kay had a new husband, and was undoubtedly enjoying introducing him to her old friends. New York City was her home, and the thrill of returning to the familiar bustle and excitement of the city must have been powerful.

CHAPTER 9

Challenges

Everybody should have a Kay Swift in their life.—Louise Carlyle

The second half of the 1950s found Swift working hard to share her music and her talents with many audiences. She explored a variety of opportunities to write in London, which returned her to her roots and allowed her to visit relatives of her mother's residing in England. In the United States, her Gershwin connection offered another professional experience. Swift was ambitious and versatile enough to explore any areas that might allow her to experiment with her creative talents.

London

The most successful of her London efforts was incidental music written for a 1958 play by Marc Connelly entitled *Hunter's Moon*. This play originated as *The Land of the Living* (1938), which was never produced, and was revised in 1952 as *There Are Two Points*. The final version premiered at Winter Garden on March 1, 1958. *Hunter's Moon* was a fantasy built around the theme that life should have solitude and meaning. The protagonist, a history professor contemplating retirement, considers the complexity and corruption of modern life against the simplicity and honesty of the past. Swift had known Connelly since his days in New York at the Algonquin Round Table. When *Hunter's Moon* opened, telegrams commended Swift's music and lyrics. There was one memorable song, a ballad entitled "Look Skyward," that occurred in several forms, once as a solo, once as a duet between two female voices, and again as incidental music. A short verse was followed by a lengthy refrain (forty measures instead of the standard thirty-two). The melody features a high, sustained pitch on the syllable "sky-," and the harmony is similar to that of her Broadway ballads. The rhythm is slow-moving and fairly straightforward. The song's character is not unlike that of the ballad from *Paris '90*, "House Where I Was Born." This lyric also refers to a magical place, although it is a bit harder to envision ("Look skyward above the town / Look to the bright full moon of green leaves"). In this lyric, the moon offers solace, inspiration, and "magic" for those who are troubled. The lyric reflects the optimism that generally permeated Swift's life. The song was recorded in New York by Teddy Johnson and published in London. A second song, "Piper in the Dew," mimics an Irish folk song in a lively 6/8 meter. Although Swift's music was successful, the play, with its lofty, utopian theme, was not, and it closed within a week. The publisher did not market either song, so her hard work brought her few benefits.[1]

A memo from Hunter Galloway to a contact in England in 1958 reveals the frustration that he and Swift must have felt after a series of unsuccessful ventures. It suggests the possibility of resurrecting *Who Could Ask for Anything More?* and staging it as a musical in London. "Know you're tired of the idea, but with Western TV films so popular here, might be able to do a good one that would have more comedy than *Oklahoma!* Think British would be sympathetic to sophisticated woman who went out and tried her best to 'make do' and always put out the top effort, etc.??" Apparently the lack of success with their new ideas turned their attention to recycling previous efforts. The time, energy, and expense of a new project was becoming prohibitive for many Broadway producers, some of whom chose to revive former hit musicals rather than risk their fortunes on an unproven show. One can assume that the production of *Who Could Ask for Anything More?* as a musical would have included all nine of the Swift pieces that were written for *Never a Dull Moment.* It is also likely that Swift approached Broadway producers with the idea before appealing to her contacts in London.[2]

Swift was making a strong effort to appeal to the British market. In addition to the production of *Hunter's Moon,* she wrote some shorter works that never achieved recognition. Several single popular songs in a more contemporary style appear in her papers, indicating that she was attempting to adapt to the rock-and-roll idiom. One song with words by Mel Howard, "Five O'Clock Feelin'," follows a twelve-bar blues pattern and is somewhat imitative of "Rock Around the Clock," the 1955 hit by Bill Haley and His Comets. Another with Howard's lyrics, "A Great Big Piece of Chalk," was written in New York but was published in London the same year as *Hunter's Moon.* Swift successfully mimicked the rock style, and with any luck these pieces could have worked as well as many other songs that did. Swift and Galloway returned to London in August to celebrate the release of its recording by Teddy Johnson. Swift later wrote, "This song had splendid reviews but resulted in no income. The publisher made an advance of $400, which was split with the lyric writer . . . and just before I left New York for London, we had invested in a demonstration recording of this song which cost $400. This, of course, cancelled out the advance made by the London publisher." Such was often the case during these years with Swift. She was not afraid to venture into unfamiliar territory and had the talent to adjust to new styles. Although she had produced a melody that seemed to be similar to current hits, the lyric may have been a bit juvenile for its target audience. It vowed to write love messages on the sidewalk with "A Great Big Piece of Chalk." In spite of the "splendid reviews," the message did not reach teenagers, even in 1958.[3]

Another song with lyrics by Mel Howard, "There's No Escape," is a slow ballad. However, "There's No Escape" is far more typical of a 1930s ballad than a 1950s "slow dance." Its long, sustained phrases and its even note values are very calming but would appeal less to fifties teenagers than to their parents. The piano accompaniment features parallel chords moving in slow triplet rhythms as an undercurrent, as well as more active countermelodies, which play against the longer note values in the vocal line. Unfortunately, the accompaniment is more interesting than the melody itself, which is rather static. Its range is less than an octave, and most of the notes lie within the narrow interval of a perfect fourth. Most of Swift's attempts to simplify her melodies and avoid large leaps unfortunately result in bland, forgettable tunes.

This lyric, moreover, is far too sophisticated for the teen-age audience, an irony considering that Howard's previous effort was a bit too juvenile. Not only was the vocabulary more advanced than most rock-and-roll lyrics ("your arms about me entwined") but the passion was too mature. Although the emotion was real in the current songs of Sam Cooke and Brenda Lee, it was more innocent than in the lyric Howard had supplied.

Perhaps "There's No Escape" was never intended for teenagers. The appeal to an older audience has already been suggested. Yet the song's existence underscores the dilemma of traditional songwriters in the postwar era who could no longer write a song and expect success without recording it first. A demonstration recording was expensive, and even such a recording did not guarantee that the song would be picked up by another artist or be played on the air. Radio play was essential to successful marketing, having usurped the importance of the Broadway show and sheet music in the creation of a hit song.

Swift would like to have mounted another successful stage production. She had repeatedly expressed interest in setting P. L. Travers's novel *Mary Poppins* as a musical, as well as *Foggerty's Fairy,* a play by W. S. Gilbert. However, she wanted someone to hire her to do so, and that never happened. A project that came closer to the London stage was a musical setting of the novel *A Candle for St. Jude,* written in 1948 by British author Rumer Godden. Set in a ballet school, Godden's novel is about finding one's identity through art. Given Swift's commitment to her art and her lifelong interest in dance, this theme would naturally have appealed to her. The reference to Saint Jude is based on an incident in the plot in which a candle has been lighted for the patron saint of lost causes during a jealous dispute between dancers. Fortunately, the dispute is soon settled and the school's reputation is saved. A screenplay of the novel had been produced for television in 1952, so prospects for converting it to a musical drama would have been encouraging. A two-year effort, however, resulted in one of Swift's greatest disappointments, after she had written seven songs for the proposed show. According to correspondence in August 1958, Godden objected to some of the lyrics in a piece entitled "Felix's Song," which was to be sung by Mr. Felix, a friend who offers sage advice to the central character, Madame Holbein, head of the ballet school. Godden felt that the lyrics should be more "distinguished." Hunter and Kay agreed and offered to hire another lyricist immediately. They also suggested that "perhaps the refrain of this song holds too much emotional content for the situation (although the verse does not) and that this music might be shifted to another part of the play—even to another character." In spite of their efforts, a note to agent Teddy Holmes of Chappell Music in London several months later reveals that the project was postponed indefinitely on the advice of Godden's agent. He apparently doubted the success of a show with such a strong emphasis on ballet, although he did say that Godden had liked the music. There is later discussion about revisions, but in a note from Swift to Godden's agent dated March 27, 1960, the ultimate failure of the project is clear. "I was disappointed to learn that *A Candle for St. Jude* won't be available for option. But I can imagine that if it is a delicate property Miss Godden probably wouldn't like the idea of any other writers working on it. We did invest a lot of time and effort. But it seemed like a good gamble at the time, and it was interesting work, though costly to us."[4]

Swift had, indeed, invested much effort, and the musical results were commendable. The opening number, "Candles," sets a very poetic text by Godden and is dignified in its treatment. Rather than a common song form, "Candles" is through-composed, with no repeated sections, more like an art song. The phrase lengths are not predictable four-bar phrases but vary from three to six measures in length, depending on the text. The key is C, although Swift uses many accidentals and emphasizes the unrelated key areas of A flat major and E major. Parallel harmonies defy traditional functional harmonic practice, and again suggest her knowledge of the impressionistic style of Debussy and Ravel (ex. 9.1).

"Lollie's Song" is one of the few songs that does include the lyric (this one by Swift) and offers her another opportunity to exhibit her knowledge of British speech idioms as well as musical practices. Since Godden was British and the play was conceived for a London audience, this is to be expected. Swift's verses are filled with authentic details and expressions that

9.1 *A Candle for St. Jude,* "Candles," measures 3–8

firmly identify the setting as England. Lollie, one of the young dancers, fantasizes what she would buy if she had "plenty of lovely pounds to spend. . . . Auntie and I could use a spot, just a spot, not a lot."

This song is far more traditional in form than "Candles," featuring the song-form arrangement AABA for the refrain. It uses regular marchlike rhythms and a smooth melody in the A section. Although some chromatic harmonies support the tune, they are largely traditional. Several elements distinguish this piece, however. First, the song opens with percussion repeating an ostinato rhythm, which the vocal line then assumes. This verse features a single-tone recitation resembling a Gilbert-and-Sullivan-like patter, a device that Swift had not used since "Etiquette" in *Fine and Dandy.* The subtle reference to the British musical tradition adds to the feeling of sophistication, while the lyric clearly establishes the setting: "Four farthings, one penny, / Twelve pennies, one shilling, / One thousand two hundred cups of tea, / Eight pounds." Second, the patter serves as a pedal tone while an accompaniment of major triads moves in parallel motion, in and out of the major key. A third unique element occurs in the form of a countermelody. The countermelody features longer note values and somewhat more syncopation than the refrain. It is sung by a male chorus echoing Lollie's desires: "Cups of tea, / Eclairs and banana sundaes, / Steak and kidney pie and chocolate cake to buy!" The first time this countermelody is sung, the accompaniment carries the original melody of the refrain (ex. 9.2). The use of the chorus as commentator introduces another Gilbert and Sullivan trait, reminding the British audience of its heritage. After its statement the melody and countermelody are sung together, lending dignity to Lollie's position since a chorus of men affirms her wishes. Again Swift is demonstrating her knowledge

9.2 *A Candle for St. Jude,* "Lollie's Song," measures 53–56

of classical techniques as she works counterpoint into the popular genre. This is yet another sign of her determination to make this a high-quality score for a project she really had hoped would succeed.

A lengthier, although incomplete movement is the "Swan Ballet," a seventy-measure fragment of an instrumental movement. The length allows Swift an opportunity to develop some of her melodic ideas rather than simply lay them out in eight-measure sections. Like "Candles" and "Lollie's Song," this piece also has elements of the impressionistic style, including ostinato patterns, quintal chords, parallelism, and a modal melody. Ballet had been a standard feature in Broadway musicals since *Oklahoma!* in 1943. Swift's use of it in *Fine and Dandy, Never a Dull Moment,* and now *A Candle for St. Jude* reflects a national trend as well as her own interest and training in dance.

It is clear that Swift was trying to promote a variety of projects, both in the United States and Britain, but producers and publishers were apparently no longer interested in her style of material. A response from her husband, Hunter Galloway, to a young composer shows their despair with the popular music industry as it had evolved in the 1950s.

Kay and others assure me that, with conditions among the publishers as they are today, a single song has really little chance. The publishers are no longer in the driver's seat; the recording men are, and they in turn depend almost entirely on the demands of individual singers. A ballad is even less likely to get anywhere, as singers now prefer either rock and roll, tunes from hit shows, or "standards." I am so sorry to sound negative, but you know you really want to hear the way things are in this admittedly miserable business, rather than have me paint a falsely rosy picture. One friend of mine has spent a lot of money on the promotion of an excellent song from an album, in the past two months, hoping for a single recording (which is what pays) without success.[5]

Never did Kay Swift convey such bitterness. Although this note was written by her husband, it must reflect a certain degree of her own frustration. In 1960 Gabriel Favoino of the *Chicago Sun-Times* interviewed Swift and sensed her discouragement with the state of popular music in America. He wrote of the changes in the popular song business from 1930 to 1960:

She is of the period of the Gershwins, of Cole Porter and Irving Berlin—an era of great American popular music. In their time it was enough to write wonderful songs and have them published. There was no need to woo the record manufacturers or court the favor of all powerful disk jockeys. "Now the entire publishing industry is on its knees to the record industry," says Miss Swift, quite frankly. Without the record, the song is dead. And since the biggest buyer of single records now are teen-agers, it is their taste that must be catered to. . . . Most of the songs thought commercial today have lyrics requiring no more than a first grade vocabulary, and deal with equally elementary themes. It is difficult to think of a more naked insult to youth." Miss Swift, who often tours the nation's high schools lecturing on music appreciation, thinks teen-agers deserve better than they are getting. "If they're exposed to good music, I've found them very responsive," she says. "The music that they're getting is contrived, controlled, fixed. I can't believe that's what they want."[6]

Both of these statements stand in stark contrast to the enthusiastic comments about writing popular music that Swift shared with interviewers fifteen years later. They convey a discouragement that is hard to dismiss.

Entertainer Bobby Short agrees that she must have been frustrated, but notes that she was not alone. "I think people of Kay's generation were all frustrated. I think Jule Styne was frustrated, I think Alan Jay Lerner was frustrated, I think all those composers of that era—Arthur Schwartz certainly was frustrated. They couldn't get to first base on Broadway. . . . I think that Kay, like many of her contemporaries, went through a terrible time." Short's comments also imply that the difficulties Swift incurred were due to her age and style rather than her gender.[7]

Her friend Alfred Stern also recalled her discouragement. When asked why Swift had not been more successful in her profession, he cited Kay's growing belief that the link to George Gershwin may have "played against her rather than for her. People thought her best music sounded like George," perhaps doubting that she had written it herself. Stern also suggested that her lack of success may have been "because of all the society stuff she was used to being involved in. Some people felt that she was a kind of dilettante. She wasn't. She was a very good musician." He went on to cite her well-known penchant for vodka and tonic, commenting that perhaps some did not take her seriously because of that. It is curious that the "society stuff" never seemed to interfere in the careers of men in the world of Broadway and, in fact, may have enhanced their images. Perhaps Swift mistakenly assumed that if she could compose the music for a successful Broadway show as men did, then she could lead as flamboyant a social life. She may not have been convinced of the double standard that applied to women in this respect, particularly after they had reached middle age.[8]

In the spring of 1959, Swift and Galloway completed a class in "Prayer, Healing and Treatment" at the New York Church of the Truth, which met at Carnegie Hall. The certificate awarded them notes its positive objective. "In the name of God, the one Power, I now reverse the pattern of seeming negativeness for this person. He is now in the full sunlight of God's successes, demonstrating God's perfect plan, finding every rich experience and complete success that is God's expression. That's the way it is. Amen. Thank you, Father." The proclamation against "negativeness" and its assurance of "complete success" indicates that Kay and/or Hunter may have been more discouraged with their difficult luck than Swift would publicly admit.

Porgy and Bess, *Part 2*

In spite of the abrupt closing of *Hunter's Moon,* Kay Swift was not idle for long. Her work on *A Candle for St. Jude,* as well as the shorter rock-style pieces, had kept her busy, if not financially secure. Perhaps because she had had difficulty generating enough income, she was more than willing in 1959 to write a statement in support of H.R. 5921, a bill that would impose fees on jukebox owners for playing recordings of copyrighted music. She wrote, "Often, as you know, a writer's best efforts result in financial loss. . . . But such losses are among the risks we all have to take in the music profession. . . . Actually, there are several things a writer must do without any hope of fast, or indeed any, reimbursement; things he could never do except for the fact that he gets royalties from commercially successful works." Swift continued, revealing that for the past twenty-five years, "my averaged phonograph record royalties have been less than $500 per year." This included the income from "Fine and Dandy," "Can This Be Love?" and "Can't We Be Friends?" Swift was a loyal member of ASCAP (one of the earliest females admitted) and an active member of the American Guild of Authors and Composers (AGAC). She was always mindful of violations of her rights, as well as those of other composers.[9]

That same year, her Gershwin connection again provided her with a project. On June 22, 1959, she and Hunter attended a press preview in New York of Samuel Goldwyn's film version of *Porgy and Bess.* Swift was delighted with the movie and felt that Gershwin himself would have been pleased that "the spirit and atmosphere" of the original work had been preserved. Gershwin's hometown audiences were extremely enthusiastic about *Porgy and Bess.* At the first public showing June 25, "police lines [kept] a seething mob from rushing to grab at the stars who were present." That evening, Swift and Galloway met at Arthur Gershwin's apartment with those members of the Gershwin family who were in New York: Frankie Gershwin Godowsky (George and Ira's sister), her husband, Leo Godowsky, and their children; Emily Paley, sister of Leonore Gershwin (Ira's wife); Leonore's brother, English Strunsky, his wife, and son; and Mabel Pleshette Schirmer, a niece of Lou Paley. Swift recalled, "Arthur still has one of George's two Steinways there, and it sounded mellow in tone when I played

'Summertime,' 'Bess, You Is My Woman Now'—and many more of the memorable songs." They telephoned Ira in California to tell him of their excitement.[10]

Although Swift was thrilled with the movie, many critics were not. They were enthralled with the music but found the film "excessive," "static," and "a stodgy bore." James Baldwin bemoaned, "Grandiose, foolish, and heavy with the stale perfume of self-congratulations, the Hollywood-Goldwyn-Preminger production of *Porgy and Bess* lumbered into the Warner theatre." Furthermore, he was concerned that the white director and producer had crafted images of blacks that were shallow and passionless, that failed to demonstrate the characters' "real agony, real despair, and real love. . . . The saddest and most infuriating thing is that Mr. Otto Preminger has a great many gifted people in front of his camera and not the remotest notion of what to do with any of them." Perhaps prompted by the negative press, several weeks later Goldwyn's public relations counselor, Lynn Farnol, called on Swift. He asked her to help promote the film by speaking to various audiences about the opera and its development, since she had been associated with *Porgy and Bess* from the beginning. This would involve her traveling and giving lectures and interviews in twelve cities across the country during a fifteen-week period. Her salary would be $150 a week while in New York and $250 a week while on the road. Enthused about the picture, she agreed to the promotional tour. It began in July with her appearance on the Tony Weitzel radio show in Chicago. Swift related the discussion:

> I described, for what was to be the first of many times, the extra-ordinarily stimulating experience of being present when the music was composed. Tony asked whether those of us who were close to the composer and lyricists knew from the start that the opera was a masterpiece; I replied that we certainly did know, and that indeed it required small awareness to perceive this fact. It was, I related, thinking of the current, exciting pennant race in both professional baseball leagues, like watching a pitcher who has a no-hitter going for him. He knows it and you know it; and, in the case of George Gershwin, as in that of the pitcher, nobody mentions the fact at the time.[11]

In spite of the composer's belief in his music and in the play, fine artistic support from Ira and both Heywards, an exceptional cast, and enthusiastic audiences, the critics had not embraced Gershwin's folk opera. When interviewer Tony Weitzel questioned Swift about the cool critical reception that *Porgy and Bess* had received in 1935, she offered her explanation. "The score was so easy to take, without dry passages where attention wandered, that some critics felt this couldn't possibly be topflight music. Later, of course, these carpers, with one or two exceptions such as die-hard Lawrence Gilman, all reversed themselves in print. By the time 1942 gave us Cheryl Crawford's revival, everybody knew the truth about 'Porgy and Bess' and about George Gershwin."[12]

As a guest on the Fran Allison television show, Swift had an opportunity to wear the antique gold bracelets George had given her after the performance of *An American in Paris* in 1928. "The cameraman would pan down to my hands, showing the button-and-buttonhole device that fastened these wide gold bands, edged with gold lace-like trimming." The bracelets were a popular topic, especially with women in the audiences. A feature writer for the *Chicago Tribune,* Lucy Key Miller, wrote an exclusive story on the bracelets published on July 20, 1959.[13]

Kay Swift had always been keenly attentive to her looks and her image, as defined by show business and *Vogue*. She suffered from poor eyesight only because she refused to wear corrective lenses. ("'No girl over the age of fifteen should wear eyeglasses,' she said. 'By that age, she should have seen everything worth seeing already.'") She loved beautiful clothing. During the Warburg years, Honor Leeming was pleased to receive her worn evening dresses. Kay had also passed designer clothes and last-year's mink coats to her close friend Mary Reinhardt. Her memoir recalls the "dream of a tailored suit" that she wore on the train to Reno. Alfred Stern admired her "marvelous leopard-skin coat." Her careful description of her costume when she and the cowboy eloped provides further insight into her priorities:

Chris [Faye Hubbard] and George [the best man] wore their regular cowboy clothes, complete with big Stetson hats, bright shirts, and high-heeled boots. I had insisted on stopping off in Washington to freshen up and change into a bright-red hat and a new Schiaparelli

print dress with a pattern of red, yellow and purple musical instruments on a black background. I had worn my mink coat, being
a perennial sissy about cold weather. Porgy, my big black French
poodle, in a gay red collar and leader that matched my hat, accompanied us.

Such details, whether true or imaginary, indicate the style Swift was accus-
tomed to (designer dress, mink coat, French poodle), as well as her outgoing
personality. The colorful print dress was certainly not standard wedding
attire, particularly when accented with a bright red hat to match her dog's
collar and leash. (It is more than a bit ironic that she had mentioned Porgy
being in attendance at all. He was a gift from George Gershwin.)[14]

In her role as a public speaker promoting *Porgy and Bess,* this attention
to her image was intensified. Swift had negotiated a wardrobe allowance
with the Goldwyn studio, which she understood to be one hundred dollars
per week for a maximum of nine weeks. Any additional purchases were to
be preapproved. Her memoirs describe her touring clothes in detail, as well
as the difficulty of keeping them clean and wrinkle-free in 1959, before poly-
ester fabrics. Apparently there was some misunderstanding about either the
procedure or the amount of money spent, evidenced by a letter that questioned the cost of six dresses and the coordinating accessories. When it became clear to Swift that the matter would not easily be resolved and that a
change in season would require another shopping trip, she terminated her
contract with Samuel Goldwyn on October 13, 1959.[15]

Nonetheless, Swift's travels for *Porgy and Bess* were so extensive and
eventful that she began a journalistic account of them and had received permission from Ira to use another Gershwin quotation, "Mornin' Time an'
Evenin' Time," for the title. Instead, Swift returned to the title from her
proposed baseball sitcom. "Here's the Pitch" was recycled and became a
chapter in her unfinished memoirs.[16]

Before she left the tour, more than one reporter had pressed for details
about George Gershwin. NBC interviewer Jack Eigen was interested in
Gershwin's personality. Swift succeeded "in establishing the fact that Gershwin was not an unhappy, restless person with overtones of tragedy. . . .
I felt compelled to scotch the impression as best I could without making

G.G. seem like a deadly Pollyanna character." Eigen closed with a very personal question. "'And now, Kay, don't you think perhaps George Gershwin carried a torch over the years? Don't you think maybe when he was writing such songs as "The Man I Love," this was what was going on in his mind?' I looked him in the eye and said I had no idea, but assumed that Gershwin, like everyone else, probably carried a variety of torches during his lifetime. I added that I, myself, had fallen in love for the first time at the age of five and had no intention of leaving off now—what about him?"[17]

Swift usually guarded her privacy and was very discreet in discussing her relationship with Gershwin. Until her last decade, she spoke about him publicly in rather aloof terms, almost as if the personal relationship between the two of them were no different than his relationships with many other women. Of course, she did not believe this, but she seemed to feel that no one else needed to know the details of their romance. It was, perhaps, her way of honoring those happy memories. In her memoirs she discussed George's magnetism.

> During my tour with the picture, I met more than one woman
> who felt, probably with reason, that she was the love of the
> composer's life. Perhaps, just as he used to sing every song with
> a peculiarly personal style, at parties, directed right to a selected
> feminine listener, he conveyed in life a concentration upon each
> of his "crushes" (horrible word, but no other comes to mind) that
> engendered in her the feeling that she was The One And Only;
> whereas, the truth probably was that she was, currently, the one,
> but not the only.[18]

There is poignancy in these words. For just as Kay Swift knew she had a singular relationship with George Gershwin, these comments seem to indicate that she recognized his lack of faithfulness or commitment. Her heart knew she was "the one," and her head knew she was probably not "the only." Yet she chose to remember the positive moments of their time together. Her respect for him and his talent, and her love for what they did share, allowed her to contribute to his legacy until she died. For this she was universally recognized and admired.

CHAPTER 10

The Show Won't Fold in Philadelphia

Never turn down any project for which someone asks you to write. You may write some of your greatest music while doing it.—George Gershwin

In the 1960s, Swift seems to have found areas of comfort in which she excelled. She had fewer professional disappointments and more successes than in the previous decade. In addition to composing single songs and piano pieces in a popular style, she resumed writing pieces in a more classical style, some of them sacred. She also became involved in writing music for a number of civic and commercial shows and World's Fairs. Musically, Swift found a niche in which she was comfortable and productive.

Swift's sixth decade had many other dimensions as well. She loved her grandchildren, grandnieces, and grandnephew and spent time with them when she could. She was playful and uninhibited. Her nephew, Shippen, recalls the time in 1964 when, at age sixty-seven, she taught his daughter to do a backward somersault on their living room carpet. She often played card games with the children. She loved to sit on the floor and play Monopoly with Katharine and John. In play as in life, however, she was "a complete bubblehead about money." Her poor performance in the game was sometimes so upsetting to her that she cried when she lost. Katharine

Weber recalls the day her mother banned Monopoly games from Ganz's activities. And she has chronicled Swift's outrageous antics in "The Memory of All That": "Going out in public with Ganz when I was growing up felt like a high-wire balancing act of pride and embarrassment. I was a mortified twelve the night that Ganz, needing to attract a waiter in a restaurant, waved her napkin high in the air and called out, 'Yoo-hoo! Waiterkins!'"[1]

Swift was loyal and compassionate. She once accompanied a friend to an Alcoholics Anonymous meeting and was so impressed with the fellowship that she reportedly stood up and exclaimed, "I wish I were an alcoholic!" Always a "champion reader-out-loud," Swift again shared this skill with those less fortunate than she. For twenty years she volunteered at the New York Association for the Blind (now Lighthouse International) at 111 East Fifty-ninth Street. There she read to visually impaired adults one-on-one, helping them absorb textbooks, business and professional materials, and literature. Her good friend Louise Carlyle sometimes went with her and they presented impromptu concerts, with Carlyle singing songs while Swift played. Swift volunteered her services to the blind for more than twenty years, from June 1967 until October 1988, when she was eighty-nine.[2]

Lee Swift, Shippen Swift's wife, recalls that in the late 1960s Kay began writing her memoirs, which she intended to publish as an autobiography. Lee would arrive to have lunch with Kay, which her housekeeper, Mattie, served in the living room. She remembered Kay working on her book, at last wearing the large eyeglasses that she had needed for so many years—but wore only in the privacy of her apartment. The memoirs, never published, comprise more than two hundred loose pages of both typed and handwritten notes and are roughly organized in thirteen chapters. Many of these chapters were revised and reorganized, as if she were in the second or third draft of its production. Its many pages were found in her apartment, scattered among her belongings, after her death.[3]

This period also had its share of sorrows. Kay and Hunter experienced difficult times financially and personally. Shippen recalls that Hunter was very nice to him and his wife, but added, "He was always . . . a sad soul. Kay always described him as being 'betwixt and between.'" Alfred Stern remembered Galloway as "a very weak guy. He became 'Mr. Swift.' She knew all the glamorous people and he knew nothing like that. We got him occasional jobs as stage manager, but he wasn't very good at it." Kay kept her office as a place to work and to receive visitors away from her husband. In 1961, Hunter lost his temper with Kay's grandson John. John's mother, Andrea, considered Hunter "unstable," and thereafter John and Katharine were forbidden to see him. Instead, they visited Kay at her office. Katharine remembers many sleepovers there with Ganz.[4]

Kay's increased activity at the Church of Truth and several sacred compositions suggest a renewed faith during these years. Her later years brought gratification to many areas of her life as well as an ability to cope with disappointments.

Industrial Shows

While Kay Swift's songs may not have made the Top Forty in the 1950s and 1960s, she had success with one genre during her mature years—the civic and industrial show. To commemorate anniversaries and festive occasions, corporations, organizations, and cities frequently commission a pageant or a play with music. Alfred Stern, the former set designer who worked with Swift at Radio City Music Hall and at the New York World's Fair, had become one of the country's premier producers of such spectacles. In addition to being a close friend, Stern respected Swift's work and her professionalism, and he hired her to write six shows between 1960 and 1974.

The first of these shows was a pageant entitled *One Little Girl* to commemorate the fiftieth anniversary of the Camp Fire Girls. With a book written by Gilbert Seldes, Doris Frankel, and Alfred Stern, it may have been the most extensive of all the industrial productions she wrote. The production allowed Swift to collaborate with some of her closest friends. Hans Spialek, who had orchestrated *Fine and Dandy*, orchestrated and conducted the pageant, Alfred Stern produced it, and Louise Carlyle starred. The show was presented at New York's Manhattan Center on November 2, 1960, and the organization was so pleased with the results that it financed the recording of the music. According to the album notes, the show relates the tale of "'one little girl' growing up among the complex problems and special joys of our Jet Stream age. . . . 'One Little Girl' is a story of today, told by the Camp Fire Girls on the occasion of their Golden Jubilee, looking fifty years back and fifty years ahead . . . with pride and humility—and, yes, with humor."[5]

Swift wrote ten songs for *One Little Girl,* in addition to the Overture and interludes. Records show that she was paid two thousand dollars for this commission, a respectable sum in 1960. Swift's music is imaginative and varied, building on her Broadway and classical backgrounds. "Camp Fire Cookout" demonstrates her contrapuntal skills as she weaves a three-part canon, or round. Three age groups of Camp Fire Girls (the Bluebirds, the Camp Fire Girls, and the Horizon Girls) begin singing the melody at two-measure intervals, a melody that has all the syncopation of "Fine and Dandy" and builds to an energetic "Square Dance." "My Favorite Campfire Girl" is an easy soft-shoe that underscores the laziness of one camper ("my favorite Camp Fire Girl / Took to the open air, Slept by a lake. / No gnat, nor bat, nor wail of brat / Could keep that girl awake!"). Alfred Stern's favorite was "She Used to Be Such Fun," a touching ballad in which a father laments, "People call her beautiful, may be, / . . . Now they say she's lovely and I agree. / But she was lovelier when she had time for me." The musical interludes demonstrate Swift's knowledge of other compositional techniques. "Theme for Mother" is a chromatic and syncopated fughetta, again displaying her skill with eighteenth-century counterpoint. The "Astronaut Theme" features complex cross rhythms and parallel triads, more contemporary elements. One piece that must have given Swift much satisfaction is "Moon Clown," an instrumental number that opens with parallel major triads winding through various keys before they settle into a familiar theme. The basic song is one that Swift had written two years earlier in anticipation of *A Candle for St. Jude.* "Moon Clown" is actually the creative "Lollie's Song" recycled, so her efforts on the previous project were not entirely lost.

By this time Swift and Galloway had formed their own publishing company, Samson Music, which did publish one number from *One Little Girl,* "In-Between Age." It is a slow ballad very much in the style of the 1930s. The opening section is a sustained, simple melody, while the contrasting bridge has quicker rhythms and a more chromatic melody. Swift apparently believed that of all the songs in *One Little Girl,* this had the most universal appeal and was most likely to be accepted by recording stars and teenagers. She wrote, "Blue days begin / When you're in that In-Between-Age, /

Ev'rything you try turns out all wrong." In an interview Swift maintained, "The lyrics don't limit the age to any special years and I have adult friends who are claiming its laments as their own." Rather than expressing the feelings of teenagers, however, the song seems to be addressing them in a maternal tone, and the music in the show is in a style familiar more to the parents and grandparents of Camp Fire Girls than to the girls themselves. In 1960 teens were more likely to be listening to "This Magic Moment" by the Drifters, "Wonderful World" by Sam Cooke, and "I'm Sorry" by Brenda Lee. Kay Swift was now sixty-two and had seven grandchildren of her own. She could cross boundaries between classical and popular music but was finding it hard to cross the generation gap.[6]

Swift made public appearances in Chicago and Detroit to promote the album, and those who met her appreciated her style and warmth. Betty Paysner, her local public relations representative in Detroit, shared the following comments about her:

> Everyone who had interviewed Kay on her previous trip for *Porgy and Bess* was eager to have the opportunity again. . . . All commented on her wit, depth, marvelous anecdotes—and genuine niceness. And Kay is the PR's dream of adaptability. She was equally engaging and entertaining when interviewed by a former history professor and by our "swingingest" deejay who speaks almost entirely in hip rhymes and was delighted to pick up Kay's spontaneous rejoinders in his lingo. I certainly hope the Camp Fire Girls realize Kay has been doing an incomparable public relations job for them.

Of course Swift was also promoting her own interests in one of the most effective manners she could.[7]

For the Seattle World's Fair in 1962, "Century 21 Exposition," Stern served as consultant, coordinator, and producer. He offered Swift a chance to write the theme music for the show entitled *The Threshold and the Threat*. This was a twenty-one-minute glimpse into the future, which envisioned a more efficient way of working and living. Swift's music was to enhance the drama, which was narrated by four sets of characters: "a knowledgeable

Guide Voice who conducts spectators on their thoughtful tour through time; the voice of a Child of Century 21 who will inherit the opportunities and dangers which the future represents; voices of a contemporary couple visiting the Seattle Fair, representing the reaction of the present to the future; and the voices of a faceless statistical family confined in a fall-out bomb shelter which represent the threatening '[future] of man between 1962 and 1999.'" Swift's orchestral music included movements like "Fanfare and Theme," a romantic "Faith in the Future" theme, the playful "Child of the Future," and "What Time Is It?" a movement that represented the uncertain future by shifting between major and minor modes. Two vocal numbers were among the compositions. "Prayer with a Beat" is an experiment for Swift. Never before had she attempted a song with a religious theme in a rock style. In ABA form, this prayer is somewhat jazzy in nature. It is written in C minor, with dotted rhythms and a walking bass. The other song, "Now and Always," is one of the most tuneful of Swift's ballads. It retains her characteristic wide leaps and the chromatic interest in the melody. Swift had taken a long time to develop this tune, for it was found in her sketchbooks with the date "1947" and the designation "G.T." for "good tune."[8]

Robert Russell Bennett orchestrated, directed, and recorded the music for *The Threshold and the Threat*, and Robert Weede, her former associate from Radio City Music Hall, sang the vocals for the demonstration records needed to illustrate the project for the committee, with very professional results. Stern recalled it being an "interesting show, ahead of its time." It always received positive comments from visitors and was reviewed in *Variety*, which pegged it, "along with the Federal Science show . . . the hit show of the fair."[9]

Stern tapped Swift again for the 1964–65 World's Fair in New York City, this time for two commissions. (She was the only composer to have two shows at the fair.) One was for the production at the Clairol Color Carousel that admitted only women. Swift describes this World's Fair phenomenon: "Forty women, teenagers and grandmothers, ride the Clairol Carousel at one time, while about three hundred wait in line to get on. Johnny Desmond sings a new song of mine, 'Nothing is Too Lovely to be True,' during the ride which runs only four and a half minutes. Four hundred people every hour, or forty-eight hundred daily, hear the music. Johnny Desmond, of course, is a composer's delight. I'm told that even the Clairol Girls still enjoy hearing him sing the song."[10]

For this ballad, Swift was able to recycle another of her efforts for the never-produced *Candle for St. Jude.* "Sixpence and a Smile" was transformed into "Nothing Is Too Lovely to Be True." Her lyric is remarkably fitting for a song that originally served a different purpose. Swift's verse follows:

When we dream by day, or when we dream by night,
They say we dream in black and white,
And what could be duller? No color!
Me, I like to think that I can choose my dreams.
So from now on, I'll refuse my dreams unless they're in color!

The emphasis on "color" in the lyric is appropriately set to "colorful" chromatic harmonies. The refrain follows the pattern ABA'C common to many popular songs, and it is similar to Swift's earlier ballads from the 1930s and 1940s in terms of harmonic language. The opening phrases are linked closely to the text. "I'll dream about a sapphire ocean / Moving in slow motion / Beneath a sky that's bluer than blue." The reference to slow-moving waves in the first two lines is set to static harmonies that alternate between C major 7 and B7 chords with a bass line moving C–B–C–B. The bass continues down to B flat and then A under "Beneath a sky that's blue." At that point, strong bass motion in fifths begins a more traditional harmonic pattern. The melody features a smoother contour and longer line, despite some very sophisticated leaps of a seventh. Overall the song is very popular in sound, more Hollywood than Broadway in character. Records show that for her six-minute musical score, which included a verse and chorus as well as background music to the script, Swift received fifteen hundred dollars.

Swift also wrote the music and lyrics for the Borden exhibit *All About Elsie.* The book was provided by Joe Oliansky, playwright-in-residence at Yale University. According to Stern, Oliansky thought they should use someone younger with fresher ideas. Stern simply replied that he wanted Kay, "and that was that." Her music proved to be a delightful counterpart to her witty lyrics. With such titles as "Doin' Fine," "Peep," "Elmer's Marvelous Ark," and "Omelet Man," the virtues of Borden products were ex-

10.1 *All About Elsie*, "Elmer's Marvelous Ark," measures 7–14

tolled. The musical settings were much like Swift's Broadway show tunes, with a touch of more contemporary popular idioms. "Omelet Man" uses jazz chords and syncopated rhythms to proclaim with a Cab Calloway swagger, "I'm a quicker draw, an' a slicker draw than any guy you ever saw! / Don't need no gun, just a fryin' pan, 'cause I'm the Instant Omelet Man!" The "Yeah, yeah, yeah" refrain, which leads into a repeat of the last line, is perhaps a salute to the Beatles, who made their U.S. debut in that year. "Elmer's Marvelous Ark" is a humorous song whose semi-serious setting underscores the subtle lyrics. "All the animals, two by two, / Enter the ark precisely. And it's holding together nicely, / Due to Elmer's Glue." Rather than employing an obvious, square 4/4 meter, which one might expect to accompany the animals marching into the ark, Swift has used 6/8 meter, which implies livelier skipping motions. Triads and seventh chords support the chromatic melody over a pedal bass (ex. 10.1). Swift notes that the show was located "in the Better Living Building (a structure that took so long to complete that we called it the Barely Living Building)" and that it played "to 49,000 people every week. As the show will run seven days a week for six months of '64 plus another six months in '65, we can't complain about any lack of exposure."[11]

An assignment for Montreal's world's fair in 1967 had Swift producing "Hello, Expo Sixty-Seven!" with husband Hunter Galloway assisting her on lyrics. The five-minute piece, background music for the carousel ride, earned her a thousand dollars.

Some composers may have perceived industrial shows as nonartistic utility writing, but Swift disagreed. "I work best when I have a definite assignment. . . . Is this inspiration? I think the songs come from inspiration. But I have to have a subject to be writing about. If I muddle about looking for one I accomplish nothing." She viewed each assignment as a challenge and worked within the given parameters to create an artistic piece.[12]

Swift did hint at the frustration that a composer experiences when working in Hollywood or for commercial ventures. William Grant Still had written the theme music for the 1939 New York World's Fair, carefully adhering to the requested time specifications. Unfortunately, "as the engineers improved their techniques in putting the show together, they gained about a minute, which in turned shortened the length of the music." Years later, in a tribute to William Grant Still, Swift sympathized with his task of cutting one minute from his composition. Wrote Swift,

> The worst sensation a composer experiences, in my opinion, is the cutting of his work in order to adapt it to some mechanical element of the show, the movie, or a TV script. . . . I dream of a day when a producer or director will say to an engineer, lighting expert or other electronic wizard, "I'm sorry, but you'll have to make some changes in your timing of special effects. The music requires more time and that has to be considered first." Of course I realize that this is not about to occur in any foreseeable future. Apparently, mechanical processes and heavy props are more impressive to the people who are in charge than the product of a pen and some manuscript paper.[13]

Swift, however, appreciated the explicit assignments, content, and timetables of industrial shows, as well as the guaranteed commissions. By 1964 she had proposed an article for *Cosmopolitan* to be titled, "The Show Won't Fold in Philadelphia," concerning "the advantages, adventures and hazards of writing music and lyrics for industrial shows." In a letter to the magazine she explained:

> An assignment as definite as are these, is a joy. Pure joy. For one
> thing, your deadline is a few months away, not a year or two, as
> is the case with theatrical productions. My boss, Alfred Stern,
> sells the top industrial brass an idea and works it out at his drawing
> board and typewriter at least a year before he calls in a writer or a
> composer. By that time the sponsor is committed (later, he may feel
> he should have been!), and you know for sure the project will not
> be scrapped. Cut, yes. Scrapped, no. In a piece running six or eight
> pages, as you suggested, I'd mention a few of the fantastic, often
> funny incidents and challenges we've met in doing industrials.[14]

With such a contract, Swift was responsible only for writing the music. Stern handled the administrative details, and the fee was not contingent on ticket sales. Stern himself preferred this business to Broadway because "productions were more regular and more lucrative." Although this arrangement could be seen as another way that Swift relinquished control of her music, after the series of thwarted projects she had tried to initiate during the 1950s, these assignments were a welcome relief. Although an article was never published, her correspondence with *Cosmopolitan* suggests that she was comfortable with these projects. She recalled a lesson learned from Gershwin: "Never turn down any project for which someone asks you to write. You may write some of your greatest music while doing it."[15]

Of the six industrial shows that Alfred Stern offered Swift, four had a distinctly feminine angle. *One Little Girl* celebrated the Camp Fire Girls; *Century 21* was the pavilion of a real estate corporation with a largely female workforce; Clairol products were directed toward women; and housewives were the main purchasers of Borden products. Although Stern used various composers for different shows and was a close friend who held Kay and her abilities in high regard, he may have felt more comfortable entrusting these projects to Swift rather than a male composer.[16]

Compositional Style

In spite of Swift's extensive background in classical music, her classical output is much smaller than her popular works. Even so, her classical works occupy an important place in her repertoire and in her life. While her focus between *Alma Mater* and *Paris '90* was on popular and stage works, she wrote one of her most significant classical compositions, *Reaching for the Brass Ring,* in the 1950s. During the 1960s, while she was earning a living by writing industrial shows, she found time to write more classically oriented pieces. Unbound by convention, she worked in the two genres until the end of her life.

Kay Swift shared Gershwin's view about the fluid boundaries between classical and popular music. "He felt, as I always have, that music is music and it doesn't matter what phase it happens to be in, just as it doesn't matter if one speaks French, Spanish, English, German, Russian. It's what one says that matters. . . . If you feel in one mood, it happens to be jazz. If it's another mood, it happens to be a sonata or a concerto." So it was that she often mixed elements of both in her classical and popular compositions.[17]

Swift drew inspiration from an eclectic group of musicians and styles. "I've listened with pleasure and delight to everybody who was good, I think. Debussy, Ravel, Bach and Brahms were strong, not so much Beethoven." She listened to both popular and classical composers, preferring those who were innovators. "I hate the predictable; I can't help it."[18]

Although Kay Swift never abandoned tonality, she certainly acquired the attitude displayed by the French and Russian composers who experimented in the early part of the century and whose works were embraced in her New York circles. Much of her music is permeated with a sense of humor, which is reflected by an interest in jazz harmonies and rhythms, blues elements, and irreverent quotations of or references to other well-known musical works. Clarity of texture is also a characteristic of her works. But above all, Kay Swift's classical and popular works maintain an emphasis on melody, the element she believed to be paramount. In February 1966, she represented ASCAP in addressing the Stephen Foster Jeanie Auditions in White Springs, Florida, and spoke of the importance of a melody that is "fresh and original." She noted that "the best music was always melodic," whether it was by Franz Schubert, Stephen Foster, or Irving Berlin.[19]

Swift also spoke with disdain about contemporary classical music trends, criticizing composers of atonal music:

> We all hear a lot of criticism these days, about the lack of melody in music that is being written. . . . [I]t's nearly impossible to remember most of it. . . . A lot of composers give a highly discouraging reason for this. They say there simply aren't any new ways left for them to use the notes and harmonies we have. So, in many cases they turn out music that is atonal, which often sounds as though it could be played backwards, starting at the end, and seem just as logical. I believe there are people who can't write a good, straightforward tune, who make this dark view an excuse to write a mindless ramble, or a mathematical-type ramble, because they feel there is nothing fresh left to be said. . . . But I honestly believe these defeated composers are wrong. So there is actually no need for us to feel that music must sound so bizarre that we can't understand what it's trying to say, or so reminiscent that it becomes an ancient story as soon as we hear it.[20]

In sharp contrast with this "bizarre" music, Swift continued to rely on well-constructed melodies and tonal harmonies in her musical compositions. Although the melodies in her classical pieces, as in her popular songs, are often disjunct and feature wide skips, they are balanced with sufficient stepwise motion. Swift admired Gian Carlo Menotti in opera, Harold Arlen in musical comedy, and Henry Mancini in movies—all of them producing original music and writing what she considered to be good melodies.[21]

Because Swift took such care writing her melodies, she was sensitive to performers who exercised too much freedom when singing popular songs. She felt that a singer's interpretation should not distort the melody and rhythm of the written score beyond recognition and was disturbed by some song stylists who took what she felt were excessive liberties. She did not mind if people elaborated on her music somewhat, but always cautioned, "Give me one clean chorus! Let me hear it once the way I wrote it."[22]

Reviewer Peter Reilly commented on three of Swift's "more 'serious'" works, excerpts from *Alma Mater,* Theme and Variations for Cello and Piano, and *Century 21,* a suite for orchestra.

> All display not only Miss Swift's solid classical training but her witty self-assurance. They are all brisk without being brittle, full of sentiment yet never sentimental, humorously and delightfully balanced between the rigors of classical form and of personal expressiveness. They are as playful and as immaculately realized as a Magritte painting, in which everyday perception is rearranged and reinterpreted even as the artist strictly observes all the rules of good draftsmanship. Kay Swift's music has that same ability to engage and parry the classical forms, to change the expected dark to the unexpected light, to toy with melody and to be seriously unserious. On the very first hearing, particularly in the dances from *Alma Mater,* the music may seem to have that too-crisp chic reminiscent of the more arid work of Les Six, but a second hearing makes it apparent that Miss Swift may be flirtatious, but she is assuredly not vacuous.[23]

Although Swift used some contemporary techniques, her music always remained grounded in tonality. This was not a surprising practice for someone of her age and background. Born at the end of the great romantic tradition, when both ragtime and impressionism were emerging, she was willing to add these new harmonies, textures, and rhythms to the classical styles in which she was so thoroughly immersed as a child.

Her ill-fated attempts to enter the world of rock and roll in 1958 were both a sign that she continued to accept new styles and to adapt to the changing tastes of the market and a signal to her that perhaps that was not a realistic endeavor. By her own admission, melody was the primary element in her songs, in spite of a generous dose of rhythmic syncopation, and her works through the 1950s had demonstrated her aptitude with such writing. In contrast, rock and roll emphasized rhythm above all, subjugating the melody to a driving bass line and rhythmic accompaniment. More important, it was transmitted by oral tradition, that is from band to band, or from radio and record player to listener. Many rock tunes were not notated, and if they were, it was often after they had become recorded hits, not before. Swift's classical approach to music began with the score, proceeded to the stage production and the publication of sheet music, and ended with the recording. Not only the elements in the music but also the process in creating a piece were reversed for her.

Her realization of this difference did not come easily, as her comments to Detroit interviewer Patricia Yaroch in 1975 reflected. Her ability to transcend several eras and styles seems to have ceased at the period of rock and roll, not so much because of her inability to write in such a manner but because of her inability to adapt to the procedure in a changing market. However, her mastery of classical eighteenth-century counterpoint, nineteenth-century operetta, early-twentieth-century styles including impressionism, and popular styles of 1930s Broadway and 1940s Hollywood, gave her a versatility that served her well as she provided music for a variety of audiences throughout the century.

Classical Works

Theme and Variations for Cello and Piano (1960) is a work written for performance by Swift with cellist Marie Romeat Rosanoff. The two had remained lifelong friends since their days at the Institute of Musical Art. Into their later years, Swift and Rosanoff would meet regularly to play chamber music for their own pleasure. According to Swift, Rosanoff kept bringing music with difficult piano parts for her to sight-read. Swift had always been able to negotiate difficult music, but as she grew older, this skill and her eyesight deteriorated. She composed this piece for the two of them to play during their afternoon salons, bringing a different variation each week. The accompaniment is not easy, but she would have been familiar with it so that reading the notes was less problematic.[24]

This is an eleven-minute piece, featuring a simple theme and four variations that reflect the many musical genres that Swift embraced. The A major theme is written, like many of her popular songs, in AABA form, and it is

10.2 "Theme" for Cello and Piano, measures 5–12

in 3/4 meter (ex. 10.2). The pentatonic character of the melody's opening phrase is reminiscent of an English folk tune. The accompaniment is somewhat romantic in character, with chromatic inflections and a simple waltz bass.

The first variation immediately breaks the folk reference and switches to eighteenth-century counterpoint, reflecting Swift's study with Percy Goetschius, when she wrote a fugue a week. The first five notes of the theme are transformed into a fugue theme in cut time that employs even rhythms (quarter notes and eighth notes), much as a Bach fugue would. The cello and piano alternate entrances at different registers and develop the texture in a contrapuntal manner (ex. 10.3).

The second variation changes character, this time employing 2/4 meter. For the A phrases, the meter divides into triplets, producing a 6/8 feeling and a blues melody. The bridge breaks into a jazz style, with regular sixteenth-note divisions of the beat. This variation pays tribute to the popular styles so central to Swift's career. The closing of this variation features the blues theme in stretto, a contrapuntal technique that overlaps entrances of the theme in different voices. This treats the blues melody in a baroque manner, again juxtaposing popular and art styles. The third variation returns to the 3/4 meter, this time playing an elegant Viennese waltz. It recalls Swift's classical roots as well as her lifelong interest in ballet and dance.

The final variation returns to 4/4, beginning in C major and moving to A minor. It introduces a repetitive, dactylic rhythmic pattern of a quarter

10.3 "Var. 1" for Cello and Piano, measures 19–24

note followed by two eighth notes, which lends the movement the flavor of a Spanish dance. It also uses harmonies that invoke Swift's familiarity with impressionistic sonorities. A return to the serene theme at the end brings unity and closure to the piece. It recalls the simplicity and directness with which Swift composes and suggests a return to her musical roots after her explorations into the classical and popular genres. All of the movements of Swift's quartet are elegant and well crafted, although contrasting in nature and style. Together they form a dynamic summary of the eclecticism and diversity that sparked Kay Swift's life. That she performed the theme and variations regularly with Marie Rosanoff gives the piece greater significance. Edward Jablonski called it "a touching memorial to a life-long friendship."[25]

In 1966 she assembled a set of five short piano pieces, *Offbeat Waltz Plus Four.* The first two, entitled "A Walk in Town" and "A Walk in the Woods," were dedicated to her granddaughter Rachel Levin. Completing the set were "Offbeat Waltz" (originally written for the ballet *Alma Mater*), "Overtones of the Past," and "Blue Note." These are intermediate-level teaching pieces. "A Walk in Town" and "A Walk in the Woods" feature Swift's typical lyrical melody against a simple linear accompaniment. "Offbeat Waltz" is a jazz waltz, with some syncopations and more difficult inner voicings.

"Overtones of the Past" introduces baroque-style counterpoint. "Blue Note" uses the syncopations and blue harmonies of which Swift was so fond. Although all the pieces are attractive, "Blue Note" is perhaps the most original of the set.

Other Endeavors

From the 1960s on, Swift produced a number of short, one-movement works. Although most continued in the popular vein, several were classical in approach, and some had sacred themes. During the 1960s, the same period in which she and Hunter were attending the Church of Truth, she wrote a high-school choral piece entitled "God Is Our Refuge," as well as the gospel style piece, "Prayer with a Beat" from *Century 21*.

"God Is Our Refuge" is an art song, well constructed and developed. An a cappella piece for five-part chorus (SSATB), it is based on a reassuring text, Psalm 46 ("God is our refuge and strength, / a very present help in trouble"). This five-minute work, signed with the pseudonym "B. F. Seale," was commissioned for a high-school choral contest in 1966 and is in three main sections, adhering to the sections of the text. Triadic harmonies abound and often move in parallel motion. The piece opens in 4/4 meter, beginning in A major and modulating quickly to F sharp major and then B minor. The B section changes to a lilting 6/8 meter ("tempo a la Barcarolle") in G major ("There is a river, the streams whereof shall make glad the city of God"). The third section in G minor is written in cut time but employs many triplet rhythms ("He maketh wars to cease unto the end of the earth"). Although the piece is basically homophonic, this section does feature some counterpoint. The coda ("Be still and know that I am God") returns to the opening key of A major.

Included in her secular music is the novelty song "The Circus Is a Family Affair," which she composed in 1966. Her humorous lyric notes how so many circus performers are related ("You take that girl and boy on a horse. / They are an aunt and nephew, of course"), and it cautions against trying to escape with one of the performing artists, since these relatives closely chaperone their young.

And the lady with the seal fairly bulges with appeal,
Man, no matter how you feel, Do take care!
She may lead a guy on, But her uncle trains the lion,
And he's handy with his whip and his chair.
Because the circus is a family affair!

There is no indication for what purpose this song was written or that it was ever performed; the piano accompaniment, however, is complete, not just a sketch. It is very much in the style of the production numbers Swift had written for the Radio City Music Hall Rockettes thirty years earlier.

Two other songs with completed piano accompaniments also seem to be from this time period, based on their characters and the handwriting in the manuscripts. Swift wrote music and lyrics for both. "Schottische" is a rhythmic dance with irregular phrase lengths (five measures plus three measures) and a lyric praising "that old fashioned tempo that always clicks." "Corny, but Nice" is "in tempo of the twenties, a la straw-hat-and-cane." The lyrics are indeed corny, yet the melody is attractive and memorable. Because there are two hand-copied accompaniments complete with an introduction, as well as a lead sheet and a typed lyric sheet, it seems clear that this tune was intended for a specific, though unknown, purpose. Both of these songs would also have made very suitable numbers for the Rockettes.

One of the greatest weaknesses in Kay Swift's later works was the lack of a consistent lyricist. Her most effective and imaginative songs were written with James Warburg (Paul James) and Al Stillman. After 1936, she either paired with lyricists sporadically or wrote her own lyrics. Although there appeared to be several superb possibilities for partners, no long-term associations were forged.

In 1967 Swift contacted lyricist Johnny Mercer about collaborating on a project. In his enthusiastic response, Mercer asked her to read *The Good Companions*, by J. B. Priestley, which he felt would convert easily to a musical that he would be in favor of writing with her. For some reason, Swift was not receptive to the idea and suggested Priestley's *Lost Empires* instead. This did not appeal to Mercer, who countered with *The Royal Family* by Edna Ferber and George S. Kaufman. Apparently the two could not agree on a book. Mercer became involved writing *Sabrina* with Henry Mancini.

He later wrote the lyrics for *The Good Companions* with André Previn, which was staged in London in 1974. Given Swift's desire for a successful production, it is hard to understand why she would not write *The Good Companions* when a lyricist of Mercer's stature was willing to commit to the project.

Another potential partner might have been Dorothy Fields, a native New Yorker who had also spent time in Hollywood and returned to the East Coast by the late 1950s. Both had the experience and the connections that would have created a formidable songwriting team. It is not clear whether the two of them even met. They might have attended some of the same theatrical parties in the 1920s, since Fields's father and brother, Lew and Herb, were both active in Broadway productions, although Dorothy Fields would have been just twenty in 1925 and did not have her first major success until *Blackbirds of 1928*. She and songwriter Jimmy McHugh left for Hollywood, and by the time she returned to New York, Swift had left for Oregon with Faye Hubbard. The late 1950s and early 1960s would have been an opportune time for Swift and Fields to connect, especially since this was a period of relative inactivity for Swift. That they never did may have been because of their personalities. Both enjoyed working with men and had spent their professional lives doing so. The prospect of working with another woman may not have appealed to either of them. The public, too, may not have been ready for an all-female songwriting team in 1960. As long as each was paired with a male, their credibility was more likely to remain intact.[26]

The most logical lyricist for Swift to have joined was, of course, Ira Gershwin. By his own admission, Swift worked in the same manner that George did and was a close friend. Yet neither seems to have considered the possibility beyond working with George's tunes. Ira was reluctant to undertake musical projects after George died and agreed only to those assignments that he felt were unique and suited to his skills. He had collaborated in 1941 with composer Kurt Weill and Moss Hart on *Lady in the Dark*, a play that was closely integrated with the music—combining light opera, musical comedy, and choral pieces. But he was not interested in simply generating more musical comedies. He wrote to Weill, "Let's not do anything unless we feel it's something that has to be done." He turned down projects that he felt someone else could have written just as easily as he. His work with Swift on *The Shocking Miss Pilgrim* was a unique project, offering him an opportunity to work again with George's music. But Swift returned to New York soon thereafter. Ira selected the music for the film *An American in Paris* (1951), which used only Gershwin pieces. His last collaborations were with Harold Arlen on songs for Judy Garland and her comeback in the film, *A Star Is Born* (1954), after which he retired from lyric writing. His next three decades were devoted to preserving and promoting the George and Ira Gershwin legacies.[27]

Swift herself suggested that a major obstacle to finding a suitable lyricist was her own early morning work schedule. "When you work with a lyricist you have to be with the other person constantly—almost have to move in together. But I work best at 5 A. M.—and I can't find anyone else who does."[28]

In 1964, Swift wrote a proposal with Henry Myers for a course on "The American Musical Theatre." Henry Myers was a former press agent for Lee and J. J. Shubert. He had written songs for *The Little Show* (1929) and *Garrick Gaieties* (1930) and had been involved with musical theater as a producer, lyricist, and librettist. His only complete score, *The Children's Crusade* (1971), was based on the novel *Our Lives Have Just Begun*, but the show closed out of town after six performances. This proposed course, which Swift and Myers wanted to teach jointly, would have covered both the history of musical comedy and instruction in production. They suggested there would be high interest among "theater-going public, young writers, composers, directors, set designers, critics, and possibly producers." While it is not clear for what institution or organization this course was proposed or whether it was ever accepted, it is a well-organized, detailed outline and yet one more avenue that Kay Swift explored as she approached seventy.[29]

Swift was active in the American Guild of Authors and Composers (AGAC, now the Songwriters Guild of America), serving on the executive committee as it planned its thirty-fifth anniversary in 1966. She was still on the committee for its fortieth anniversary in 1971, when she designed a brochure to promote AGAC, describing its history and defining its benefits. In her breezy prose, she wrote, "Happiness is an AGAC contract that is signed, countersigned and working 365 days a year for you over a period of 28 years plus renewal, all by means of 23 protective-filled paragraphs created to warm a writer's heart." She clearly felt that membership in this organization as well as in ASCAP was a privilege and a responsibility necessary to preserve the rights of present and future composers.[30]

Personal Affairs

These years were a difficult time for Swift and Galloway, a troubled man. Katharine Weber remembers Hunter with fondness. He was fun-loving and kind to her and taught her to juggle. "A door-opener and a chair-puller-outer," he was a charming escort for her grandmother but lacked a strong character. By this time in their marriage, Hunter's spending habits had exceeded his income, and Kay was obliged to cover his debts. In 1961, she was forced to sell *The Charing Cross Bridge,* an oil painting by André Derain of 1905–6 that she had inherited from her mother. The work sold for eighty thousand dollars, a substantial sum. This was the same year, when Katharine was six and John was ten, that their mother forbade them to have further contact with Hunter.[31]

Yet Swift remained positive about their marriage. In an outline for a chapter of her memoirs written around 1966, she speaks of a "common philosophy" that kept them together "come rain, come shine, and bring-'em-on." She spoke of Hunter's "background, military and theatrical. The disciplines he acquired, both in the army and later on, have stood him in excellent stead. At any rate, I am grateful for his tastes, his mentality, his judgment, and most of all, for his company." His "judgment" was dubious when Kay questioned a bill from a local jewelry store for a seven-hundred-dollar bracelet that she never received. Nephew Shippen had the unfortunate task of determining that the bracelet had been presented to another woman. Hunter claimed to be dating the current Miss Venezuela, to whom he had presented the gift, but she did not return his favors—or the bracelet.[32]

It was also in 1966 that Swift parted with some of her treasured Gershwin scores, eventually acquired by the Library of Congress—the *1932 Songbook,* as well as a black notebook that has been touted as one they had shared. George supposedly started from one end of the book and filled the first eleven pages, and Kay inverted the notebook and wrote her notes from the other end. In fact, they could never have shared this notebook unless the earliest of her pages had been removed. Swift's first notation is dated 1952, fifteen years after Gershwin's death. The notebook includes some early sketches for *A Candle for St. Jude,* including "Lollie's Theme," along with sketches from *Hunter's Moon* (1958). It would have been typical of Kay, who was somewhat disorganized and impulsive, to have run out of manuscript paper and have grabbed the first blank paper she could find. The first page of the Swift end was actually cut from the book with scissors.[33]

Galloway's unstable behavior was highlighted by an incident reported on the front page of the *New York Times* on November 11, 1967. He had attended an art sale at Parke-Bernet and successfully bid $467,775 for ten paintings, later admitting that he could not pay for them. (Apparently Hunter did not understand the protocol and believed that he could resell some of the paintings at a profit to pay for the others.) The auction house asked the consignors to sell the paintings to the underbidders at the auction and sued Galloway. Although Swift managed to keep her name out of the newspaper, she bore the brunt of the expense. Her royalties from "Fine and Dandy" and the Warburg trust fund were her most stable income, and she lived comfortably but was not wealthy. Galloway's actions forced her to give up several more valuable paintings. The incident was devastating. In a note to a friend several weeks later, Swift wrote, "He [Hunter] is now handling himself calmly—always has after a scare—and will, he says, *look for a job.* Which sounds great. His statement in the Times was the *truth.*" This note is significant for several reasons. First, it suggests that this was not an isolated occurrence and that a pattern of crisis and recovery had been established. Second, it reveals Swift's impatience that, after more than twenty years of marriage, Hunter had never been employed. In the months that followed, Galloway moved out of their apartment. Kay's impatience and, one would speculate, her shattered faith led to their divorce soon afterward. The action cited "mental cruelty and abandonment," and the divorce was final in 1968. On February 14, 1969, Valentine's Day, Galloway died suddenly. The death certificate cited "occlusive coronary artery disease" as the cause, although family and close friends acknowledge that it was suicide. Kay was visiting her daughter Kay Levin at the time of the tragedy. A memorial service was held in the apartment of Kay's close friend Mary Lasker. To Swift's credit, she continued to support Minerva Stanley, Hunter's mother, until Stanley's death five years later, another sign of her compassionate nature.[34]

Kay and Hunter had had a lengthy association with the New York Church of the Truth, beyond their class in "Prayer, Healing and Treatment" in 1959. In June 1963 they received a certificate from Dr. Ervin Seale, whom Swift considered "a remarkable philosopher." It recognized them "for perfect attendance of a three-year course of instruction in Divine Science and Metaphysics." Notebooks with copious notes show that their attendance at Wednesday night Bible study at the Church of Truth continued in 1964 and again in 1967. In the months following Hunter's death, Swift made a donation to the church. However, documentation of her participation in that organization stops in 1969.[35]

Kay Swift's maturity in the 1960s reflects an understanding of her skills and strengths. She recognized the advantages of her classical knowledge and training and did not hesitate to combine this genre with her love of popular music. Composing for industrial shows was not only lucrative but challenged her imagination and creativity. Swift's talents and determination gave her strength to move forward through personal adversity with a positive attitude.

CHAPTER 11

Keep on Keepin' On

I think my mother equipped me with a disappointment adjustant.
—Kay Swift

Compositions and Musical Activities in the 1970s

Kay Swift remained active throughout the 1970s in her work and in her social life. For a septuagenarian, she was remarkably productive. Even though she may not have been working at her former pace, she continued to compose and pursue her musical activities. As in the 1960s, she wrote fewer popular songs and compositions and tended to write more pieces, both secular and sacred, that were classical in style. She also added to her cycle of children's songs, with "Shoana," a tribute to April's granddaughter, who was born in 1970.

Swift returned in these years to her early practice of setting poetry. Early in the decade she wrote "Man, Have Pity on Man," a song for solo voice with a text based on a poem by Ursula Vaughan Williams, the second wife of composer Ralph Vaughan Williams. Number eight in a cycle of nine poems that told the story of Noah's Ark, the piece was performed with orchestra in 1972. Its dark, philosophical text and clashing harmonies were unusually severe for Swift. As Vaughan Williams questions what will remain on earth after the forces of destruction have run their course, Swift's parallel triads deny a single tonal center, moving through the keys of B flat, C, A, and G major. The harsh dissonances are balanced by a regular 3/4 meter and a fairly conjunct melody, with a few well-placed leaps for interest.[1]

A sacred song begun in 1972 is incomplete but worth mentioning for the contrast it offers to "Man, Have Pity on Man." This biblical text is much more uplifting: "Think on these things, and the God of peace shall be with you. Rejoice in the Lord always." Perhaps these two sacred efforts helped Swift face and deal with some of her personal disappointments.

In the secular category is a song written in 1972 and based on a poem by Carolyn Kramer, a friend of her daughter Andrea. "The Bee Song" is a novelty verse that contains musical references. Although the melody and text are complete, the accompaniment again is only sketched. Several features, however, are notable in this late song. There are meter shifts and key changes, and the chorus is interrupted with a quotation from Richard Wagner's "Bridal Chorus" that underscores a budding romance between two bees. Swift was obviously intrigued by the text and put her creativity to work, illustrating the verbal puns with musical text painting. It is typical that she would complete the melody, which was the portion of the music she felt was most important, and never finish the piano part. She could accompany the lead line at sight without completing the tedious task of writing out each note. There is no evidence that this song was ever performed publicly, but Louise Carlyle may well have read through it with Swift at the piano.

Another unfinished piece from this period demonstrates Kay Swift's continued experimentation. The title, "Yes, I Shall" (1972), for trombone and orchestra, reflects her determination to be productive and is innovative in its use of 5/4 and 6/4 meters. The unfinished piece totals seventy-five measures and consists of two large sections. The opening section in 5/4 features an erratic rhythmic theme with octave leaps and syncopation. The contrasting middle section harmonizes a subdued, romantic melody in straight 4/4 meter in the key of E major. The score exists in keyboard format, but notations indicate orchestration plans and rehearsal letters. Although the orchestrations were not completed, the piece did undergo a transformation. A piano piece from 1973 that bears the title "New Tune" is actually this middle section transposed to the key of F major. Thirty-four bars long and in ABAC format, "New Tune" is in the style of her popular songs, without words. The sinewy melody, a gradually ascending line, is harmonized with full, lush chords that create a bit more dissonance than her earlier popular songs.

Swift's last commissioned show, *Dr. Rush Pays a House Call,* was for the 1974 celebration of the American Medical Association as the nation's Bicentennial approached. The drama centered on the four physicians who signed the Declaration of Independence, with Dr. Benjamin Rush, surgeon general of the Continental Army, as the central character. Swift provided incidental and background music for the drama. There are no lyrics. Again Robert Russell Bennett orchestrated and conducted, continuing a respectful collaboration.

Much of Swift's professional life continued to center on her knowledge of George Gershwin and his music. Various biographers of Gershwin, including Lawrence Stewart, Robert Kimball, and Edward Jablonski, consulted Swift not only as Gershwin's close friend and companion but as a respected musician. At "The Gershwin Years," a concert event staged in 1971 at Lincoln Center by the American Academy of Dramatic Arts, she and Louise Carlyle presented a medley from *The Shocking Miss Pilgrim.* The show also featured appearances by Ethel Merman, Ginger Rogers, Ruby Keeler, and Bobby Short.

Merle Armitage had invited Swift to write an essay for a volume of tributes to George Gershwin in 1938, but she had felt it was too soon after his death to respond. Edward Jablonski and Lawrence Stewart had consulted her extensively for their volume, *The Gershwin Years* (1958). However, by 1973, when Robert Kimball and Alfred Simon produced their coffee-table volume, *The Gershwins,* Swift was very generous with her memories, her photographs, and her memorabilia. Kimball, now artistic consultant to the Ira and Leonore S. Gershwin Trusts, was a former curator of the Yale University Collection of the Literature of the American Musical Theatre and a recognized authority on the American musical. Alfred Simon, a Gershwin scholar and director of light music at the New York Times radio station, WQXR, lived in Swift's apartment building on East Fifty-ninth Street and had served as a rehearsal pianist for *Of Thee I Sing.* Swift's contributions to *The Gershwins* mark the first time that she herself had written about Gershwin or his music. Several months later she published these recollections of Gershwin as the article "Remembering George Gershwin" in the *Saturday Review of the World*.[2]

For *The Gershwins*, she shared two photographs of herself from the early 1930s. One features her in a slim, white evening gown, wearing the gold bangle bracelets that George had purchased for her after the performance of *An American in Paris* in 1928. The second depicts a carefree Kay Swift lounging on a beach in a bathing suit and shorts, enjoying the sun. Photographs of documents, now in the Library of Congress, included pages from Gershwin's 1921 notebook, which he had given to her, and the dedication from his *1932 Songbook* that read, "For Kay—These manuscripts and of course—Best. George. Oct. 26, 1931." Again, "Best" was their code word for "love."[3]

Swift continued to use her memory of Gershwin tunes to facilitate their performance. Robert Kimball remembered that she would frequently play the songs "Freud and Jung and Adler" from *Pardon My English* (1933), as well as the "Meadow Serenade" from the 1927 version of *Strike Up the Band*, both of which had been lost. Entertainer Bobby Short relied on her expertise when he recorded his double album, *Bobby Short Is K-ra-zy for Gershwin*, in 1973. To choose the final selections for this album, he consulted Robert Kimball, Alfred Simon, and Kay Swift, "three good friends who probably know as much about a Gershwin song as anybody." It was Swift who suggested he sing "Hi-Ho," which had been written in 1936 for Fred Astaire to sing in the film *Shall We Dance* but was never used. The song had not been published until 1967 and was little known. Swift remembered playing the second piano obbligato with Gershwin, and she played it with Short on the recording in the same manner. In addition, Short wanted to sing the unpublished "Comes the Revolution," from *Let 'Em Eat Cake*, so Kay simply taught it to him from memory. She also taught him "K-ra-zy for You," a song from the Gershwins' first flop, *Treasure Girl* (1928), which generated the album title. (It also inspired the 1992 adaptation of *Girl Crazy*, retitled *Crazy for You*.) Short admired her musical talents, her perspective, and her sensitivity. He also recalled her being very generous with her time and her gifts. During one of their rehearsals Swift pulled a folded piece of manuscript paper from her pocket and said, "Here, I think you should have this." It was the beginning of the second theme of Gershwin's *Concerto in F*, a pencil sketch written in his own hand.[4]

Probably the most poignant Gershwin moment occurred in 1976. For the Bicentennial, Sherwin Goldman was considering a touring production of *Porgy and Bess* in its entirety. When Goldman consulted Kay Swift early in the discussions, she assured him that the work should be presented as an opera rather than a musical and that Gershwin had never been happy with all the cuts that had been made for the New York opening. Goldman began working with David Gockley, director of the Houston Opera. Swift elicited a promise that if the new production ever made it to Boston, it would be produced in the Colonial Theatre and she would be invited to the premiere. (Her own musical, *Fine and Dandy,* had played at the Colonial in 1930 before its Broadway run.) The opera opened in Houston on July 1, 1976, and then moved on to Philadelphia, Wolf Trap, Ottawa, Toronto, and Boston. Goldman complied with Swift's insistence on the Colonial Theatre, even though the orchestra would not fit into the pit since the theatre's remodeling in 1935. Some box seats had to be removed for this production. Goldman explained her keen interest in the project.

> Kay . . . told me what seats she wanted on opening night. She
> wasn't quite sure exactly which ones, so I blocked off several. They
> were toward the back of the house. When we came to the theatre
> she remembered the seats and we sat together. "Now you've given
> me my gift," she said. "So many years ago I sat with George in
> these seats. I was in tears because of all the cuts that were being
> made in his work. 'George,' I said, 'they're not going to hear and
> see what you wrote.' He told me, 'Someday, Kay, you'll sit in that
> same seat and you'll hear what I wrote, I promise you.'"

For forty years, Kay Swift had remembered his promise. This performance allowed her the opportunity to have it fulfilled.[5]

Robert Kimball appreciated Swift's musical talents as well as her knowledge of Gershwin. In December 1974, he, Alfred Simon, and Kay Swift went into the Nola Sound Studios and recorded all the songs from *Fine and Dandy.* Kimball and Swift sang while Swift and Simon played the piano. The recording was by no means of commercial quality. Kimball said later that they simply wanted to preserve the songs as Kay had remembered and played them. As a historian of American musical theater, he recognized Kay's contribution to the Broadway musical tradition and wanted to capture this piece of history. Because only seven of the thirteen songs from the show had been published as sheet music, Kay had to renotate the others to teach Kimball and Simon. Only "Fine and Dandy" had been recorded. This tape not only preserves the compositions for posterity but represents the joy that three friends found in Swift's music.[6]

Others also began to realize what a gift Kay Swift had given the music world. Vivian Perlis interviewed Swift in 1975 for the American Music Oral History Project at Yale University, which records the thoughts of contemporary composers, performers, and patrons for future scholars. Swift was joining such major figures in American music as Eubie Blake, John Cage, Leo Ornstein, and Claire Reis with this interview. Several newspapers featured stories about Swift, and she had an opportunity to share her memories, not just of Gershwin, but of her experiences as a composer. An article reflecting on her career and her association with Gershwin appeared in the *Philadelphia Evening Bulletin* when she attended a production of *Porgy and Bess* there in 1976. A reporter from *Newsday* focused on her positive attitude and high energy level, citing her disregard for her advancing age and her exercise routine that included thirty-six push-ups daily. And a feature article in the *Long Island Press* concentrated on her songwriting career as a woman and her plans for future works.[7]

In 1975, after battling Parkinson's disease, her brother, Sam, died. Swift was now reflecting on her own life and works, and she decided to record a number of her compositions on a double album. Entitled *The Music of Kay Swift: Fine and Dandy*, it featured an assortment of her best-known works. The album sold its first pressing quickly. Swift is the only female composer represented in the Mark 56 series, which includes "collectors' items by George Gershwin and Harold Arlen." Edward Jablonski wrote the extensive liner notes. In addition to comments about the music, the notes contain biographical material and several photographs of Swift and her musical associates. The album features both popular and classical selections of Swift's work. These include her most successful songs ("Fine and Dandy," "Can

This Be Love?" "Calliope," "Once You Find Your Guy," "Up Among the Chimney Pots," and "Can't We Be Friends?"), as well as some of her instrumental music, including three dances from *Alma Mater*, with Vincent Abato, clarinet and saxophone, Homer Mensch, bass, Bradley Spinney, percussion, and Milton Kraus and Kay Swift, pianos. The album also includes Theme and Variations for Cello and Piano, performed by lifelong friends Marie Rosanoff and Kay Swift. Her industrial compositions were represented by "Can't Win 'Em All," a piece from the Borden show at the 1964 World's Fair that Swift now arranged for saxophone and rhythm section; and *Century 21*, a suite for orchestra from the 1962 World's Fair in Seattle, orchestrated by Carol Huxley and conducted by John Lesko. Finally, nine songs from *Reaching for the Brass Ring* are recorded. Seven of these were orchestrated and directed by Robert Russell Bennett with Louise Carlyle as soloist, as mentioned earlier. Kay Swift herself presented the other two, accompanying herself at the piano. Peter Reilly observed in *Stereo Review*, "As fine as Miss Carlyle's performances of the others are, Kay Swift's renditions, replete with her devil-may-care but gallant sense of vocal pitch, have the authentic joyousness of a lady communicating her loving." Reilly characterized Swift's album as "unexpected, civilized pleasure. . . . [It] demonstrates wonderfully well how hard she has worked and how completely she has succeeded in getting the best of everything out of her own considerable talents."[8]

Personal Notes

In spite of her many professional accomplishments at this advanced age, Kay Swift had other interests besides music. She spent precious time with her daughters and her grandchildren and was thrilled to go places with them. Yearly she traveled to Rome to spend Christmases with April and her family. When her granddaughter Katharine Kaufman married Nicholas Weber in September 1976, she arranged special music for their wedding, including a Bach bourrée and a version of the Gershwin song "Love Is Here to Stay" for flute and trombone—an unlikely combination but one that suited their chosen personnel. This would be a particularly poignant afternoon for Swift, because Katharine and Nick were married at Bydale. Although James Warburg had died in 1969, his third wife, Joan Melber Warburg, still lived there and consented to host his granddaughter's wedding in sight of the guest cottage where Gershwin had composed *An American in Paris*. This was Kay Swift's first and last return to the Connecticut estate.[9]

Ever a baseball fan, she continued to root for the Dodgers, now based in Los Angeles. In 1981 and 1985, she visited her daughter Andrea and grandson John in Los Angeles, attending Dodgers games on both trips. While there in 1981, she also met with Ira Gershwin and Michael Feinstein. She wrote about that meeting to her friends the composer William Bolcom and his wife, singer Joan Morris, pleased that Ira had found someone with whom to share his memories and thoughts of George. "I'm certain that Michael's the best thing that's happened to Ira since George's death. Wonderful guy."[10]

Kay Swift led a very active social life. Friends and family members often lunched at her apartment. Her housekeeper, Mattie, would prepare "generous drinks" and serve the meal. She hosted parties for her friends from the music and theater worlds, among them Cornelia Otis Skinner, Alfred Stern, Louise Parker, and Gershwin associates Alfred Simon (who lived in her building), Mabel Schirmer, and Emily Paley. William Bolcom and Joan Morris remember evenings in her apartment with six or eight guests gathering for an informal buffet dinner. Rarely did they sit at the dining table, most often balancing their plates in their laps and listening to one of the guests play the piano. More frequently they went to one of Swift's favorite neighborhood restaurants, the Double Dolphin. Bolcom recalls, "There was nothing 'Old Lady' about her." He remembers Kay's meticulous grooming, classic tastes, and fondness for beautiful scarves. She had many friends and loved to socialize. Robert Kimball remembers how generous she was. He, too, frequented the Double Dolphin with her, and she always insisted on picking up the check. Kimball and his wife, Abigail, hosted a party with Kay for her eightieth birthday in 1977 at his residence. Nearly eighty people, including many musicians, helped her celebrate the occasion.[11]

Swift's looks and actions belied her advancing age. She was a petite woman who carefully maintained her figure. For a sixtieth reunion photograph of her class at Miss Veltin's in 1977, she prided herself on being able still to sit on the floor. Swift continued her daily exercise routine into her eighties. Katharine Weber remembers how limber her grandmother remained, doing yoga on the living room floor in her pajamas. She watched her extend her leg and raise her knee to her ear while sitting in a kitchen chair. She also recalls that in order to avoid gaining weight, Swift ate little, even when her "perpetual cup of coffee" turned into her "perpetual vod ton" at cocktail hour. Alfred Stern remembered, "Kay wanted to be younger all the time. Her hair was always terribly blond." He also recalled that she enjoyed the company of younger men. She never admitted her age and was occasionally known to report a false birth date. She also had three facelifts in the 1980s.[12]

This streak of vanity was long-standing. In 1966 the British Broadcasting Company had asked to interview Swift for an upcoming television program that would feature Larry Adler playing Gershwin's music on the harmonica. Swift responded positively and participated in the program. Her acceptance letter, however, illustrates the fact that she never lost her concern for her image. She added the following postscript: "P.S. At the risk of sounding like a prima donna, I would greatly appreciate being photographed without the tight close-ups and only full-face shots." She was sixty-nine at the time.[13]

Kay loved attending the theater, the ballet, and dining at Sardi's on West Forty-fourth Street. As a young woman in the 1920s, she had developed a love of parties, dancing, and socializing that stayed with her late into her life. Whenever her granddaughter Katharine and her husband, Nicholas, took "Ganz" out for an evening, Swift, even in her eighties, insisted on having a proper escort. The age of her escort was irrelevant, but his presence was not. "What would people think? And what if there's dancing?!" The Webers sometimes provided one of their contemporaries, aged thirty-something, as her "date."[14]

One final anecdote illustrates her sense of humor, mischief, and flirtatious nature, even in her later decades. Nicholas Weber used to stay at Swift's apartment when he had business in New York. After one visit, when Swift was in her eighties, Weber sent her a bouquet of flowers. Knowing that she would delight in the joke, he signed the card, "From the man who spent the night." As he expected, Swift proudly displayed the bouquet in her hallway with the card carefully propped against the vase. Moreover, Mattie reported that when the flowers wilted, she replaced them with a fresh bouquet! Clearly this was a woman who was young in spirit and full of energy, who loved life and was eager to share it with friends and family.[15]

11.1 "For Betsy," measures 1–6

In May 1979, sudden tragedy stunned Kay Swift's family, when her twenty-eight-year-old granddaughter, Betsy Levin, was struck and killed by a truck while riding her bicycle to graduate classes in Eugene, Oregon. Swift wrote, "Her death has cut like a scythe across the lives of all her relatives and friends. For, Betsy was a very special girl." Betsy's mother, Kay Levin, wrote an article about death, musing, "Surely there must be as many ways to grieve as there are to love. Not all grief is bitter, but it all does seem so unexpected, so unexplainable. Above all, it is so endless." Swift's grief ultimately manifested itself in a piano piece, "For Betsy," which she completed in 1983, four years after the accident. Just as Swift had written songs celebrating the births of all her grandchildren, she now found herself commemorating the death of one of them.[16]

"For Betsy" is just twenty-four measures long, a brief memorial, but several of its features are significant. It is the one of the only pieces Swift ever wrote in D flat major. It has two themes, the first of which quotes several characteristic motives from "Smiling Betsy," the song from *Reaching for the Brass Ring* in her honor (see ex. 8.3). The melody in measures 3 and 4 of "For Betsy" quotes measures 10 to 12 of "Smiling Betsy," although the meter has been altered to a more sedate 4/4. The first theme of "For Betsy" uses parallel triads in the right hand against a bass line that features tonic and dominant pitches in syncopated rhythms, giving it a popular tone (ex. 11.1).[17]

Midway through the piece Swift modulates to the unrelated key of G major, a distant tritone away from D flat. The shift from D flat major to G major, an awkward transition, may not only symbolize the emptiness and disorientation felt by the family at Betsy's death; it might also be read as the emergence from despair to hope, as the music moves from the relatively obscure key of five flats to the very common key of one sharp. The second theme is from "Reaching for the Brass Ring," another song in the cycle. Although it was written for Betsy's older brother, Davey, Betsy is mentioned in it, so the melody was special to both of them. This second theme introduces more intricate rhythms, chromaticism, and counterpoint between the voices. The melody occurs in canon and is then accompanied by the first theme, which has been moved to the left hand. Swift intertwines the two melodies at the end, a technique at which she was accomplished and which she had previously used to highlight various songs, although not recently. Chromatic sequences return to the original key of D flat major. It is not coincidental that "Smiling Betsy" began in the key of C, and modulated to D flat major. It seems clear that Swift's choice of this unusual key for her memorial was an intentional echo of Betsy's original song.

Saddened as she was by this tragedy, Swift did not let the accident consume her life. That same year, she received an invitation for two to cruise on the Rhine River in Germany. She invited her close friend Louise Carlyle who was thrilled to accompany her. Carlyle had vivid memories of the trip, although Swift never mentioned it in her memoirs. Among the party of forty guests was Maurice Levine, conductor and founder of the musical theater series "Lyrics and Lyricists" that he had produced at the Ninety-second Street Y since 1970. Also invited were Levine's wife, singer Bobbi Baird, and Bob Lang, who had once sung with the Satisfiers, a back-up group. Carlyle elaborated on the trip:

> While we were on board Maurice Levine and Kay decided to have a "Lyrics and Lyricists" evening for the benefit of all on board. When we got to a certain port, we would do the show for whoever got on board. I was singing "I'm all at sea, can this be love?," which is a song of Kay's. Maurice is doing the dialogue, which he does so well. And Kay Swift played every single number—WITHOUT MUSIC.

It was a Kay Swift–George Gershwin evening. Nobody knows about this one! I just wish it had been on tape somewhere. Bobbi Baird sang, I sang. . . . Later Bob Lang sang.[18]

It is a testament to Kay Swift's amazing memory and stamina that at the age of eighty-two she could play every night for hours, remembering the songs as well as she did. Carlyle continued, "Maurice is asking Kay all these questions about George. That would be an interview that isn't in any books. She gave such wonderful answers that she answered, but didn't answer, if you know what I mean." That she managed to resist such inquiries during a week of partying at her age is even more remarkable, knowing how much she enjoyed her vodka and tonic. She seemed to be determined to keep her times with George Gershwin private, at least in public venues. However, close friends Joan Morris and Bill Bolcom recall that she spoke freely about him and her relationship with him.[19]

During this decade Swift reflected on her life in several ways. Not only had she recorded the double album of her music, but she continued to work on her autobiography. Although incomplete, the memoirs offer insight into her family, her musical training, her professional experiences, and personal anecdotes. Some of the memoirs are dated as early as 1966. She referred to them in a 1976 interview with Doris Wiley and probably continued to revise them until the early 1980s. Some topics remain off-limits. Not surprisingly, she wrote little about George Gershwin, except in professional terms. She mentioned the bracelets he had purchased for her only because she had worn them during the promotional tour for *Porgy and Bess* and they were an item of great interest to audiences. The snow bank episode after *Der Meistersinger* was a rare glimpse into their personal relationship and the fun they had together. The memoirs reveal little emotional involvement with any of her husbands or lovers and less of the frustration she must have undergone personally and professionally at various times. She spoke of Hunter briefly with fondness; at the time they were still married. She was most sentimental when describing her parents and Bertha Tapper. She had idolized both her father and Tapper, and they had had tremendous impacts on her young life. Both receive lengthy attention and repeated references in the manuscript.[20]

Her memoirs demonstrate her sense of humor, her ability to laugh at herself, and her positive attitude. She never dwelled on the negative, a trait confirmed by several of her friends. Louise Carlyle recalled, "She was always so positive. She never had a negative word about anybody. Always made you feel good, even in the worst of circumstances." William Zeffiro remarked, "She would never say a mean word about any of her husbands to me. She always said . . . I loved them, and it was great while it lasted." Swift herself admitted, "I'm never disappointed, really. . . . I'm so Pollyanna. . . . The truth is, I think my mother equipped me with a disappointment adjustant [sic]. . . . Balance, a compass." Her refusal to brood about the past helped her through difficult events, including her granddaughter's death. Carlyle maintained that her faith also helped her through tragic times. "Kay was such a believer in God, which is what pulled her through all that. . . . She had a very good philosophy about life, that we go on somewhere else. It all worked out. Such a positive thinker. Everything will always be fine."[21]

Swift was a complex woman whose personality and circumstances both enhanced her talents and limited the ways in which she used them. She was very sensitive to the label "woman composer," denying that gender bore any relation to creativity. Swift had always maintained she had an equal opportunity to compete in a musical world dominated by men. Columnist Phyllis Battelle reported Swift's feelings in 1976. "We never had the feeling we weren't equal. . . . I don't remember ever losing any chances because I was a woman, not at all." In her interview with Vivian Perlis, Swift expressed similar feelings. "I never had any trouble in any job in being a woman. I have always had any job I wanted; I never even thought about there being any difference, and I think I have always been paid as much as anybody. . . . [W]here equal jobs are done and women are paid less, I think that's really so unbelievably old fashioned. . . . I agree with people who go in for Women's Lib. I don't happen to, it doesn't affect my work in any way."[22]

Although Swift mentions her support of "Women's Lib," she tries to separate herself from the ideology. She maintained a traditionally feminine image and way of life and publicly denied that the women's movement affected her work. Yet privately she enjoyed an atypical career that was, to an extent, fostered by the forward thinking of her family and teachers. Her musical successes were not duplicated by many other female composers of the time.

In her interview with Battelle, Swift cited such successful songwriters as

Mabel Wayne ("In a Little Spanish Town"), Ann Ronell ("Willow Weep for Me"), and Dana Suesse ("My Silent Love"), all of whom enjoyed royalties from their few hits for many years. Swift joked, "It's a good business, writing hit songs. . . . I wonder why more women today don't go into it." Obviously she recognized the flaw in her statement. She continued, "You can't sit down and say, 'Now I'm going to write a pop standard.' Nobody's ever done that, man or woman. Not even Cole Porter, not even George Gershwin."[23]

What Swift did not mention is that although Ann Ronell, Dana Suesse, Ruth Lowe, and she herself each had two or three hit songs, their male counterparts (Rodgers, Berlin, Gershwin, Porter) each had hundreds. Even the lesser-known male composers, such as Arthur Schwartz, Hoagy Carmichael, and Burton Lane, have volumes of their published pieces that are available today.

Swift's denial of discrimination against herself as a female composer in 1976 was due both to her own personality and perhaps to anti-feminist backlash. Her granddaughter comments on Swift's determination. "She would not admit that anything was difficult. She wouldn't admit that it was difficult to get a taxi. . . . If anyone began a question, 'As a woman composer,' she would not have listened to the rest of the question. She was not interested." Furthermore, it was not unusual for successful women of her generation to be grateful for their good fortunes and opportunities rather than to question what more they might have become without succumbing to certain assumptions and roles. This attitude would be congruent with Swift's optimistic philosophy. Later, however, she came to understand that being female played an important role in how her life and career developed. In spite of her protests, the fact that she was a woman was of great significance to her as a musician. Katharine Weber maintained, "She was incredibly flirtatious. She was one of the most deeply female people I've ever known, and she had a lot of sexual relationships with a lot of people that complicated everybody's lives. How could she say being female had no bearing? She was totally female and it had a lot of bearing on her career."[24]

Although Swift's public comments from the 1970s deny that male and female composers had different experiences, Swift's memoirs suggest she was rethinking that position throughout the decade. The tone here is somewhat more philosophical. Swift mused privately:

Time was when I used to be impatient about any comment that began with the premise, *WHY ARE MEN* or *WHY ARE WOMEN*. It was hard for me to admit that in any creative area there could be basic differences between men and women. . . . But at last I see what seems a valid reason for the lack of recognizable success among . . . creatively talented women. . . . It is my belief, now, that women often allow their talents to dwindle because of the fact that they . . . are all too apt to be incurable romantics. I ought to know, because that's what happened to me. For a while, that is . . . . We often let our gifts grow rusty for lack of exercising them. And this, I believe, is something we're free to choose. It is not, I would say, a sin to fail to compose the Great American Symphony, or to write the Great American Novel. But it is good, if one makes the choice, to know why one makes that particular one. And, this fact has not been fully recognized by me. I think there must be many other women who have failed, equally, to see the nitty gritty of the situation facing them.[25]

With these thoughtful words, Swift seems to have reconsidered her earlier statements, acknowledging that women composers did, indeed, have less success than men and that often that was because of choices the women themselves had made. She personalized the situation by recognizing that she had made this mistake herself. "This is not to say that I am running down romance, as such. Never. It's only that I believe that the active pursuit of it—even in cases where the pursuit is only mental; perhaps, *especially* in these latter situations—takes much time and energy from the dogged pursuit of excellence in any given specialty." Swift did not make conscious choices to interrupt her career. She simply pursued other interests. As her daughter April suggested, "She had much more talent than she ever showed. She was too busy living. She did exactly what she wanted."[26]

Swift offered an alternative for being such an "incurable romantic." "Years ago, at a moment when I felt bereft because a man, about whom I felt strongly, had turned away, a wise English lady suggested to me, 'Why on earth don't you fall in love with your work, for a change?'" Swift acknowledged the possibilities, noting that in the world of show business, this is essentially what happens. One becomes consumed by the current show, its production, its schedule, its personnel. "The only people you want to see are other show business people, who understand your preoccupation." She indicated that she had acquired this professionalism later in life, perhaps after the distraction of husbands and family.[27]

Swift went on to maintain that among creative work, show business was particularly well suited for a woman because of its disciplined schedule. "Of course, show business is easier for a woman than many other fields of creative work, because it involves a deadline. And a deadline is essentially masculine, unyielding, and immovable. That's meat and drink to a woman writer, composer or lyricist." Although many would question this generalization today, her comment explains the comfort she felt with accepting assignments for industrial and commercial shows. Swift felt it was easier to be assigned a deadline by an outside party than for her to assign a deadline to herself. She preferred the passive role of taking instructions rather than the active role of giving them. She believed that women possessed talent equal to men's but that they often lacked the resolve to pursue their ambition.[28]

In a related section of her memoirs, Kay Swift mused whether her love for taking lessons in piano, composition, or dance was "in fact a part of that longing to please—to please a teacher, a lover, a husband, the public, one's children—that sometimes causes one's personal ambition to dwindle. If the person or persons to be pleased require that one perform, or write, or whatever, then one does so. If not—then a woman sometimes retires into a background from which she emerges, inevitably, to a fresh challenge."[29]

The pattern of Swift's output would tend to substantiate this theory. Her compositions declined in number when she was not enrolled at the Institute of Musical Art. Only the brief nursery songs remain from the year in which she studied privately with Charles Martin Loeffler in Boston, and there are no references to other pieces she wrote under him. She talked about taking in "bits of whatever I was working on" but did not indicate that any of them were ever completed. Neither Warburg nor Loeffler, it seems, was pressuring Swift to compose more music, probably because she had three young daughters. Swift, likewise, was not pushing herself during those years, so the quantity of her writing between 1922 and 1926, all classical, is very limited.

Swift's compositional activity between 1926 and 1937, the years she knew

Gershwin, is less logical. From 1926 to 1930, she wrote many popular songs, including the show *Fine and Dandy*, a significant achievement that indicates that Gershwin, Warburg, and her close friends encouraged her. Warburg could share in the creation of popular songs by writing the lyrics. The abrupt hiatus in her composition between 1930 and 1934 would not seem to reflect Gershwin's wishes. If, however, he expected her to be listening and reacting to his works during this prolific period of his, her available time and energy may have been sapped. In 1935 and 1936, while Swift was working at Radio City, she produced many popular songs at regular intervals. Of course, there she had a weekly deadline. When she left Radio City to take an administrative position with the World's Fair, Gershwin went to Hollywood and her composition seems to have ceased for several years. With the weekly deadline gone, she did not create one for herself. The cowboy, with no musical background, would certainly not have had high expectations that she compose. Instead he may have urged her to adapt to his way of life, a scenario that her miniscule output during those years reflects. Hunter Galloway, by contrast, was a great encourager and cheerleader. Swift wrote many kinds of works as she sought some success during the two decades of their marriage. That hers was the sole income would have been uncomfortable for her, but she had determination and energy enough for both of them.

CHAPTER 12

Finale

Saturday, August 9, 1980, 2 P.M.—It's a pleasant day, hot outside, cool in my apartment; a peaceful day, and one in which I might manage to alleviate the guilt I feel on awakening each morning. This feeling of guilt results from the fact that I haven't been working for the past couple of weeks.—Kay Swift

Kay Swift's work ethic pushed her to continue composing and contributing to the world of music late in life. She often worried that she had not done enough with her gift, and retirement was not an option she seems ever to have considered. When a friend once commented with enthusiasm, "You must have had such an interesting life!" Swift bristled and snapped, "I'm still having it!"[1]

In the summer of 1980, when she was eighty-three, Swift again teamed with Robert Kimball, this time to teach a class on American musical theater at New York University. Originally, the six-week summer workshop was to be divided among the music of three composers, Stephen Sondheim, Eubie Blake, and Kay Swift. Two weeks were to be devoted to *Fine and Dandy*. But when the course began, Sondheim was busy working on a new project and Blake could not attend class because of a health problem. So the class spent all six weeks on *Fine and Dandy*. Kay had written out from memory some of the songs from the show that had not been published. Kimball and Swift took turns lecturing, while pianist Paul Trueblood played and the entire class sang songs from the musical. Kay won the students' hearts as she delivered lessons on life along with the lectures on music. Kimball recalls that Swift "had a great time, and the students adored her."[2]

In 1982, hundreds of lost scores, lyrics, and songs by some of Broadway's classic composers were discovered at the Warner Brothers warehouse in Secaucus, New Jersey. Music from obscure shows by Jerome Kern, George Gershwin, Cole Porter, and Richard Rodgers had been misplaced for decades and was now rescued from oblivion. Although it took several years to catalog the newly found materials and settle disputes over possession and copyrights, the find generated tremendous interest. Among Gershwin scholars, it led to a renewed quest to revive the Gershwins' hapless *Let 'Em Eat Cake.*[3]

Ira had donated the piano-vocal score for the show to the Library of Congress as early as 1963, although manuscripts for three numbers ("Comes the Revolution," "The Union League," and "First Lady and First Gent") were incomplete. From memory Swift had notated "Comes the Revolution" for Bobby Short to record in 1973. Her memory proved to be infallible: the same song with different lyrics had been used in *Pardon My English,* the 1933 flop whose score was among those found in Secaucus. Titled "Watch Your Head," this version of the song was harmonized, and it matched Kay's piano copy exactly.[4]

As conductor Michael Tilson Thomas arranged for a concert production of *Let 'Em Eat Cake,* Swift acted as a consultant, filling in melody and harmonies when necessary. She completed a version of "Union League" as well as the song "First Lady and First Gent." In the few instances when she could not remember the music as Gershwin had played it, she approximated his style and created a plausible substitution. Michael Feinstein, representing Ira Gershwin's interests in the Secaucus find, acknowledged Kay Swift's significant role in re-creating the missing elements in *Let 'Em Eat Cake* and noted that she contributed some original material to works attributed to George. He later wrote, "Kay Swift actually composed the verse and final sixteen bars of a song called 'First Lady and First Gent' but was not given credit. The only music that existed for the song was a lead sheet in Gershwin's hand of the first few bars. The rest of the song, including harmonies, was created by Kay. What would it have hurt to give her credit?" Given her demeanor and devotion to Gershwin, Swift probably refused to be acknowledged. Mark Steyn muses, "Like Ira, at times she was content to neglect her own career to serve what she saw as George's genius." Eventually Maurice Levine arranged and wrote the narrative for a 1987 concert version of *Let 'Em Eat Cake* that was presented at the Brooklyn Academy of Music. Orchestrator Russell Warner devised new orchestrations based on the piano-vocal score, and Tilson Thomas directed a recording of the production.[5]

Among some of the lesser-known findings at Secaucus were the music and lyrics to five numbers from Kay Swift's *Fine and Dandy* ("Machine Shop Chant," "I'll Hit a New High," "Etiquette," "Jig Hop," and "Rich or Poor"). Conductor John McGlinn, who had been so instrumental to many show revivals and re-creations, suggested to Russell Warner that *Fine and Dandy* itself should be restored. Warner wrote and received a grant from the National Endowment for the Arts to restore *Fine and Dandy,* and although the Secaucus material included just five numbers, he was thrilled that "some of them had Hans Spialek's little notations for the orchestrations!" Warner recalls, "Of extraordinary value to me was the fact that Kay had one surviving full score from the show still in her possession. This number was 'Nobody Breaks My Heart,' orchestrated by Hans Spialek, and from it we learn with certitude the exact make-up of the orchestra used in the pit in 1930. I have no idea why or how it survived the 60 years till I got a copy." He remembered her collection of manuscripts. "All her personal music 'archives,' by the way, were in her closet on the floor. In a pile. She was not one to worry about the past—she was very much living in the present. Fortunately, she did keep a Gershwin manuscript she had—an orchestration of his own song, "Freud and Jung and Adler,"—but of course, she kept it 'safely' on the floor of her closet with everything else. So casual!" The first phase of *Fine and Dandy* was completed in 1998, including the script, piano-vocal score, and a supplement. Orchestrations were completed in 2003, and Tommy Krasker, cofounder of PS Classics, agreed to produce a recording. Aaron Gandy conducted recording sessions months later.[6]

Swift remained vital, engaged in her surroundings, and involved with her music and her friends well into her nineties. Maurice Levine, host of the "Lyrics and Lyricists" series at the Ninety-second Street Y in New York, invited Swift to appear on his program. On January 29 and 30, 1984, she was his special guest on the episode "The Golden Decade of Song: The Tuneful Thirties."

In March 1986, she flew to Ann Arbor, Michigan, where William Bolcom and Joan Morris were rehearsing for a review of Swift's songs for *An American Tribute,* a celebration of American music and dance to be held at the University of Michigan's Power Center. Swift coached her friends on the seven songs, which were choreographed by Bill De Young and danced by ten students from the University of Michigan Dance Department. The songs included "Up Among the Chimney Pots," "Calliope," "Nobody Breaks My Heart," "Fine and Dandy," "Once You Find Your Guy," "Can't We Be Friends," and "Sawing a Woman in Half." For the occasion, Swift penned a new verse for the reprise of "Fine and Dandy," specifically for her Michigan audience. ("Maize and blue, / Fine and Dandy, / I'm so happy, . . . / Let's all 'Go Blue!'") Also a football fan, Swift apparently loved watching the University of Michigan marching band and had begun writing "The Michigan Band," a rousing piece for male voice with band accompaniment that warned, "Stand by for the Michigan Band, / Hold on! You'll be gone!"

Swift appeared in a film produced in 1987 by the BBC, *George Gershwin Remembered,* which was later broadcast in the United States on the Arts and Entertainment Network. Swift's musical gifts and her loyalty to Gershwin made her a unique and valuable asset to Ira and the Gershwin estate as they made every effort to preserve and prolong his legacy as an American composer.

Singer and entertainer William Zeffiro had been a Gershwin enthusiast since his college days. He had also admired Kay's songs and was fascinated by her association with Gershwin. An opportunity to meet her arose from a project in 1982, and although he was sixty years younger than she, he and Swift established an immediate rapport. It would be two more years before he asked her to lunch to learn more about her experiences as a composer and as a colleague of Gershwin's. Always eager to meet people, she responded enthusiastically, "Well, if the sky doesn't fall—and it probably won't fall—why don't you come over on Tuesday?" When he arrived at her apartment, she invited him to have a drink in Swiftian fashion: "Will you have something straight or something drunken? I'm having something drunken." Their friendship, which began over a vodka and tonic, flourished between 1984 and 1988. She hired him to organize her papers and manuscripts, a task of monumental proportions, given the disarray. In the process they resurrected several other unpublished works, "One Last Look" and "Look Skyward," for Bill to sing in his cabaret act. He also admired her piano playing, "especially the precision—harmonically, lyrics, with phrasing. You'd hear her play and you knew every eighth note counted. And you knew every little inner voicing."[7]

It was Zeffiro who first took Swift to the Marble Collegiate Church on Twenty-ninth Street and Fifth Avenue, where she became a member in 1985. She enjoyed the fellowship as much as the worship. On Sunday mornings, she would call him and ask, "Are you going to *l'église?*" When Marble Collegiate staged its Homecoming Celebration later that year, she was very much a part of the festivities. In the program, she accompanied Bill as he sang "Can't We Be Friends?" and "Fine and Dandy." With soprano Kim Fairchild, he sang "Look Skyward," from *Hunter's Moon* and "Let's Go Eat Worms in the Garden." Even at her advanced age, Kay Swift was not timid in her approach to the piano accompaniments, which she played from memory. Nor was she content to sit silently at the piano while the singers commanded all the attention. Equipped with a microphone, she alternated some of the lines of "Fine and Dandy" with Bill, singing-speaking with gusto. She introduced each number, often with self-deprecating humor. As she contemplated the introduction for "Look Skyward," she muttered, "If I don't get the right key, I'm dead!" In the piano introduction that followed, however, she began to play "Fine and Dandy" again, until Bill discreetly walked over and reminded her of the correct song. She joked, "As I told you, I left my brain at home." She maneuvered out of the key and the introduction she had begun and into that for "Look Skyward," which she then played flawlessly, including the half-step modulation on the final verse. Her humor surfaced again in the introduction for the last number, as she rolled a G major arpeggio. Recognizing she had made an error, Zeffiro gently asked, "Will you play an A minor chord for us?" Swift looked down, corrected herself, and quipped, "It was right next to where I was!" Her quick thinking, as well as her assured playing, endeared her to the audience.[8]

This event prompted Zeffiro to suggest a concert of Swift's compositions, an idea she relished. As her ninetieth birthday approached, and with the encouragement of family and friends, Kay Swift planned a celebration of her life's work. The concert was to be held at Merkin Hall in New York City on October 14, 1986, and was to feature a variety of her favorite works, including classical and popular songs and orchestral compositions. She sent letters to a few people in June 1986, seeking their support and assistance in planning the program. "As a blessing and a talisman, I am asking a few close friends and colleagues to lend their names to a small committee for this event." Many agreed to serve on the planning committee, an indication of their respect and love for her. The committee included songwriter Ann Ronell and Lucinda Dietz, widow of composer Howard Dietz. Even Broadway composer Stephen Sondheim agreed to lend his name to the committee, though he declined any duties.[9]

Longtime friend Alfred Stern was the show's producer, and William Zeffiro handled much of the organization. Several pieces had to be re-scored for different instrumentation, and parts copied, tasks Swift herself oversaw. While she worked with singers and performers individually in her apartment, rehearsals in Merkin Hall took place on Wednesday, October 8, between noon and 5:00 P.M. and on the day of the performance, Tuesday, October 14, between 10:00 A.M. and 5:00 P.M. Tickets, priced at fifteen dollars each, were sold out, and Swift received letters from friends expressing their disappointment at having to miss the performance. Michael Charry rehearsed and directed the orchestra. The show itself, two and a half hours long, was hosted by her good friend, composer and pianist William Bolcom. Friend and composer Burton Lane presented Swift with a citation on behalf of ASCAP commemorating her many years of membership in that organization. A review in the *New York Post* on October 16, 1986, by Robert Kimball noted the "packed house of enthusiastic well-wishers," which included singers Celeste Holm and Margaret Whiting, ballerina Tamara Geva (who had danced in the original production of *Alma Mater*), and Frances Gershwin Godowsky, sister of George and Ira. Friends and associates of Kay's were the performers, including Bolcom and Joan Morris, singers Julie Wilson, Bobbi Baird, Kim Fairchild, William Zeffiro, and singer-pianist Steve Ross, cellist David Christensen, and Swift herself. Entertainer and close friend

Bobby Short and singer-pianist Michael Feinstein were scheduled to perform but canceled at the last minute and sent telegrams of congratulations that were read aloud from the stage.[10]

The commemorative event was presented in two acts, arranged for musical variety rather than chronologically or by genre. Act 1 opened with an orchestral overture from *Paris '90,* followed by Joan Morris singing "Fine and Dandy" and Bobbi Baird presenting "Up Among the Chimney Pots." The Radio City Music Hall days were represented by William Zeffiro's rendition of "Sawing a Woman in Half." Bobbi Baird sang "Sagebrush Lullaby" from *Never a Dull Moment* and then was joined by Zeffiro in "Let's Go Eat Worms in the Garden" from *Fine and Dandy.* David Christensen and pianist Alex Rybeck played the Theme and Variations for Cello and Piano, after which a small ensemble and a sextet of dancers presented three selections from *Alma Mater.* Act 1 closed with Julie Wilson singing "Can't We Be Friends?" accompanied by Billy Roy.

Act 2 opened with the torch song "Nobody Breaks My Heart," performed by Joan Morris and William Bolcom. Next were four excerpts from *Reaching for the Brass Ring* ("Reaching for the Brass Ring," "My Teeny Restaurant," "The Sleepy Song," and "John Likes It When the Wind Blows"), sung by Louise Carlyle with the orchestra. "Once You Find Your Guy" was presented as a duet by Bobbi Baird and Kim Fairchild, followed by "One Last Look," by William Zeffiro, "I'm All Washed Up On Love," by Louise Carlyle, "Man, Have Pity on Man," sung by Kim Fairchild, and "Look Skyward," from *Hunter's Moon,* sung by Kim Fairchild and William Zeffiro. The vocal selections were followed by a saxophone performance of "Can't Win 'Em All" and a piano piece entitled "Rumba." Both were accompanied by bass and drums and featured dancers. Steve Ross then presented three songs, "Rich or Poor," "The House Where I Was Born," and "Can This Be Love?" followed by William Bolcom's introduction of Kay Swift. Swift played two piano selections, "For Betsy," the composition written after her granddaughter's death, and "Keep on Keepin' On," the last piece she composed. Following that, a Bolcom-Morris version of "Calliope" led to the introduction of Burton Lane, who presented a citation from ASCAP on behalf of its president, Morton Gould, and Swift's acceptance. The finale was none other than a reprise of her signature song, "Fine and Dandy," with numerous verses sung by the full company. It was "a lovingly prepared tribute" to Kay Swift and her lifetime of compositions.[11]

The final two pieces that Kay Swift wrote, "For Betsy" and "Keep on Keepin' On," were particularly meaningful to her. Both are piano pieces, or "instrumentals," as she called them. "For Betsy" has already been described. "Keep on Keepin' On" returns to the song form of her popular works and employs march and ragtime rhythms. As in all of her music, the melody dominates. It opens with an ascending arpeggiated line, perhaps symbolizing her determination to keep advancing. With the inscription, "For Z. One," this piece was dedicated to William Zeffiro, a recognition of the support and care he showed her. (There were three people in her life whose last names began with Z, to whom she referred as "Z. One," "Z. Two," and "Z. Three." It was yet another example of her trademark abbreviations.) In the Merkin Hall concert, she began to play the final piece with assurance but floundered as she apparently suffered a memory lapse. She never stopped, however, and her vast experience allowed her to improvise until she regained her composure—many in the audience were never aware of her difficulty.[12]

Louise Carlyle reminisced about Kay's excitement as she prepared for this major event in her life, this rite of passage for senior composers. The extramusical details were not to be overlooked. Since concert attire was "evening dress for ladies and tuxedos for gentlemen," Swift had an elegant red dress made in Greenwich Village, and Carlyle accompanied her for numerous fittings. But Swift understood the premier reason for the program and was personally involved with numerous musical rehearsals and decisions until the night of the production. This was the ultimate celebration, with Swift and her music the center of attention. Carlyle remembered, "Everything had to be perfect. And it was."[13]

That is, everything was thoroughly prepared through the last minute of the concert. But no one had thought to make plans for a celebration afterward. Although all three daughters had flown in for the event, each had assumed that someone else was seeing their mother home. A friend of the composer spotted Kay Swift on a nearby street corner after most of the crowd had left. She was alone, hailing a taxicab after her music ended.[14]

Swift performed "For Betsy" and "Keep on Keepin' On" at Merkin Hall in 1986, when she was eighty-nine. Perhaps these pieces were intended to bring her full circle to an understanding of who she really was. Not only did they include a compendium of her musical techniques, but they represented the things that were important to Kay Swift. Devotion to her grandchildren and perseverance in the face of adversity were two of the strongest values in her life. Her performance, though not perfect, embodied her determination, professionalism, and ability to cope with the unexpected—just as she had done throughout her life. More important, these pieces are evidence that Swift was composing in her last decade of life, motivated only by her desire to do her best. After discussing her "desire to please" in her memoirs, Swift later penciled the following comments in the margin: "Perhaps, in the last analysis, one tries to please what has been called 'The Deep Self.' Some people have referred to that as God. I am inclined to agree with them."[15]

Kay Swift's perseverance was commendable. Among the many ideas for projects that were found among the Kay Swift Papers was a brief typewritten proposal for a revue entitled *Dancers in the Dark*. The one-page abstract outlines a show using the music of Kay Swift with a book based on "reports in the tabloids and theatrical newspapers of the 1930s and 1940s." There is no date on the proposal, but it suggests using Swift's more popular songs, as well as "Keep on Keepin' On," which was completed in 1985. Its mention indicates that even into Swift's late eighties she continued to develop ideas for creative projects. The use of "Keep on Keepin' On" as a conclusion in the show "embodies the refocused optimism" of the characters, Swift wrote in her notes. Likewise, the proposal for *Dancers in the Dark* embodied the refocused optimism of Kay Swift. *Dancers in the Dark* may have been a preliminary sketch for the Merkin Hall concert. But her ambition did not stop with Merkin Hall. Zeffiro contends that she wanted to write a completely new Broadway musical and talked about doing so as late as 1987. After years of unrealized dreams and unproduced theatrical works, she never abandoned the thought of returning to Broadway.[16]

Zeffiro mused, "One of the things I loved most about Kay was that she was always positive. She was always looking into the future. . . . She reminisced with me, but she was here . . . looking forward." He recalled sitting at the table with Kay one day as she went through her mail. She would read the note, and then discard it. He exclaimed, "Kay! You're throwing away your mail!" to which she answered, "My mother always said, 'Letters are for today.'"[17]

Louise Carlyle and Kay Swift shared a fast and true friendship that lasted more than forty years. Carlyle recalled the early 1980s with fondness. Her husband had died in 1980. On Friday nights she would come to the city from her home in Upper Montclair, New Jersey, to meet Swift, Alfred Stern, and Baldwin (Beau) Bergerson, an entertainer and composer who lived in Kay's apartment building. The four would go to dinner or simply stay home and talk. Until Swift became ill, Carlyle often stayed for the weekend. Carlyle said of Swift, "She lifted you up at all times. She wasn't so pleased about things in her own personal life, but she always had something good to say about everything."[18]

Swift had the greatest respect for Louise Carlyle both as a singer and as a person. She would always introduce her as "My favorite singer, Miss Carlyle." Kay recognized Louise's talent and constantly urged her to resume her performing, which had been interrupted by her husband's accident, disability, and subsequent death. Eventually Carlyle did return to the stage, something she had long felt she should do, and sang with the Montclair (New Jersey) Operetta Club. In the late 1980s, she played the title role of *Mame*, and Swift attended one of the performances.[19]

Shippen and Lee Swift would occasionally come down from Redding, Connecticut, to take Kay to lunch. One of her favorite restaurants was La Marmiton, on Forty-seventh Street. Recalls Shippen, "She loved it there—particularly the way the bartender served her 'Vodtonias.'" This was the same restaurant where he had entertained Kay and an elderly client of his several years earlier. When the guest left to visit the men's room, Kay remarked, "If he touches my knee one more time, I'm going to belt him!" Shippen reflected, "Quite an experience to be chaperoning a pair in their eighties!"[20]

On April 19, 1987, Kay Swift celebrated her ninetieth birthday. Her three daughters, April, Andy, and Kay, came to town. They treated her to an evening at the Café Carlyle to hear Bobby Short sing. Two days later, Louise Carlyle threw a surprise cocktail party at Sardi's. The restaurant has been a landmark for Broadway theatergoers since 1927 and is distinguished by its celebrated show-business clientele who dine in the restaurant and whose caricatures adorn the walls. For the surprise party, Swift's daughters were in attendance, as were Katharine and Nicholas Weber, Bobby Short, Bobbi Baird, and Maurice Levine. Carlyle had arranged to have Swift's caricature drawn and hung on the wall, a symbol of her successful career. She later recalled the evening. "She was so surprised. That's when I had the picture hung. They [Sardi's] knew her long before they knew me. They were delighted to be a part of it. It was done [hung] when they were closed. She was so surprised, and she autographed it. It was just a cocktail party, but never mind—it was very nice. . . . I toasted her: 'Here's to Kay, whom we all love. I don't know how old she is, but I'm certainly glad she lived this long.' Swift maintained her coyness about her age by signing the caricature: 'To Sardi's—on my _____ birthday! Love, Kay Swift.'"[21]

Two tragic events interrupted Kay Swift's last years, and she never fully recovered from them. In July 1988, she stepped off a curb and was hit by a taxicab. Although she was not severely injured, she broke her wrist and instantly lost her sense of independence. Katharine Weber maintains that her grandmother never fully recovered from that accident, even after the arm had healed. It eventually became necessary to hire additional care, which meant that strangers passed through her apartment regularly. In this home where a lifetime of compositions, scripts, photographs, jewelry, and Gershwin memorabilia were strewn, confusion reigned, and losses occurred. Katharine Weber did show her grandmother how to hide her precious gold bangle bracelets above the back leg of the grand piano, where they remained safe.[22]

Yet another tragedy occurred when her youngest daughter, Kay Levin, contracted pneumonia and died on December 13, 1989. Her article about death, written when her own daughter, Betsy, was killed, mused, "How do you say goodby to one of your own children. . . . Our children live on after we, ourselves, die. Right?" Levin had expressed feelings of helplessness. "It's almost as hard to accept powerlessness as it is to accept the loss itself." And so, as Gertrude Horton Dorr Swift had had to bury six babies and her grown son, Samuel, and as Kay Levin had mourned the loss of Betsy, so Kay Swift said good-bye to her youngest daughter. Perhaps she found comfort in her daughter's words: "If grief never really ends, what does change, I suppose, is our ability to cope with it. Friends help immeasurably."[23]

As late as Easter 1990 she attended Marble Collegiate Church with William

Zeffiro and his wife, Lynne, Louise Carlyle, Jack Wrangler, and Margaret Whiting. Soon after that, signs of a developing Alzheimer's disease were noticeable in Kay Swift. Her checkbook reveals that she had a routine in her last years and frequented several businesses in her neighborhood of East Fifty-ninth Street and First Avenue. Checks were written regularly to the corner grocery and the neighborhood wine shop. Other recipients were her trusted housekeeper of forty years, as well as a man whom she considered her "manager." He visited her every Friday for lunch and she paid him two hundred dollars each week to "manage her affairs," although she did not really have such funds at that stage in her life. She seemed to assign a professional status to these regular meetings that was apparently worth the fee to her. One afternoon Bobby Short, who lived near her, encountered her wandering a block from her home, carrying a doll. Although Short was a friend and colleague, Swift did not recognize him that day. He gently took her hand and walked her back to her building, where the doorman took her up to her apartment.[24]

Swift's great friend Louise Carlyle played several more shows after *Mame*, including *Me and My Girl*, *70 Girls 70*, and *Inherit the Wind*, but Swift was unable to attend them. "It seemed to me as if I was losing the best friend I ever had. To watch her deteriorate . . . . We used to meet. I used to spend time with her. Sometimes we went to lunch, or would just sit and talk. I would always say, 'Let's sing.' She wasn't really doing much of that and I knew how important it was to her. She was just getting older, that's all."[25]

Late in 1992, Kay Swift was moved to the Alzheimer's Resource Center in Southington, Connecticut, one of the first homes to specialize in patients with this disease. Katharine Weber remembers visiting her shortly after she had moved there. They had taken a walk around the hall and returned to her room. Outside every room was a glass case where mementos of each resident's life were displayed, with

> artifacts that signified who these people had been. . . . Most people had family photos and such. . . . In her case I had put the Kimball-Simon book open to the page with her formal portrait in the white dress. We looked at that for a moment, and discussed the bracelets. Then we started to go into the room. . . . She was so senile she

really had no idea she had a roommate. They ignored each other totally. . . . And next to each door there were name markers indicating the names of the residents. There were two name plates, one over the other, for each of these double rooms. So we started to go into her room, as at an office . . . and she pointed at her [name plate], which was over Olive's (I had no idea she could see this well without her glasses, or even notice that there were name plates), and said triumphantly, "Look! Top billing!" and then grandly proceeded into her room.

Her indomitable spirit prevailed even as the memories of her life had faded. Kay Swift died there on January 28, 1993, at the age of ninety-five.[26]

Kay Swift was highly respected by her peers as a musician, pianist, and composer. She had immense talent, extraordinary intelligence, a whimsical imagination, and a keen sense of humor. A member of ASCAP since 1931, she observed a disciplined work ethic throughout her long career. She followed her passions and pursued a profession when many women did not in a discipline dominated by males. Orchestrator Russell Warner reflects, "She was a wonderful, lively woman. She never needed Gloria Steinem." Despite her vanity and eccentricities, she was well loved by many who admired her generosity, her love for her daughters and grandchildren, and her loyalty to her friends. Her humor, style, energy, and sense of adventure carried her well into her nineties, even though Alzheimer's disease eventually eroded her memory. Louise Carlyle spoke the thoughts of many when she said, "I can only wish that everybody has a Kay Swift in their life."[27]

Kay Swift's devotion to George Gershwin was uncompromising, based on their ten-year romance and her admiration of his genius. She knew him as a person with needs and desires and was confident in the strength of their relationship. Yet it was a relationship that she kept very private. In the last decade of her life, William Zeffiro delicately asked her, "Was George Gershwin the love of your life?" Ever on guard, she retorted, "Well, I was the love of his!" In an interview in 1973, she did acknowledge that George was "probably the most profound influence on my life except for my father. . . . When George died a great many people felt not only sad but bored. He loved every aspect of life, and made every aspect of life loveable. People thought they could never sense that special joy again." Kay admitted to her close friends that she had loved George deeply. Yet she was determined to focus her energy on living, finding pleasure in her friends, her family, and her work. We cannot know if she ever again sensed the "special joy" that Gershwin brought her; but she spent her life vigorously seeking it.[28]

Those of us never fortunate enough to have met Kay Swift will always be able to enjoy her music, her memoirs, and her contributions to the Gershwin legacy, as well as the loving and humorous reminiscences of her family and friends. Secondhand, we can catch glimpses of her creativity, her spirit, and her resilience. We can appreciate her efforts to be a woman and a composer at a time when the two roles were not easy to reconcile. Her choices may not always have been wise, but there is no doubt that they were her own. Arguably, they were choices made in the difficult attempt to balance her extreme passions. Among those passions was to remain young at heart. Swift fought the aging process with more determination than many nonagenarians, and her self-deprecating wit helped to palliate the inevitable. Found amid her papers was the following anonymous prayer:

> Lord, Thou knowest better than I know myself that I am growing older, and will some day be old.
>
> Keep me from getting talkative, and particularly from the fatal habit of thinking I must say something on every subject and on every occasion.
>
> Release me from craving to try to straighten out everybody's affairs.
>
> Make me thoughtful, but not moody, helpful, but not bossy. With my vast store of wisdom, it seems a pity not to use it all—but Thou knowest, Lord, that I want a few friends at the end.
>
> Keep my mind from the recital of endless details—give me wings to get to the point.
>
> Seal my lips on my many aches and pains—they are increasing, and my love of rehearsing them is becoming sweeter as the years go by.
>
> I ask for grace enough to listen to the tales of others' pains. Help me to endure them with patience.

Teach me the glorious lesson that occasionally it is possible that I may be mistaken.

Keep me reasonably sweet; I do not want to be a saint—some of them are so hard to live with; but a sour old woman is one of the crowning works of the devil.

Help me to extract all possible fun out of life. There are so many funny things around us, and I don't want to miss any of them.

Amen.

To the end, Kay Swift celebrated life. She pursued her passions with determination and confidence. She felt free to ignore constraints that others may have preferred she observe. And she met adversity with resilience and creativity. Her final composition, "Keep on Keepin' On," was a testament to her spirit and her optimism, her "disappointment adjustant" that enabled her to persevere. Life may not always have been "fine and dandy," but she would never have admitted it.

Chronology

1897   Katharine Faulkner Swift is born April 19 in New York City to Samuel
       Swift, a music critic for the *New York Mail and Express,* and his wife,
       Ellen Faulkner Swift.

1903   Katharine's brother, Samuel Swift, Jr., is born January 19.

1905   Katharine begins piano lessons at the Institute of Musical Art with
       Bertha Fiering Tapper. She attends the Metropolitan Opera House
       with her family.

1906   Katharine enrolls in Miss Veltin's School.

1909   Katharine begins composition lessons with Arthur Edward Johnstone.
       Her earliest surviving composition is "My Thoughts Are Like the Little
       Birds," set to a poem by Grace Duffield.

1914   Katharine's father, Samuel Swift, dies July 14 of complications after
       gall bladder surgery.

1915   Bertha Tapper dies. Katharine graduates from Miss Veltin's School.
       She again enrolls in the Institute of Musical Art, studying piano with
       Anna Lockwood Fyffe and counterpoint with Percy Goetschius.
       Katharine receives a Certificate of Graduation from the Institute of
       Musical Art.

1916   Katharine receives a scholarship for additional study.

1917   Katharine receives her piano teachers' diploma from the Institute of
       Musical Art. On graduation she performs with the Edith Rubel Trio.
       That summer she meets James Paul Warburg, and they are engaged.

1918   Katharine Swift and James Warburg are married June 1. Warburg is
an officer in the Naval Reserves, and they settle in Washington, D.C.
He takes a position with the Metropolitan Bank.

1919   The couple's first daughter, April, is born in April. The Warburg family
relocates to Cambridge. Katharine begins piano study with Heinrich
Gebhard and composition with Charles Martin Loeffler.

1920   Katharine accompanies Louise Homer, Jr., in several voice recitals.

1921   Katharine, James, and April return to New York. James joins his father's
International Acceptance Bank. Katharine re-enrolls in the Institute for
Musical Art, resuming study with Percy Goetschius. She first hears the
popular songs of George Gershwin.

1922   Katharine's brother, Sam, Jr., graduates from the Milton Academy
in Massachusetts. The couple's second daughter, Andrea, is born
September 29.

1924   The Warburgs purchase a country home, Bydale, in Greenwich,
Connecticut. Their third daughter, Kay, is born November 26.

1925   George Gershwin attends a party at the Warburgs' with Pauline Heifetz,
and Katharine and George meet.

1926   Gershwin and Swift become close friends after he returns from a European tour. He encourages Katharine to change her name to "Kay." She
acts as his musical secretary, sounding board, and confidante.

1927   Swift begins composing popular songs, her husband writing the lyrics
under the name "Paul James." She is the rehearsal pianist for Richard
Rodgers's *Connecticut Yankee*.

1928   Swift's mother dies of breast cancer July 4. Gershwin finishes writing
An American in Paris at Bydale. He purchases gold bracelets for Kay
after the premiere of *An American in Paris*. The first Swift-James songs,
"Little White Lies" and "When the Light Turns Green," are interpolated into the revue *Say When*.

1929   "Can't We Be Friends," the Swift-James collaboration's first hit, is sung
by Libby Holman in *The Little Show*. Two other songs, "Up Among the
Chimney Pots" and "How Would a City Girl Know?" are interpolated
into the *9:15 Revue*.

1930   Following the *Garrick Gaieties*, in which Swift and James's song,
"Johnny Wanamaker," is sung, they write the score for *Fine and Dandy*.
The show opens on Broadway, September 23. Less than a month later,
the Gershwins present *Girl Crazy*.

1931 James Warburg is occupied with the family business, traveling frequently to Germany. The Swift-James collaboration is over. Swift turns her attentions to Gershwin and his works. *Of Thee I Sing* premieres, and Swift hosts the party afterward.

1932 Swift's father-in-law, Paul M. Warburg, dies January 24. Gershwin dedicates his *Song Book* to Kay.

1934 After a four-year hiatus, Swift writes the music for the ballet, *Alma Mater,* the first American ballet choreographed by George Balanchine. She misses its premiere, having traveled to Reno for the six-week residency required to obtain a divorce. Swift's divorce from Warburg is finalized December 20.

1935 Swift takes a position at Radio City Music Hall as staff composer. She writes show tunes for the Rockettes with lyricist Al Stillman. Her daughters live with Warburg after he remarries.

Swift is involved with all aspects of writing, casting, and rehearsing Gershwin's *Porgy and Bess.* It opens October 10 at the Alvin Theatre.

1936 Swift leaves Radio City to become director of light music for the 1939 New York World's Fair. George and Ira Gershwin leave New York for Hollywood to write music for films. Swift and Gershwin agree not to see each other for a year.

1937 George Gershwin is stricken with a brain tumor and dies.

1939 Swift, as director of light music for the World's Fair, elopes with a cowboy from the rodeo at the fair, Faye Hubbard. They move to a ranch in Oregon, the Faye-and-Kay.

1943 Swift publishes *Who Could Ask for Anything More?* an autobiographical novel of a city girl's life in the West. She sells the rights to RKO Pictures and writes eight songs for a film.

1946 Swift and Hubbard divorce in June.

1947 Swift marries May 19 for the third and last time. Her husband, Hunter Galloway, describes himself as a radio personality with theatrical experience. He is twelve years younger than she.

1948 Swift and Galloway return to New York City.

1949 Kay's first grandchild, Guido, is born to April.

1950 A movie based on her book is released. *Never a Dull Moment* stars Irene Dunne and Fred MacMurray. Only three songs are used.

Swift writes the score for another Broadway show, a one-woman show for Cornelia Otis Skinner entitled *Paris '90.* She accompanies the road tour.

1953   Swift composes a set of songs, *Reaching for the Brass Ring,* for each
        of her seven grandchildren. They are performed by the Philadelphia
        Orchestra.

1958   Swift writes incidental music for a Marc Connelly play, *Hunter's Moon,*
        which opens in London and closes within a week.

1959   Swift goes on speaking tour to promote the film version of Gershwin's
        Porgy and Bess.

1960   Alfred Stern engages Swift to write music for a commercial show, *One
        Little Girl,* commemorating the fiftieth anniversary of the Camp Fire
        Girls. He will hire her to write six shows over the next sixteen years.
        Swift writes Theme and Variations for Cello and Piano, to play with her
        friend Marie Romeat Rosanoff.

1962   Swift writes music for the pavilion *Century 21* at the Seattle World's Fair.

1964   Alfred Stern hires Swift to write for two productions at the New York
        World's Fair, *All About Elsie* (Borden) and "Nothing Is Too Lovely to
        Be True" (Clairol).

1967   Swift writes music for *Expo '67!*

1968   Swift and Galloway are divorced.

1969   Galloway commits suicide, February 14.

1975   A double album of Swift's music, *Fine and Dandy: The Music of Kay
        Swift,* is produced.
        Vivian Perlis interviews Swift for Oral History, American Music Project
        at Yale University.

1976   Swift writes her last commercial show, *Dr. Rush Pays a House Call,* for
        the American Medical Association.

1980   Swift teaches a class in American musical theater with Robert Kimball
        at New York University.

1986   A concert of Kay Swift music is held at Merkin Hall, New York,
        October 16. She performs two piano numbers.

1987   Swift's friend Louise Carlyle hosts a party for her ninetieth birthday
        at Sardi's Restaurant, where her caricature is framed and mounted.

1988   Swift falls and breaks a wrist in July. She never fully regains
        independence.

1989   Swift's youngest daughter, Kay, dies of pneumonia, December 13.

1992   Swift is stricken with Alzheimer's disease. She is moved to the
        Alzheimer's Resource Center in Southington, Connecticut.

1993   Kay Swift dies January 28.

Musical Works by Kay Swift

STAGE WORKS

Say When (1928)

    Little White Lies

    When the Lights Turn Green

Whistling in the Dark, lyrics by Paul James

The First Little Show (1929)

    *Can't We Be Friends?, lyric by Paul James

Nine-Fifteen Revue (1930)

    *Up Among the Chimney Pots, lyric by Paul James

    How Would a City Girl Know?

Fine and Dandy (1930), lyrics by Paul James

    Overture

    Machine Shop Chant

    *Rich or Poor

    *Fine and Dandy

    Wheels of Steel

    Mechanical Ballet, original music by Eugene Grona

    *Starting at the Bottom

    *Can This Be Love?

    *I'll Hit a New High

* = published

Giddiup Back
Fordyce (Picnic Song)
*Let's Go Eat Worms in the Garden
Etiquette
*Jig-Hop
*Nobody Breaks My Heart
Wedding Bells
Waltz
I'm Afraid I'll Have to Fall in Love
Not used:
    Say, Joe
Fine and Dandy (1930), complete score, reconstructed by Russell Warner (1997);
    orchestrations completed, 2003
Alma Mater, ballet (1934)
    Introduction
    Invitation to the Bicycle
    Hero
    Snake Dance
    Villain
    Angry Dance
    Big Waltz
    Dream and Bride Theme
    Wedding Procession
    Offbeat Waltz
    Funeral Procession
    Morning . . . Sweeping the House
    Nightmare
    Comic Strip
    Salvation Army Sal
    Finale
Songs from Radio City Music Hall (1935–36), lyrics by Al Stillman (Alfred
        Silverman)
    Fine and Dandy (1930)
    Sunny
    Roxyettes
    Up Among the Chimney Pots (1929)
    Professor, How Could You? (February 21, 1935)
    Collegiate Number
    Forever and a Day (February 28, 1935)

Waltz for a Ballet
Physical Culture (April 4, 1935)
Masseur Incident
March for Rockettes
There's Gold in Them Thar Hills (May 9, 1935)
Intro and Typewriter Interlude
Headlines (May 9, 1935)
Young Man of Manhattan
I've Gotta Take My Hat Off to You (June 20, 1935)
Black and White
Coney Island by the Sea (July 25, 1935)
*Sawing a Woman in Half
Up Among the Chimney Pots (1930)
Footnotes from the Greek
Blonde or Brunette (August 29, 1935)
We've Got a Ticket for the Sweepstakes (Sept. 19, 1935)
Road Show
The Little Church Around the Corner (Sept. 26, 1935)
Waltz for a Dancer
I'm All Washed Up on Love
Put It Down on Paper (October 31, 1935)
At the Golden Calf (December 30, 1935)
The Wooden Horse of Troy (March 13, 1936)
Graduating Gibson Girls (March 26, 1936)
I'd Walk a Mile for You
Previously composed and used at Radio City Music Hall:
Up Among the Chimney Pots
Fine and Dandy
Parade (1935)
I'm All Washed Up on Love
Sarah Was There (c. 1948)—songs for proposed television series; lyrics by
Ralph Freed
Donna Sarah's Recitative
Donna Sarah's Tango
The Napoleon Song (no lyric)
Sarah Was There
Vienna
Never a Dull Moment (1950)—film
*Once You Find Your Guy

The Man with the Big Felt Hat
Sagebrush Lullaby
Not used:
    Down Crooked River Way
    Gate to Nowhere
    He's a Pretty Fair Hand
    Some of the Time I'll Miss You
    Me and My Jam-Up Friend
    Nightmare in the Desert (Dance Pantomime)

Paris '90 (1952)
Songs
    *Calliope
    The Waltz I Heard in a Dream
    The House Where I Was Born (Peaceful Theme)
    Lend Me a Bob Till Monday
    Madame Arthur, music by Yvette Guilbert, lyrics by Kay Swift
    Turn, My Little Mill Wheel, music by Paul Delmet, lyrics by Kay Swift
Instrumentals
    Overture
    The Nou-Nou
    A Lady of Fashion
    The Duchess of Verprès
    La Belle Conchita
    Oh Look, Mon Trésor
    La Bicyclette
    The Angel
    The Laundress / Tourne Mon Moulin
    A Boston Schoolteacher
    A Woman of Virtue
    A Professor's Wife
    Avec mes Sabots
    La Goulue
    Can-Can
    Lion Tamer
    St. Lazare
    Berthe la Sourde

A Candle for St. Jude (1958)—never produced
    Candles, lyric by Rumer Godden
    Lollie's Song
    Felix's Song (no lyric extant)

Hilda's Song (no lyric extant)
Madame's Song (no lyric extant)
Sixpence and a Smile (no lyric extant)
When We Dance (no lyric extant)
Hunter's Moon (1958)
  *Look Skyward!
  The Piper in the Dew
One Little Girl (1960)
  Overture
  *In-Between Age
  Fughetta (Theme for Mother) (instrumental)
  When You Ride Your Bike
  When You Hear a Song in Waltz Time
  She Used to Be Such Fun
  Astronaut Theme (instrumental)
  Lunar Theme (instrumental)
  Moon Clown
  Camp Fire Picnic
  Square Dance
  My Favorite Campfire Girl
  Interview on the Moon
Century 21—The Threshold and the Threat (1962)
Songs
  Prayer with a Beat
  Now and Always
Instrumentals
  Child of the Future
  Fanfare and Theme
  Faith in the Future
  What Time Is It?
Clairol Color Carousel (1964)
  Nothing Is Too Lovely to Be True
All About Elsie (1964)
  Doin' Fine
  Audition Song
  Ice Cream Kids
  The Star You Are (Elsie, You're in Clover)
  Elmer's Marvelous Ark
  Instant Omelet Man
  Peep

Expo '67
  Hello, Expo '67! lyric by Hunter Galloway
Dr. Rush Pays a House Call (1975)—incidental music for AMA
  Busy Doctor
  Contemporary M.D.
  Dr. Rush Theme
  Rainy Night on Second Avenue
  Sad Yankee Doodle

SONGS WITH ORCHESTRAL ACCOMPANIMENT
Reaching for the Brass Ring (1953)
  Reaching for the Brass Ring
  Smiling Betsy
  My Teeny Restaurant
  I've Got a Horse
  Bath Time
  Ridin' His Bike
  Upside Down
  The Sleepy Song
  John Likes It When the Wind Blows
  Rachel Is the Singing One (1954)
  Three Balloons (1955)
A Wonderful Day for a Picnic (1953), lyric by Ralph Freed
Man, Have Pity on Man (1972), on a text by Ursula Vaughan Williams

SONGS WITH PIANO ACCOMPANIMENT
Popular Songs
  Birthday Suite (1941)
    Happy Birthday, Dear Andy
    If I Could Write a Melody
    When Are You Comin' Out West?
  *Fighting on the Home Front Wins! (1942)
  One Last Look (c. 1948)
  *A Great Big Piece of Chalk (1958), lyric by Mel Howard
  There's No Escape (1958), lyric by Mel Howard
  Five O'Clock Feelin' (1958), lyric by Mel Howard
  Baseball, Baseball (c. 1958), lyric by Ralph Freed
  The Most Beautiful Time of the Year (c. 1958), lyric by Ralph Freed

What If I Should Haunt You with a Minor Strain? (c. 1958), lyric by
    Ralph Freed (music also set to lyric, When You Hear This Music,
    Remember Me)
Schottishe (c. 1960)
They Say Waltzing Is Old-Fashioned (c. 1960)
The Circus Is a Family Affair (1966)
Corny, but Nice (1966)
I Hate the Bard (c. 1965), lyric by Kay Swift and Hunter Galloway
Which Comes First, the Words or the Music?
Write a Song for Me (1967), lyric by Hunter Galloway

Art Songs
My Thoughts Are Like the Little Birds, on a text by Grace Duffield (c. 1910)
Boots (1911), on a text by Rudyard Kipling
Impression Fausse: Dame Souris Trotte, on a text by Paul Verlaine (c. 1916)
Nursery Songs (1921), lyric by James Warburg
    Doggy
    Kitty
    Piggie
    Sleep
Why Don't Fishes Have Feet? (c. 1925), lyric by April Warburg
Velvet Shoes (1940), on a text by Elinor Wylie
Poems in Praise of Practically Nothing (c. 1948), on a text by Samuel
    Hoffenstein
Shoana (1970)

PIANO MUSIC
Mazurka (1926)
Furlana (1926)
Nevermore (1956)
Off-Beat Waltz Plus Four (1966)
    Morning Walk
    A Walk on the Town
    Off-Beat Waltz
    Overtones of the Past
    Blue Note
New Tune (1970)
For Betsy (1983)
Keep on Keepin' On (1985)
Rumba

CHORAL WORKS
God Is Our Refuge (SSATB) (1966)

INSTRUMENTAL MUSIC
Theme and Variations for Cello and Piano (1960)
Can't Win 'Em All—for alto saxophone and piano (1975)

CHAMBER MUSIC
A Song for String Quartet (c. 1936)

MISCELLANEOUS
Spring Again (c. 1950)—music by Giacomo Puccini, lyric by Kay Swift,
    arranged by Deems Taylor (never produced)
Waiters Have a Wonderful Time
You're Impossible to Please
Once in a Dream World
Lonely
Call It Love
I'd Forgotten
Maurice's Air
Twilight Is Falling
Without a Guiding Star
*The Dark Wind Plays a Lonely Tune (1953)—music by Roger Machado,
    original Spanish text by Leyenda de la Petenera, English lyric by Kay Swift

Notes

The Kay Swift Papers (MSS 65) are housed in the Gilmore Music Library Archival Collection at Yale University. Catalogued by James Leve, they include her music manuscripts and published music, as well as scripts, writings, photographs, articles, correspondence, and miscellaneous material. They are hereafter abbreviated KS MSS. Recordings of some of Kay Swift's music and selected interviews with her are in the Historical Sound Recordings of the Gilmore Music Library at Yale. They are abbreviated HSR Yale.

CHAPTER 1 *Prelude*
1. Swift family tree, KS MSS.
2. Nancy Tatnall Fuller, *Joseph Swift: In the Wild West* (privately published, 1997), 96. One child was stillborn, four lived no longer than six months, and a son, John, died at age five.
3. Gertrude Horton Dorr Swift, diary, KS MSS.
4. Joseph Swift's activities: Fuller, *Joseph Swift,* 96. Samuel Swift's: G. H. D. Swift, diary, KS MSS.
5. My thanks to Jo Thompson, director of the Holy Trinity (Old Swedes) Church Foundation in Wilmington, Del., for providing the Reverend Henry's first name. Swift's organist position in Wilmington is noted in "Samuel Swift Dead," *New York Times,* July 22, 1914, 9. His later employment is described in G. H. D. Swift, diary, KS MSS.
6. K. Swift, "Seven Lives So Far," KS MSS.

7. Wedding details: G. H. D. Swift, diary, KS MSS. Katharine's birth certificate incorrectly identifies her as "Katharine Eleanor Swift," and her mother as "Ellen M. Swift." KS MSS.

8. Swift remembered that her mother "read any musical score" in "Seven Lives," KS MSS. The Swifts' financial position, "unburdened by wealth": K. Weber, "Kay Swift." S. Swift, "Summer Music in New York," 663. In this article he summarizes the light musical fare available in the city when the regular concert season is over. Because much is incidental music for theater productions, operetta, or vaudeville and is presented in dinner theaters or beer gardens, he writes, "it is not wise to take summer music in New York too seriously."

9. G. H. D. Swift, diary, KS MSS.

10. G. H. D. Swift, diary, KS MSS.

11. G. H. D. Swift, diary, KS MSS.

12. K. Swift, "Seven Lives," KS MSS.

13. K. Swift, "April Day," KS MSS.

14. K. Swift, "Seven Lives," KS MSS.

15. K. Swift, "Veltin 1915," Contribution to Veltin School Class of 1915 newsletter, 1978, personal copy.

16. K. Swift, "Veltin 1915."

17. Kay Swift, memoirs, n.d., personal copy.

18. The New York *Mail and Express* became the *Evening Mail and Express* in 1904. "Hedges and green pastures": Samuel Swift, letter to Adeline Dorr, August 22, 1905, KS MSS.

19. K. Swift, "Seven Lives," KS MSS.

20. Samuel Swift's employment: "Samuel Swift Dead." "At a serious loss," "showed a great desire to help her father," and "delightful, ready to help others": G. H. D. Swift, diary, KS MSS. "My mother did a lot of research": K. Swift, interview by Perlis.

21. Although Gertrude Horton Dorr Swift refers to her publications in her diary, I have not yet found any records of them. Samuel Swift's religious practices and "His religious views": G. H. D. Swift, diary, KS MSS. "The man who hid his talents": K. Swift, memoirs.

22. Katharine Weber, interview by author, New Haven, Conn., June 11, 1998.

23. K. Swift, "Baseball."

24. "The best schoolboy first baseman": K. Swift, "Baseball." "Tim Cassiday" reported by Shippen Swift, interview by author, Hancock, Me., June 13, 2001.

25. "She plays a little piece": G. H. D. Swift, diary, KS MSS. "When I added several variations": K. Swift, memoirs.

26. "Complete musicians": Damrosch, Address at Opening Ceremony, *Institute of Musical Art Lectures, Recitals and General Occasions, Oct. 11, 1905–June 12, 1906*. Information about institute founders: Olmstead, *Juilliard*, 38. Katharine Weber has a letter from Walter Damrosch to Samuel Swift asking for "the little family." K. Weber, e-mail to author, August 28, 2002.

27. Information about Bertha and Thomas Tapper from Oja, *Making Music Modern*, 13, and Nicholas Slonimsky, ed., *Baker's Biographical Dictionary of Musicians*, centennial ed., s.v. "Tapper, Thomas." The history book Tapper co-wrote is Percy Goetschius and Thomas Tapper, *Essentials in Music History* (New York: Charles Scribner and Sons, 1914). Information on Leo Ornstein is offered by Oja, *Making Music Modern*, 12, and Olmstead, *Juilliard*, 38.

28. K. Swift, memoirs.

29. "Boot camp": K. Swift, memoirs. "Everything went with it": K. Swift, interview by Perlis.

30. Memories of the piano recital: G. H. D. Swift, diary, KS MSS. "A stimulating, happy occasion": K. Swift, "Seven Lives," KS MSS.

31. Horatio Parker: Olmstead, *Juilliard*, 36, 9. "When I put on record that Mr. Parker": G. H. D. Swift, diary, KS MSS.

32. "Each of these occasions": K. Swift, "Seven Lives," KS MSS. Ornstein: Olmstead, *Juilliard*, 38. The photograph is published in Oja, "Women Patrons and Crusaders for Modernist Music," 246, and Oja, *Making Music Modern*, 13. Nine other students are unidentified.

33. Memories of Ornstein's performance are related in Oja, *Cultivating Music*, 244–46. Samuel Swift's association with the MacDowell Club and New Music Society is noted in "Samuel Swift Dead."

34. Johnstone's book is Arthur Edward Johnstone, *Instruments of the Modern Symphony Orchestra and Band* (New York, 1917; rev. ed., 1948). His biography is included in *Baker's Biographical Dictionary of Music and Musicians*, s.v. "Johnstone, Arthur." "When one writes at the piano," and "It's a wonderful discipline": K. Swift, interview by Perlis.

35. "They told my parents": K. Swift, memoirs. The penmanship in "My Thoughts Are Like the Little Birds" is much less controlled than in "Boots," thus my supposition that it is earlier by a year or two.

36. K. Swift, memoirs. Swift retells this story three times, each for a different birthday. It is unclear whether it was her thirteenth, fourteenth, or fifteenth birthday, but it must have certainly occurred.

37. Katharine's descriptions of her dancing and of Madame Bonfanti: K. Swift, "Seven Lives," KS MSS. "Marie Bonfanti," in Selma Jeanne Cohen, ed.,

International Encyclopedia of Dance (New York: Oxford University Press, 1998).

CHAPTER 2   *Professional and Personal Choices*

1. K. Swift, memoirs.
2. K. Swift, memoirs.
3. K. Swift, memoirs.
4. G. H. D. Swift, diary, KS MSS.
5. K. Swift, memoirs.
6. K. Swift, memoirs.
7. Student records, Lila Acheson Wallace Library Archives, Juilliard School of Music. Recital information from *Institute of Musical Art Lectures, Recitals and General Occasions, Oct. 11, 1915–June 2, 1916.*
8. Description of Level V: *Institute of Musical Art Catalog, 1915–16*, Lila Acheson Wallace Library Archives, Juilliard School of Music, 20. Swift credits Arthur Johnstone in "Seven Lives," KS MSS. "Katharine played beautifully": G. H. D. Swift, diary, KS MSS.
9. Distinction between the two courses is made in the *Institute of Musical Art Catalog.* "In the Teachers' courses two grades of pedagogy are required in addition to the advanced work in technical and theoretic lines. For the Artists' diploma not only are high grades of scholarship and skill demanded, but the candidate must have given proof of his maturity in successful public recital, and before musicians of standing who are not connected with the Institute." The piano teachers' course would have included piano, music theory, and ear-training, as well as pedagogy with Frank Damrosch. *Institute of Musical Art Catalog, 1915–16.* The anecdotes about "Mme. Goiter" and her accompanying experiences are included in Swift's memoirs.
10. *Institute of Musical Art Lectures, Recitals and General Occasions, Oct. 16, 1916–June 6, 1917.*
11. N. Weber, *Patron Saints*, 247. Nicholas Weber is married to Katharine Kaufman Weber, one of Kay Swift's granddaughters. With her he is co-trustee of the Kay Swift Memorial Trust.
12. *Institute of Musical Art Lectures, Recitals and General Occasions, Oct. 15, 1917–June 5, 1918.* Level VII described in *Institute of Musical Art Catalog, 1915–16*, 20.
13. *New Grove Dictionary*, s.v. "Goetschius, Percy." Swift's description of Goetschius is included K. Swift, interview by Perlis.
14. Dvořák's philosophy is detailed in Tibbetts, ed., *Dvořák in America*, 7. Loomis is cited in Adrienne Fried Block, "Dvořák's Long American

Reach," in Tibbetts, ed., *Dvořák in America,* 163. Swift continues her assessment of her work with Goetschius in K. Swift, interview by Perlis.

15. National trends provided by Citron, *Gender and Musical Canon,* 61. Institute statistics: Olmstead, *Juilliard,* 24, and *Institute of Musical Art Catalog, 1907–08,* Lila Acheson Wallace Library Archives, Juilliard School of Music.

16. Judith Tick notes women's limited public exposure in *Ruth Crawford Seeger,* 20. Specific duties of women teaching at the institute are detailed in Olmstead, *Juilliard,* 24–26.

17. Warburg family history is detailed by Chernow, *Warburgs,* 53–56, 90, 130–40. Comments about Warburg religious tradition are provided by Warburg, *Long Road Home,* 19.

18. Comments about Jimmy are in Chernow, *Warburgs,* 182. Comments by Jimmy are in Warburg, *Long Road Home,* 44–45.

19. Chernow, *Warburgs,* 182, 183.

20. Warburg, *Long Road Home,* 45–46.

21. Women's employment is discussed by Scharf, *To Work and to Wed,* 13. Warren Susman covers Henry Ford in *Culture as History,* 137. Lawrence Erenberg analyzes ballroom dancing in *Steppin' Out,* 161–62. Lary May details changes in movies in *Screening Out the Past,* 110–125.

22. "Ensign Warburg Weds Miss Swift," *New York Times,* June 2, 1918, 16.

23. Family attitudes toward the marriage of Katharine and James were discussed by Katharine Weber in a 1998 interview; Warburg in *Long Road Home,* 46; and Chernow in *Warburgs,* 185. It is Chernow who comments on Swift's "shabby-genteel poverty."

24. K. Weber, interview, 1998.

25. Warburg, *Long Road Home,* 60.

26. Chernow, *Warburgs,* 314.

27. *New Grove Dictionary,* s.v. "Gebhard, Heinrich."

28. "Young Artists Gave Concert," n.p., n.d. [Geneva, N.Y., 1920], personal copy provided by Ben Sears and Brad Conner. My thanks to them for providing me a copy. They received the two articles from Louise Stires Curtis, daughter of Louise Homer Stires, after her death.

29. Louise Homer's recital, accompanied by Katharine Swift Warburg, is recounted in "Miss Homer Heard in duPont Recital," n.p. [Wilmington, Del.], n.d., personal copy provided by Ben Sears and Brad Conner. Recitals of Louise Homer, Jr. and Sr., are described by Anne Homer in *Louise Homer and the Golden Age of Opera,* 365.

30. K. Swift, interview by Perlis. Swift later told Ellen Knight that her lessons were every other Saturday, which seems more likely. Knight, *Charles Martin Loeffler*, 215.
31. K. Swift, memoirs.
32. Knight, *Charles Martin Loeffler*, 12.
33. Swift's comments about Loeffler's consideration of her work are found in Knight, *Charles Martin Loeffler*, 12.
34. Knight discusses Loeffler's many interests, *Charles Martin Loeffler*, 3. Warburg describes his attraction to him in *Long Road Home*, 55.
35. "The arts were good hobbies": N. Weber, *Patron Saints*, 250.

CHAPTER 3 *Highbrow/Lowbrow in New York City*
1. Warburg shares his reactions to Hoover in *Long Road Home*, 56.
2. Chernow notes that Katharine's professionalism defies Warburg tradition in *Warburgs*, 185. "Lady's maid" is described by Katharine Weber, interview by author, New Haven, Conn., June 29, 2000.
3. K. Swift, memoirs.
4. *Institute of Musical Art Lectures, Recitals and General Occasions, 1921–22.*
5. Shippen Swift, interview by author, Hancock, Me., June 13, 2001. Katharine Weber, e-mails to author, July 30, 2001, and March 30, 2003.
6. Esther Leeming Tuttle, telephone interview by author, February 4, 2003. "Mink coats": K. Weber, e-mail to author, March 17, 2003.
7. Warburg, *Long Road Home*, 56–61.
8. Gaines, *Wit's End*, 30. *Current Biography* 1941, s.v. "Woollcott, Alexander," and "Adams, Franklin P."
9. Warburg, *Long Road Home*, 62–63.
10. Warburg, *Long Road Home*, 63.
11. Details on the renovation of the townhouse are offered by Warburg in *Long Road Home*, 68. Nursery stories were related by April Gagliano, telephone interview by author, May 30, 2000. Katharine Weber's comment appears in her essay, "Memory of All That," 21.
12. K. Weber, interview, 2000.
13. Tuttle, interview; Chernow, *Warburgs*, 316; Warburg, *Long Road Home*, 69.
14. *Current Biography*, s.v. "Astaire, Fred and Adele," "Lillie, Beatrice," "Field, Marshall," and "Harriman, William Averell."
15. *Current Biography*, "Rodgers, Richard, and Lorenz Hart," 1940, 1941, 1945. Rodgers, *Musical Stages*, 45. Chernow, *Warburgs*, 244, addresses the friendship between Gerald Warburg and Richard Rodgers, as well as Katharine's support for Gerald's musical career.

16. Warburg's descriptions of the Damrosches' parties are found in *Long Road Home,* 64; Connelly's, in *Voices Offstage,* 69–70.

17. Chernow, *Warburgs,* 316; Warburg, *Long Road Home,* 67.

18. April Gagliano recalled the music lessons in her interview. Chernow relates the Brearley story in *Warburgs,* 317.

19. "Married: J. V. N. Dorr and Ellen Faulkner Swift," *New York Times,* June 22, 1924, 31. K. Swift describes their marriage in her memoirs.

20. Chernow, *Warburgs,* 316

21. Gagliano, interview. Andrea's contrasting attitude was shared by K. Weber, interview, 2000.

22. Warburg, *Long Road Home,* 68. His reference is to Thorstein Veblen's "conspicuous consumption," discussed in Veblen's *Theory of the Leisure Class: An Economic Study of Institutions* (1899; New York: Modern Library, 1961), 52–76.

23. There are several conflicting versions of when and where Swift and Gershwin met, but all agree that it took place in 1925. George Gershwin's accomplishments before their meeting are detailed in Jablonski, *Gershwin,* 38–39, 44, 75. Katharine's attitude toward popular music and then to Gershwin's popular songs appears in Kimball and Simon, *Gershwins,* 64. The remarks by Swift in that book were later published as an article, "Remembering George Gershwin," *Saturday Review of the World,* October 9, 1973. William Bolcom and Joan Morris talked about Swift's frequent attendance at *Shuffle Along* in an interview by the author, Ann Arbor, Mich., March 28, 2002, tape recording.

24. Peyser, *Memory of All That,* 117–18.

25. Kimball and Simon, *Gershwins,* 66.

26. Heyward's comments: Alpert, *Life and Times of Porgy and Bess,* 84.

27. These early engagements are reported in a variety of Gershwin biographies, including Ewen, *George Gershwin,* 144; Jablonski, *Gershwin,* 48, 127, 298; and Peyser, *Memory of All That,* 118–19. Swift's memories are recorded in Kimball and Simon, *Gershwins,* 116.

28. Jablonski discusses Gershwin's appreciation of Berlin in *Gershwin,* xi. Swift shared her enthusiasm for "At the Devil's Ball" with Robert Kimball, telephone conversation with author, April 6, 2003. Kimball and Simon mention Hoagy Carmichael in *Gershwins,* 66.

29. Jablonski discusses the Preludes in *Gershwin,* 135–37.

30. Dvořák's use of spirituals is discussed in Tibbetts, ed., *Dvořák in America,* 6.

31. Knight, *Charles Martin Loeffler,* 236.

32. Swift's membership in the union: Rosemary Brent, "A Swift Success," *Popular Songs Magazine,* December 1935, 8. Esther Leeming Tuttle

remembered that Kay and her sister worked for Norman Bel Geddes. Peyser writes of Gershwin's generosity to young musicians, *Memory,* 176. She told Robert Kimball how she had met Rodgers.

33. Brent, "Swift Success."

34. Published poetry by James Paul Warburg includes "Fame," *Century,* September 1920, and "Sonnets," *Century,* January 1921. Ron Chernow, in *The Warburgs,* reports that Warburg had a sonnet published in the *Atlantic Monthly,* 315. Warburg later published two volumes under the name Paul James, *And Then What?* (New York: A. A. Knopf 1931) and *Ships and Shoes and Sealing Wax* (New York: A. A. Knopf, 1932). As James P. Warburg, he published *A Book for Jimmy, Jennifer and Philip* (Greenwich, Conn.: Privately published, 1955). His secret writing ambitions are shared in Warburg, *Long Road Home,* 51.

35. *Say When* is included and critiqued in Bordman, *American Musical Theatre,* 439–40. Song titles, their introductions, and other details are listed in Bloom, ed. *American Song,* s.v. "Say When."

36. Engel, *American Musical Theater,* 45, 66.

37. Mordden, *Make Believe,* 85.

38. Information about *The Little Show* is in Baral, *Revue,* 278. Jon Bradshaw includes the Libby Holman anecdotes in *Dreams That Money Can Buy,* including "torch singer par excellence," 73, and Wilder's reaction, 72.

39. See Bradshaw, *Dreams That Money Can Buy,* for Dietz's comment ("had a lot of visitors"), 114, Swift's support ("I knew she was right for the part"), 113, and the Smith Reynolds murder, 45, 171. Adding to the sensationalism of Holman's indictment was that she was pregnant with Reynolds's child. Swift always insisted that Holman was innocent. F. Scott Fitzgerald, "A New Leaf," in *Bits of Paradise: Twenty-One Uncollected Stories by F. Scott and Zelda Fitzgerald* (New York: Charles Scribner's Sons, 1973), 298–314. Fitzgerald's reference, "She sang him Libby Holman's 'This is how the story ends,' in a soft low voice,'" is on p. 308.

40. Allen Forte notes Western European traditions as well as African-American traditions in American popular music in *American Popular Ballad,* 7–8. David Levering Lewis addresses the white interest in African-American culture and the subsequent invasion of Harlem, *When Harlem Was in Vogue,* 162, 164. Gershwin himself conducted *Strike Up the Band* (1930), with Benny Goodman, Glenn Miller, Jimmy Dorsey, Gene Krupa, and Jack Teagarden in the pit; Jablonski, *Gershwin,* 197. For *Girl Crazy* the band was under the direction of cornetist Red Nichols; Rosenberg, *Fascinatin' Rhythm,* 190. "I Got Rhythm" has since become a standard for jazz improvisers. Not only is the tune widely played, but the sequence of chords

is itself the basis for such other jazz compositions as Duke Ellington's "Cottontail," Dizzy Gillespie's "Shaw 'Nuff," and Lester Young's "Lester Leaps In"; Gridley, *Jazz Styles,* 170.

41. Discussion of "blue subdominant": Forte, *American Popular Ballad,* 161.
42. William Bolcom and Joan Morris, interview by author, Ann Arbor, Mich., March 28, 2002, tape recording. Brooks Atkinson admired Etting's performance in his review, "'Nine Fifteen Revue' Is Noisy and Speedy," *New York Times,* February 12, 1930.
43. Brooks Atkinson, "The Garrick Gaieties," *New York Times,* June 5, 1930.

CHAPTER 4 Fine and Dandy

1. "My grandparents had a Broadway musical": Katharine Weber, telephone conversation with author, New Haven, Conn., July 21, 1995. Kay Swift composed the entire score except for one dance number, "Mechanical Ballet," which was composed by Eugene Grona. When Russell Warner restored the full score for *Fine and Dandy,* that music had not been located, so Swift suggested that music for another number, "Machine Shop Chant," be used for the dance. As of this writing, the Grona piece still has not been found.
2. Erlanger's Theatre history: Morrison, *Broadway Theatres,* 153.
3. N. Weber, *Patron Saints,* 249.
4. *New Grove Dictionary,* s.v. "Spialek, Hans."
5. Tichi, *Shifting Gears,* 25–26.
6. Lyric in Kay Swift and Paul James, "Machine Shop Chant," *Fine and Dandy,* unpublished score, restored and edited by Russell Warner, 1997. "Rhythm of the turning machines": Donald Ogden Stewart, *Fine and Dandy,* unpublished script, restored and edited by Russell Warner, 1997, 1.1.1. References are to act, scene, and page number.
7. With the character of George Ellis, "a recent Yale graduate and son of the plant manager," Donald Ogden Stewart, a Yale graduate, takes a subtle swipe at James Warburg, a Harvard man.
8. Stewart, *Fine and Dandy,* 1.1.19, 1.1.30, 1.1.34, 1.3.1.
9. Allen Forte analyzes the verse as well as the refrain in *Listening to Classic American Popular Songs,* 69–70.
10. This would be classified as a Schenkerian "5-line" descent, since after the initial arpeggiation in phrase A, the overall progression of the melody moves stepwise from c2 down to f1.
11. "Amos 'n Andy" reference in Allen, *Only Yesterday,* 293. "Check and double check": *Fine and Dandy,* 1.1.28. *Check and Double Check* was also the name of a movie starring the Amos and Andy characters in their first

talking motion picture. It was released in 1930 and featured appearances by the Duke Ellington Orchestra. *Check and Double Check,* Nostalgia Family Video, 1997.

12. K. Swift and P. James, "Fine and Dandy" (New York: Harms, 1930). Bordman, *American Musical Theatre,* 513.

13. Stewart, *Fine and Dandy,* 1.1.16.

14. Stewart, *By a Stroke of Luck,* 184.

15. "Can This Be Love?" is significant enough to have been included among Allen Forte's selected ballads of the era, which he discusses in *American Popular Ballad,* 310–15. "Let's write a little something": Kimball and Simon, *Gershwins,* 116.

16. "Pitch painting": Forte, *American Popular Ballad,* 28. Stewart, *Fine and Dandy,* 1.5.8, 1.5.24.

17. The additional verses were found in the Warner Brothers warehouse in Secaucus, N.J., in 1982. They are now located in the Music Division, Library of Congress. Thanks to Charlotte Kaufman, whose presentation at the Sonneck Society annual meeting in March 1999, in Fort Worth, Texas, addressed the importance of these refrains. She spoke about the verses concerning the Harvard-Yale rivalry and Gandhi. Thank you to Michael Bloomquist ('03), Harvard crew Web-master, for verifying the results of the crew races from those years.

18. "Honey Fitz": David Wallechinsky and Irving Wallace, *The People's Almanac* (Garden City, N.Y.: Doubleday, 1975), s.v. "John F. Fitzgerald." Both Curley and Fitzgerald vehemently attacked the Ku Klux Klan for its anti-Catholic views, even though the Klan was not particularly active in Massachusetts. Curley went so far as to stage cross-burnings during his political speeches. See Victor Laskey, *J.F.K.: The Man and the Myth* (New York: MacMillan, 1963), 34. The cross-burnings may explain the choice of the word "blazes." Both Curley and Fitzgerald were Irish, and not quite accepted by the Boston Brahmins, who indeed may have viewed their rhetoric as "homely."

19. *Current Biography,* s.v. "Gandhi."

20. Philip Furia, *The Poets of Tin Pan Alley: A History of America's Great Lyricists,* 2d ed. (New York: Oxford University Press, 1992), 110.

21. "Here today, gone tomorrow": Kay Swift, interview by Jim Morris, *The American Musical Theater,* WCBS-TV, New York City, October 29, 1960. Tape recording in HSR Yale.

22. Feature on Art Metrano in "Da-da-DA Da-da-DA-DA," *New Yorker,* July 31, 1971, 26. Warburg, *Long Road Home,* 65.

23. Brooks Atkinson, "Presenting Joe Cook," *New York Times,* September 23, 1930, 26, col. 1. Donald Ogden Stewart, *A Parody Outline of History* (New York: George H. Doran, 1921). *Current Biography,* s.v. "Stewart, Donald Ogden."

24. Stewart, *Fine and Dandy,* 1.1.3.

25. Stewart, *Fine and Dandy,* 1.1.8, 1.1.14.

26. Allen, *Only Yesterday,* 172. Stewart's golf interest: *By a Stroke of Luck,* 159.

27. Stewart, *Fine and Dandy,* 2.1.2, 3. It is not clear who actually sang this song in the show. Russell Warner assigned it to Joe.

28. Jablonski, *Gershwin,* 143.

29. Stewart, *Fine and Dandy,* 2.1.3.

30. K. Swift, synopsis of *Fine and Dandy,* KS MSS.

31. Tichi, *Shifting Gears,* 88.

32. Davis, *Blues Legacies,* 17–20.

33. Stewart, *Fine and Dandy,* 2.3.10. Donald Ogden Stewart, *Fine and Dandy,* unpublished script, restored and edited by Russell Warner, 1997.

34. Tichi, *Shifting Gears,* 88.

35. ASCAP requirements are detailed in Ryan, *Production of Culture,* 11.

CHAPTER 5 *Stagestruck*

1. Broadway statistics from Bordman, *American Musical Theatre,* 425–68. Warburg outlined his advisory capacity to FDR in *Long Road Home,* 112. His publications include *The Money Muddle* (New York: Knopf, 1934); *The Monetary Problem* (Washington, D.C., 1934); *Hell Bent for Election* (Garden City, N.Y.: Doubleday, Doran, 1935); and *Still Hell Bent* (Garden City, N.Y.: Doubleday, Doran, 1936). Warburg would publish more than fifty volumes during his lifetime.

2. "Despite her own": Arvey, "George Gershwin," 11.

3. N. Weber, *Patron Saints,* 250.

4. Warburg's concerns about "the effects on the children" are expressed in *Long Road Home,* 159. That Zilboorg treated Gershwin, Swift, and Warburg is reported in Jablonski, *Gershwin,* 292–93. Swift's sexual experiences with Zilboorg are detailed in Peyser, *Memory,* 263.

5. "I had a happy career": Peyser, *Memory,* 124. "Well-known treatment": K. Swift, interview by Perlis. "Mrs. J. P. Warburg in Reno for Divorce: Banker's Wife Arrives There to Establish Residency in Order to Bring Action," *New York Times,* November 6, 1934, 28.

6. "Ludicrous parody": N. Weber, *Patron Saints,* 245. The only recording of *Alma Mater* to date is on the double album *Fine and Dandy: The Music*

of Kay Swift. "Gould was forever grateful": Robert Kimball, telephone conversation with author, April 6, 2003.

7. K. Swift, notes to *Alma Mater,* KS MSS.

8. K. Swift, notes to *Alma Mater,* KS MSS.

9. Nicholas Fox Weber offers a complete account of *Alma Mater*'s origin and its opening night in *Patron Saints,* 245–59.

10. "Horseplay at Harvard," *Time,* December 17, 1934, 66. "The ultimate carryings-on of the smart set" and *Washington Post* quotation reported by N. Weber, *Patron Saints,* 258.

11. K. Swift, memoirs.

12. "A visit paid to Charleston": K. Swift, memoirs. Gershwin's 1934 attendance at a church service is reported by Jablonski, *Gershwin,* 273.

13. "Chorus of crows": reported by Sharley, "Gershwin's Friend Kay Swift," 19. Description of the "unforgettable experience": K. Swift, memoirs. In actuality, DuBose Heyward probably was not present much of the time. He preferred to remain in South Carolina and collaborate from a distance.

14. Ann Brown, who played Bess in the premiere, confirmed Swift's attendance at rehearsals and casting decisions with Katharine Weber at the Commemoration of George and Ira Gershwin Room, Coolidge Auditorium, Library of Congress, Washington, D.C., March 15, 1998. K. Weber, e-mail to author, July 30, 2001. "She wrote faster and more neatly": K. Weber, e-mail to author. Description of sketch, "I Got Plenty o' Nuttin," by Johnson, "Gershwin's Sketches for *Porgy and Bess.*" Description of fugue by Shirley, "Reconciliation on Catfish Row," 162.

15. Swift's role in Boston opening: Jablonski, *Gershwin,* 288. Relationship between Natica Nast and Gerald Warburg shared by N. Weber, *Patron Saints,* 250. Description of Condé Nast, his apartment, and his parties: "Condé Nast," *Time,* September 28, 1942, 50, 56. *Current Biography,* 1940, s.v. "Paley, William." "I remember taking whole days making lists," and presentation of silver tray: Jablonski and Stewart, *Gershwin Years,* 231. "Soliciting signatures": Swift, telegram to Norman Bel Geddes, Norman Bel Geddes Papers, Harry Ransom Humanities Research Center, University of Texas, Austin.

16. Swift's lectures on *Porgy and Bess* are reported in Kimball and Simon, *Gershwins,* 188. "She had memorized the entire score": I. Gershwin, *Lyrics on Several Occasions,* 70. Jablonski describes Gershwin's article in *Gershwin,* 289–90.

17. "A magnitude and splendor," "demonstrating his faith in the American future," and "flocked to legitimate theaters": Francisco, *Affectionate History of Radio City Music Hall,* vii; descriptions of Radio City stage shows: 33.

"The Howl," K. Swift, memoirs. Movie theaters in the 1920s are described by May, *Screening Out the Past*, 148–66.

18. "A chance to write": Kay Swift, interview by Martha Dean, WOR "Woman's Program," New York City, March 19, 1935, tape recording, HSR Yale. "I wrote a song a week": Kay Swift, interview by Margaret McBride, WEAF, New York, August 17, 1943, tape recording, HSR Yale. Radio City staff is described in Francisco, *Radio City*, 17. Swift is listed in Radio City Music Hall programs, 1935, Radio City Music Hall Corporate Library, New York. Stern shared his memories of Radio City in his interview with James Leve, New York, March 1, 1995, tape recording, personal copy. Name change from Al Silverman to Al Stillman, K. Weber, interview by author, New Haven, Conn., June 11, 1998. "Al proved the easiest": K. Swift, memoirs. *Current Biography*, 1985, obituaries, "Peerce, Jan," 472. *Current Biography*, 1972, obituaries, "Weede, Robert," 473.

19. Kay Swift folder, Radio City Music Hall Corporate Library, New York.

20. "Kay Swift was very social, very chic": Stern, interview by Leve. "Other more serious music": K. Swift, interview by Perlis.

21. Warburg's memories of "her work in the theater," as well as the stable and happy home life attributed to Phyllis are recounted in Warburg, *Long Road Home*, 170, 238. Katharine Weber shared that "Phyllis and April did not get along" but affirmed that "the two younger daughters embraced their stepmother," interview, 1998. James and Phyllis Warburg were divorced in 1947. He married Joan Melber in 1948, and they had four children. James Warburg died in 1969.

22. Music from Radio City Archives, KS MSS. Two of the songs found were arrangements of earlier pieces Swift had written, "Up Among the Chimney Pots" and "Fine and Dandy." Apparently Swift's entire output has not been preserved, since at least seventy-five weeks comprise the eighteen months she was on staff. Several factors may account for this discrepancy. Often in 1935 and 1936, movies were held over a second week, and so was the stage show. And if a number was particularly successful, the routine might be repeated several months later. (These may have been the scores that survived.) Another composer, Maurice Baron, contributed numbers as well as Swift, although some weeks they were writing for the Ballet as well as for the Rockettes. The Radio City Records, however, list many distinctive stage show themes (for example, Fiesta Mexicana, In a Quaint Old Quaker Town) that do not correspond to any of Swift's surviving music. The number of stage shows without corresponding titles might simply indicate that those titles were not preserved. Radio City Records, Radio City Corporate Library, New York.

23. "We have an old cat head": K. Swift, memoirs.

24. "Nola" was a piano composition by Felix Arndt published in 1915. Vincent Lopez popularized it during his performances at the Pekin Restaurant. He later formed his own orchestra, which broadcast live from the Hotel Pennsylvania, and "Nola" became his signature song; Ewen, *American Popular Songs*. Katharine Weber recalls that her grandmother sang an alternate lyric to the third line: "And you crave something faster than gin or canasta." Swift penciled in this lyric on her own copy of the music.

25. "Sawing a Woman in Half," Kay Swift, music, and Al Stillman, lyrics © 1935, Edward B. Marks Music Company. Copyright renewed. Used by permission. All rights reserved.

26. "Weede, as a magician, sang it": K. Swift, memoirs. Cabaret singers Brad Connor and Ben Sears, who presented a program of Swift and Gershwin songs in Lexington, Massachusetts, were surprised when, during the performance of "Sawing a Woman in Half," a woman in the audience sang along to this little-known gem. She knew the piece because her husband is an amateur magician and told them that the song is still sung at magicians' conventions. Bolcom and Morris are not nightclub singers; they perform classic popular songs in concert settings.

27. Lindhe, "You Can't Draw a Line."

28. Thanks to my colleague Ann Sears for her observations regarding the quartet.

CHAPTER 6 *Gershwin Obsession*

1. K. Weber, "Memory of All That," 17.

2. Details of Gershwin's life are well documented in several biographies. I have relied on Jablonski, *Gershwin;* Jablonski and Stewart, *Gershwin Years;* Kimball and Simon, *Gershwins;* Ewen, *Journey to Greatness;* and Goldberg, *George Gershwin*. James Warburg's life is chronicled in Chernow, *Warburgs*, as well as in his autobiography, Warburg, *Long Road Home*.

3. Jablonski, *Gershwin*, 6.

4. Gershwin's residences, Jablonski, *Gershwin*, 5, 109.

5. "'I'd bet on George,'" reported in Ewen, *Journey to Greatness*, 236.

6. "His joyous delight": Kimball and Simon, *Gershwins*, 140. "An encourager, an enthusiast": Burt Korall, "George Gershwin," n.d., typescript, 12, KS MSS.

7. "So it happened": Arvey, "George Gershwin," 11. "Spanish Prelude": Jablonski, *Gershwin*, 136.

8. "In a Mandarin's Orchid Garden": Chernow, *Warburgs*, 317. "I knew just enough": William Zeffiro, interview by author, New York, August 11, 2000, tape recording.

9. Williams and D'Amico, *George Gershwin Remembered*.

10. "He had had affairs with other women": Chernow, *Warburgs*, 315. "Kay and George were a glamorous couple": K. Weber, "Memory of All That," 23.

11. "Gershwin reported to Damrosch": Jablonski, *Gershwin*, 173. That Warburg was "remarkably obliging": Chernow, *Warburgs*, 318.

12. Warburg, *Long Road Home*, 71.

13. Description of Gershwin and Swift attending *An American in Paris:* Jablonski, *Gershwin*, 180. "Antique gold bracelets": K. Swift, "Here's the Pitch," KS MSS.

14. "April and Andy!" Jablonski, *Gershwin*, 198. "It had a wonderful opening night": Kimball and Simon, *Gershwins*, 140.

15. Frankie's wedding: Jablonski, *Gershwin*, 131. Gershwin's dedication to Swift: Jablonski, *Gershwin*, 229, and Kimball and Simon, *Gershwins*, 180. "To K.S.," James Warburg (Paul James), *Shoes and Ships and Sealing Wax* (New York: A. A. Knopf, 1932).

16. Jablonski, *Gershwin*, 240.

17. K. Swift, interview by Perlis.

18. Jablonski, *Gershwin*, 262. Thanks to Mark Trent Goldberg, executive director of the Ira and Leonore Gershwin Trusts, for information about the Gershwin radio show; telephone conversation with author, August 12, 2003. Scripts for "Music by Gershwin" series are in Gershwin Archives, San Francisco.

19. Arvey, "George Gershwin," 27.

20. "Poodle named Porgy": Jablonski, *Gershwin*, 225. "Blue cornflower": K. Weber, interview by author, New Haven, Conn., June 18, 2002. "She waited backstage": Chernow, *Warburgs*, 318. "'Best' was their code word for 'love,'" K. Weber, interview by author, New Haven, Conn., June 11, 1998. "She knew it would be concealed": Feinstein, *Nice Work*, 115. "If there was one woman": Ewen, *Journey to Greatness*, 144.

21. "She was going with Gershwin": Esther Leeming Tuttle, telephone interview by author, February 4, 2003.

22. "He had several affairs and flirtations" and "I always felt I held a unique position": William and D'Amico, *George Gershwin Remembered*. Interest in Rosamund Walling is mentioned in Kimball and Simon, *Gershwins*, 138. The allegations of an affair with Molly Charleston and having a son, Alan, are made in Peyser, *Memory*, 110–11. Katharine Weber reports that Swift received a telephone call in her presence from someone she later identified as Alan Gershwin. He had supposedly asked Kay to verify his identity, to which Swift answered, "I can't do that." It is not known whether she did not believe that he was Gershwin's son or whether she was simply adhering

to the Gershwins' preferences. Interview by author, New Haven, Conn., June 18, 2002.

23. "The future Miss Kay Swift": Mark Steyn, "George's Best Girl," London *Telegraph,* October 6, 1985, KS MSS. "He didn't want to be responsible for them": Feinstein, *Nice Work,* 64. "He was fond": Williams and D'Amico, *George Gershwin Remembered.* Kimball, telephone conversation with author, April 6, 2003.

24. Shippen Swift, letter to Katharine Weber, May 17, 1998, personal copy.

25. Kimball and Simon, *Gershwins,* 151.

26. Jablonski maintains that Kay and George did not discuss marriage, *Gershwin,* 298. Swift describes "a chic twenty-seven-year-old," and "Both girls are on their way": K. Swift, "Reno," KS MSS.

27. Katharine Weber remembered that her grandmother had gone to Reno with her close friend Mary Reinhardt (later Mary Lasker) and that, according to tradition, they had thrown their wedding rings off the Truckee Bridge. K. Weber, interview by author, New Haven, Conn., June 29, 2000, and e-mail to author, March 17, 2003. "It was on the train, with its steely rhythms": Goldberg, *George Gershwin,* 139. Swift left the volume to William Zeffiro in her will. The inscription from Gershwin reads, "For Kay. Best. George. Oct. 1, 1931." William Zeffiro, interview by author, New York, August 11, 2000, tape recording. It seems that James Warburg had already been searching for a new bride; he married Phyllis Baldwin Browne four months later, in April 1935. Warburg, *Long Road Home,* 161. "She just wanted it to be easier for them to be together": Zeffiro, interview.

28. Rodgers's story is found in Kimball and Simon, *Gershwins,* xii. Swift's divorce was reported in the newspaper: "Divorce Granted," *New York Times,* December 21, 1934, 26.

29. K. Swift, memoirs.

30. "Postpartum letdown": Jablonski, *Gershwin,* 292. "Did he ever propose?" Doris B. Wiley, "Gershwin's Gal: It Never Got to 'Toothbrush Time,'" *Philadelphia Evening Bulletin,* July 21, 1976, 17A. Clarification of "toothbrush time" by William Bolcom and Joan Morris, interview by author, Ann Arbor, Mich., March 28, 2002, tape recording. William Bolcom and Arnold Weinstein, "Toothbrush Time," in Bolcom and Weinstein, *Cabaret Songs: For Medium Voice and Piano* (New York: Edward B. Marks, 1985), vol. 2, poetry by Arnold Weinstein.

31. "They planned to assess their relationship": Jablonski, *Gershwin,* 299. "I never saw him after that photograph": Kimball and Simon, *Gershwins,* 200.

32. George's inquiries about Kay are mentioned in Jablonski, *Gershwin,* 313, as are his interests in Simon and Goddard, 305, 317. "Weeping cocktail time":

Alfred Stern, interview by James Leve, New York, March 1, 1995, tape
recording, personal copy. "When I knew he was in the hospital": Wiley,
"Gershwin's Gal," 17A. "George is gone": Williams and D'Amico, *George
Gershwin Remembered*. The fate of their correspondence is reported by
Feinstein, *Nice Work*, 66.

33. K. Weber, "Memory of All That," 18, 30. "George approached life":
Burt Korall, "George Gershwin," KS MSS.

CHAPTER 7 *New Frontiers*

1. "Anyone who came from Radio City": Alfred Stern, interview by James
Leve, New York, March 1, 1995, tape recording, personal copy.

2. Warren Susman discusses the fair at length in "The People's Fair: Cultural
Contradictions of a Consumer Society," in *Culture as History*, 211–29.
Whalen's comments are in Tyng, *Making a World's Fair*.

3. "Festival of sight and sound" and other comments by Susman, in *Culture
as History*, 216. Hall of Music information is outlined in "Music Festival
Plans," *New York Times*, March 12, 1939, 1. Russell B. Porter writes about
"bands of strolling players" in "Fair Will Stress Appeal to 'Masses,'"
New York Times, May 6, 1939, 1.

4. Ira Gershwin recalled Grover Whalen's initial charge in his notes in
George Gershwin's *Tune Book*, Gershwin Room, Library of Congress, 2.
His comments about Kay Swift are found in I. Gershwin, *Lyrics on Several
Occasions*, 70. Furia's comments are found in his *Ira Gershwin*, 194. The
recording of George Gershwin, "Dawn of a New Day" (New York:
Chappell Music), 1938, is available on *From Gershwin's Time: The Original
Sounds of George Gershwin 1920–1945*, Horace Heidt and His Musical
Knights, originally recorded January 26, 1939, Sony Classical MH2K 60648.

5. Descriptions of the fair are in Appelbaum, *New York World's Fair*, 3. Alfred
Stern's comments were made in the interview by James Leve, New York,
March 1, 1995, tape recording, personal copy. Still's response is reported in
Smith, *William Grant Still*, 74. "Which he carried out with style": K. Swift,
memoirs.

6. "Music Program Canceled by Fair," *New York Times*, May 25, 1939, 30.

7. "To preserve and save the best of modern civilization": Tyng, *Making a
World's Fair*, introduction by Whalen.

8. The description of the Parachute Jump is in "Amusement Area Offers
Freaks, Peeks and Rides," *Life*, July 3, 1939. The description of the
American Jubilee is found in the *Official Guide Book*, 133. Faye Hubbard's
colorful insights are in "Dancin' and Horses—Bad Habits Linger,"
Colfax (Wash.) Gazette, August 21, 1975, Kay Swift Papers.

9. Cawelti, *Adventure, Mystery, and Romance,* 230–37.
10. Malone, *Country Music,* 89.
11. The fate of "Don't Fence Me In" is detailed by McBrien, *Cole Porter,* 190. Billy Hill is discussed in Malone, *Country Music,* 151.
12. Fuller, *Joseph Swift,* 1.
13. K. Swift, *Who Could Ask,* 3, 4, 209.
14. K. Swift, *Who Could Ask,* 209.
15. K. Weber, interview by author, New Haven, Conn., June 11, 1998.
16. Comments by Andrea Warburg Kaufman and Katharine Weber were related in Weber's 1998 interview. April Gagliano's comments are from her telephone interview by the author, May 30, 2000.
17. Julia McCarthy, "Western Man the Master, Says Kay," *New York Daily News,* n.d. [1943], KS MSS.
18. The physical description of Hubbard was offered by Katharine Weber, telephone interview by author, July 28, 1995. April's comments are from her telephone interview, and Shippen Swift's memories were shared in the interview by author, Hancock, Me., June 13, 2001, tape recording. Hubbard admitted his alcoholism in "Dancin' and Horses."
19. S. Swift, interview; K. Weber, interview, 1998.
20. S. Swift, interview.
21. K. Swift, *Who Could Ask,* 8–9.
22. K. Swift, *Who Could Ask,* 209.
23. Finger exercises are included in Kay Swift, Unidentified Sketches, KS MSS.
24. S. Swift, interview.
25. Kay Swift, "Happy Birthday, Dear Andy," September 29, 1941, tape recording, personal copy. An incomplete manuscript (no accompaniment) is in the Kay Swift Papers.
26. Explanation of Fritz Hoppe's presence at the recording session was offered by Katharine Weber, "Kay Swift," paper presented at Commemoration of George and Ira Gershwin Room, Coolidge Auditorium, Library of Congress, Washington, D.C., March 15, 1998.
27. Kay Swift, "Fighting on the Home Front Wins" © 1943 (Renewed) Chappell and Co. All Rights Reserved. Used by Permission. Warner Bros. Publications U.S. Inc., Miami, Florida 33014.
28. "Amiable and beguiling": critique of book found in *Book Review Digest* 1943, 791. "Super-sophisticated New Yorker" is Margaret McBride's description in her interview, WEAF, New York, August 17, 1943, tape recording, HSR Yale. Swift's comments about western men are reported by Helen Harrison, "Comeback of the Horse-Ridin' Romeo," *New York Journal America,* September 11, 1943, KS MSS.

29. Weber's comments about John Wayne were made in the 1995 telephone interview. Characteristics of westerns are discussed in Cawelti, *Adventure, Mystery, and Romance*, 192–93.

30. Kay Swift, "Once You Find Your Guy" © 1950 (Renewed) Chappell and Co. All Rights Reserved. Used by Permission. Warner Bros. Publications U.S. Inc., Miami, Florida 33014.

31. K. Swift, *Who Could Ask*, 31.

32. "Eighty-six" and "H. C.": K. Weber, in "Memory of All That," 25. April's comments about "L & D" were offered in her interview.

33. K. Swift, memoirs.

34. Brown Derby: suggested by K. Weber, interview by author, New Haven, Conn., June 29, 2000. Marc Connelly recalled the restaurant (or perhaps a different site) as Chasen's Southern Barbeque Pit in *Voices Offstage*, 128.

35. Steyn, "George's Best Girl"; Feinstein, *Nice Work*, 179; I. Gershwin, *Lyrics on Several Occasions*, 70.

36. Jablonski, "What About Ira?" 257. The prelude has been published as George Gershwin, "Prelude (Sleepless Night)," in Alicia Zizzo, ed., *The Complete Gershwin Preludes for Piano* (New York: Warner Bros., 1996).

37. Feinstein, *Nice Work*, 179. Steyn, "Kay Swift" *(London) Independent*, February 2, 1993, 25, KS MSS. Ben Sears and Brad Conner shared their thoughts in a conversation with author, Lexington, Ky., March 9, 2002. Swift's comments ("The music is all Gershwin") are in Steyn, "George's Best Girl."

38. Swift discussed their fascination with California in her interview by Perlis. Residency in California is apparent because royalty checks, which had been sent to Kay Swift in Bend, Oregon, for the last quarter of 1945, were, for the first and second quarters of 1946, sent to her in Hollywood, c/o Mrs. Dorian Otvos. In the third quarter, they were sent to Beverly Hills. Hubbard's union status was detailed in "Dancin' and Horses." Swift's description of their social life in California is in her memoirs.

39. Swift's version of the breakup is presented by Jean Mandelker, "A Composer Whose Life Is 'Fine and Dandy,'" *Newsday*, August 29, 1975, 11A, KS MSS. Hubbard's is related in "Dancin' and Horses," 12. The move to Benedict Canyon is told by Swift in "A Little Western," KS MSS.

40. Hunter Galloway, court action, KS MSS.

41. This anecdote was related by K. Weber, interview, 2000.

42. William Zeffiro, interview by author, New York, August 11, 2000, tape recording.

43. Bobby Clark, letter to Kay Swift, January 8, 1948, KS MSS.

44. George Oppenheimer, letter to Kay Swift, July 6, 1949, KS MSS.

45. *Sarah Was There*, videotape pilot, HSR Yale.

CHAPTER 8 *She'll Have Manhattan*

1. K. Swift, memoirs.
2. The mink coat story is told by Katharine Weber, e-mail to author, March 17, 2003.
3. K. Swift, memoirs.
4. *New Grove Dictionary,* s.v. "Taylor, Deems." A typical adaptation of a classical piece for popular purposes, Harry Carroll, words, Joseph McCarthy, music, "I'm Always Chasing Rainbows" (New York: Robbins Music, 1918). "She opened an office": K. Swift, memoirs; Shippen Swift, interview by author, Hancock, Me., June 13, 2001.
5. The authenticity of the Toulouse-Lautrec nobility is questioned by Sweetman, *Explosive Acts,* 22–24. Other biographical details are offered by Heller, *Toulouse-Lautrec,* 7, 10, 19, 20, 21, 106.
6. "Candy box blonde" and "dowdy, ridiculous frump": *Paris '90,* liner notes, Sonic 12-2625 ss, HSR Yale. *New Grove Dictionary,* s.v. "Bennett, Robert Russell."
7. K. Swift, interview by Perlis.
8. "Calliope," by Kay Swift © 1952 Chappell & Co. (Renewed). All Rights Reserved. Used by Permission. Warner Bros. Publications U.S. Inc., Miami, Florida 33014. "Whirled breathlessly": Buckman, *Let's Dance,* 123. The 1952 recording of *Paris '90* has been re-released on CD. Cornelia Otis Skinner, *Paris '90,* music by Kay Swift, directed by Nathaniel Shilkret (1952; DRG 19034, 2003).
9. Davis, *Blues Legacies and Black Feminism,* 33–41.
10. Schonberg, "Symbolism and Impressionism," 465. Reference to Reynold's in Lockspeiser, *Debussy,* 136.
11. "The House Where I Was Born," by Kay Swift © 1952 (Renewed) Chappell & Co. All Rights Reserved. Used by Permission. Warner Bros. Publications U.S. Inc., Miami, Florida 33014. "Prestige platter": Bing Crosby, letter to Cornelia Otis Skinner, August 24, 1952, KS MSS.
12. Jean Bouret, *The Life and Work of Toulouse-Lautrec: Court Painter to the Wicked* (New York: Abrams, n.d.), 126.
13. Touring schedule: K. Swift, memoirs. Records as Christmas gifts: K. Swift, memoirs. *Paris '90,* conducted by Nathaniel Shilkret (1952; Columbia ML-4619). Reviews of show: W. Gibbs, *New Yorker,* March 15, 1952; "Cornelia Otis Skinner," *New York Times Magazine,* March 16, 1952; Brooks Atkinson, *New York Times,* March 5, 1952, all in KS MSS.
14. K. Swift, "Seven Lives," KS MSS. Jablonski, liner notes for *The Music of Kay Swift,* Mark 56, 1975, HSR Yale.

15. They were performed in 1957 by the New Orleans Symphony Orchestra at Robin Hood Dell and taped for broadcast by the Norddeutscher Rundfunk Orchester in Hamburg, Germany, with D. Bruno Schneider conducting and Louise Parker as soloist. Parker also performed the songs in the Netherlands and Norway in 1957. A performance by the Cleveland Orchestra was conducted by Michael Charry.

16. Al Jolson, Buddy de Sylva, and Joseph Meyer, "California, Here I Come!" (Warner Bros.–Seven Arts Music, 1924), in Nat Shapiro and Bruce Pollock, eds., *Popular Music, 1920–1979* (Detroit, Mich.: Gale Research, 1988). Jack Norworth and Albert von Tilzer, "Take Me Out to the Ballgame" (York Music, 1908), in Barbara Cohen-Stratyner, ed., *Popular Music, 1900–1919* (Detroit, Mich.: Gale Research, 1988).

CHAPTER 9 *Challenges*

1. The plot of *Hunter's Moon* is summarized in Paul T. Nolan, *Marc Connelly* (New York: Twayne, 1969), 108–10.
2. Hunter Galloway, letter to Darlo, KS MSS.
3. K. Swift, statement in support of H.R. 5921, KS MSS.
4. Thoughts about *Mary Poppins* and *Foggerty's Fairy:* K. Weber, telephone conversation with author, June 9, 2003. Summary of *A Candle for St. Jude:* Lynne Rosenthal, *Rumer Godden Revisited* (New York: Twayne, 1996), 33–35. Screenplay, Rumer Godden, *Studio One Presents "A Candle for St. Jude,"* producer Worthington Miner, director Paul Nickell, adaptor Elizabeth Hart, broadcast February 4, 1952. TV script, Popular Culture Library, Bowling Green University, Bowling Green, Ohio. "Distinguished": Rumer Godden, letter to K. Swift, KS MSS. "Perhaps the refrain": K. Swift, letter to Godden, KS MSS. "I was disappointed to learn": K. Swift, letter to Miriam Howell, March 27, 1960, KS MSS.
5. Hunter Galloway, letter to Ellen Gould, KS MSS.
6. Gabriel Favoino, "The Pop Side," *Chicago Sun Times,* December 4, 1960, KS MSS.
7. A 1976 interview was conducted by Phyllis Battelle, "Royalties Are 'Fine and Dandy': Composer Has Had a Noteworthy Career," *Long Island Press,* August 10, 1976, 10. Bobby Short, interview by author, New York, June 13, 1999, tape recording.
8. Stern, interview by James Leve, New York, March 1, 1995, tape recording, personal copy. I am grateful to Jack Santino for suggesting this double standard.
9. K. Swift, statement of support for H.R. 5921.
10. K. Swift, "Here's the Pitch," KS MSS. K. Swift, memoirs.

11. "Excessive": John McCarten, "Gershwin with All Stops Out," *New Yorker*, July 4, 1959, 65; "Static": Philip T. Hartung, "'And Nuttin's Plenty for Me,'" *Commonweal*, August 14, 1959, 425; "A stodgy bore": Stanley Kauffmann, "Two Preminger Premieres," *New Republic*, July 13, 1959, 23. "Grandiose, foolish, heavy": James Baldwin, "On Catfish Row," *Commentary*, September 1959, 246–48. "I described . . . the extraordinarily stimulating experience," K. Swift, memoirs.

12. K. Swift, memoirs.

13. K. Swift, memoirs.

14. "No girl over the age of fifteen": Jean Mandelker, "A Composer Whose Life Is 'Fine and Dandy,'" *Newsday*, August 29, 1975, 11A. "Last year's mink coats": K. Weber, e-mail to author, March 17, 2003. "Marvelous leopard-skin coat": Stern, interview by Leve. Description of her wedding attire, K. Swift, *Who Could Ask*, 2.

15. Reference to wardrobe allowance: L. Arnold Weissburger, letter to Ralph Wheelwright, October 13, 1959, KS MSS. Misunderstanding about expenses: Lynn Farnol, letter to Kay Swift, September 8, 1959, KS MSS. Resignation: Weissburger, letter to Wheelwright.

16. I. Gershwin, letter to Kay Swift, KS MSS.

17. K. Swift, "Here's the Pitch."

18. K. Swift, memoirs.

CHAPTER 10 *The Show Won't Fold in Philadelphia*

1. Shippen Swift, interview by author, Hancock, Me., June 13, 2001, tape recording. K. Weber, interview by author, New Haven, Conn., June 29, 2000. K. Weber, "Memory of All That," 25–26.

2. "I wish I were an alcoholic" and "champion reader-out-loud": K. Weber, interview by author, New Haven, Conn., June 11, 1998. Memories of singing for the blind were offered by Louise Carlyle, interview by James Leve, New York, March 1, 1995, personal copy.

3. Lee Swift, interview by author, Hancock, Me., June 13, 2001, tape recording.

4. S. Swift, interview. Alfred Stern, interview by James Leve, New York, March 1, 1995, tape recording, personal copy. "Unstable": Katharine Weber, e-mail to author, July 30, 2001.

5. Kay Swift, *One Little Girl*, conducted by Hans Spialek, 12/33 Camp Fire Girls D-81, 1960, HSR Yale.

6. Swift, interview by Patricia Yaroch, "Writes with Song in Heart," Detroit, Mich. (source unclear, [1975]), KS MSS.

7. Betty Paysner, letter to Bill Doll, n.d., KS MSS.

8. Description of show by K. Swift, publicity for *Century 21:* KS MSS. "G.T." designation: Kay Swift sketches, KS MSS.

9. Stern, interview by Leve. The reference to the review in *Variety,* July 12, 1962, appeared in Swift's letter to Bernie Green, n.d. [c. 1967], KS MSS.

10. Kay Swift, letter to James Palmer, August 4, 1964, KS MSS.

11. Stern, interview by Leve. K. Swift, letter to Palmer, KS MSS.

12. Yaroch, "Song in Heart."

13. K. Swift, "None but the Brave," 189, 191.

14. K. Swift, letter to Palmer.

15. Stern, interview by Leve. Gershwin quoted in Yaroch, "Song in Heart."

16. I wish to thank my colleague Jan Younger for calling this point to my attention.

17. K. Swift, interview by Perlis.

18. K. Swift, interview by Perlis.

19. Kay Swift, "Everywhere I Roam," address for Stephen Foster Jeanie Auditions (White Springs, Fla., February 1966), KS MSS.

20. K. Swift, "Everywhere I Roam."

21. K. Swift, "Everywhere I Roam."

22. William Zeffiro, interview by author, New York, August 11, 2000, tape recording.

23. Reilly, "Kay Swift."

24. K. Swift, interview by Perlis.

25. Jablonski, liner notes for *The Music of Kay Swift,* Mark 56, 1975, HSR Yale.

26. Thanks to my colleague Charlotte Greenspan for her thoughts on this possible collaboration. Winer, *Sunny Side,* 34–41.

27. Rosenberg, *Fascinatin' Rhythm,* 377, 384.

28. Yaroch, "Song in Heart."

29. K. Swift and Henry Myers, letter to Warren, July 27, 1964, KS MSS.

30. K. Swift, AGAC brochure, KS MSS.

31. K. Weber, interview, 1998.

32. Swift's tribute to Galloway is in "Fresh Woods and Pastures New," KS MSS. Shippen Swift's discovery was shared in his interview with the author.

33. K. Swift and G. Gershwin, black notebook, Gershwin Archives, Library of Congress.

34. Milton Esterow, "Art Buyer 'Sorry,' but He Can't Pay $467,775 Bill," *New York Times,* November 11, 1967, 1. Swift's need to sell paintings was recalled by Shippen Swift in his interview. Swift's reaction was recorded in her letter to "John," KS MSS. Acknowledging Galloway's suicide were Shippen Swift, Katharine Weber, and Alfred Stern in their interviews. "A memorial service": K. Weber, e-mail to author, March 17, 2003.

35. K. Swift, memoirs. It is unknown whether Dr. Seale was the inspiration for the pseudonym B. F. Seale, which she used for her choral piece "God Is Our Refuge," although this could have been a subtle tribute to the man she so admired. Perfect attendance was acknowledged by Ervin Seale, certificate for Divine Science and Metaphysics, Church of Truth, KS MSS.

CHAPTER 11 *Keep on Keepin' On*

1. Ursula Vaughan Williams, "Noah's Ark," in her *Silence and Music* (Fair Lawn, N.J.: Essential Books, 1959), 70.
2. Merle Armitage, ed., *George Gershwin* (New York: Longmans, Green, 1938; reprint ed. with introduction by Edward Jablonski, New York: Da Capo Press, 1995); Jablonski and Stewart, *The Gershwin Years;* Kimball and Simon, *Gershwins.* Her first interview about Gershwin had been with Verna Arvey, "George Gershwin Through the Eyes of a Friend." K. Swift, "Remembering George Gershwin," *Saturday Review of the World,* September 9, 1973, 18+.
3. Kimball and Simon, *Gershwins,* 140.
4. Robert Kimball's memories of Swift were shared in a telephone interview with the author, August 13, 2001. The recording on which Swift assisted Short is *Bobby Short Is K-ra-zy for You,* 1973, Atlantic 608-2, 1990. "Three good friends" is from the liner notes. His recollections of her assistance and generosity were shared in his interview with the author, New York, June 13, 1999, tape recording. My thanks to Robert Kimball for noting the transformation from "K-ra-zy for You" to "Crazy for You," telephone interview by author, April 6, 2003.
5. Alpert, *Life and Times of Porgy and Bess,* 297, 303.
6. Kimball, telephone interview, 2001.
7. Doris B. Wiley, "Gershwin's Gal" *(Philadelphia) Evening Bulletin,* July 21, 1976. Jean Mandelker, "A Composer Whose Life Is 'Fine and Dandy,'" *Newsday,* August 29, 1975, 11A. Phyllis Battelle, "Royalties Are 'Fine and Dandy': Composer Has Had a Noteworthy Career," *Long Island Press,* August 10, 1976.
8. "Collectors' items by George Gershwin and Harold Arlen": Ken Drisko, "Fine and Dandy: The Music of Kay Swift," *Massachusetts Apartment and Condominium Living,* n.p., n.d., KS MSS. Reilly, "Kay Swift," 108.
9. Christmases in Rome: Mandelker, "Composer." The wedding at Bydale was described by K. Weber, telephone conversation with author, June 9, 2003.
10. Her continued love for the Dodgers: Swift, "Baseball." K. Swift, letter to William Bolcom and Joan Morris, October 1, 1981, personal copy.

11. "Generous drinks" were reported by William Zeffiro and Shippen Swift in interviews with author (New York, August 11, 2000, tape recording; Hancock, Me., June 13, 2001, respectively). The guest list was for a party that was canceled April 30, 1971, after Swift's brother, Samuel, was hospitalized following an accident, KS MSS. "There was nothing 'Old Lady' about her": William Bolcom and Joan Morris, interview by author, Ann Arbor, Mich., March 28, 2002, tape recording. Kimball described the birthday party in his interview, 2003.

12. K. Weber, interview by author, New Haven, Conn., June 18, 2002. Alfred Stern, interview by James Leve, tape recording, New York, March 1, 1995, personal copy. An incorrect birth year was published in "Kay Swift," in Virginia Grattan, ed., *American Women Songwriters: A Biographical Dictionary* (Westport, Conn.: Greenwood Press, 1993).

13. K. Swift, letter to BBC, August 8, 1966, KS MSS.

14. K. Weber, telephone interview by author, July 21, 1995. This is also recounted in K. Weber, "Memory of All That," 28.

15. K. Weber, telephone interview, 1995. This is also recounted in K. Weber, "Memory of All That," 28–29.

16. K. Swift, "Seven Lives," KS MSS. Kay Levin, "Death Doesn't Play Fair," *Insight*, n.d., KS MSS.

17. My thanks to Katharine Weber for calling this reference to my attention.

18. Louise Carlyle, interview by James Leve, New York, March 1, 1995, personal copy.

19. Bolcom and Morris, interview.

20. I am deeply grateful to Katharine Weber for sharing these memoirs with me.

21. "She was always so positive": Carlyle, interview by Leve. "She would never say a mean word about any of her husbands": Zeffiro, interview. "Disappointment adjustant": K. Swift, interview by Perlis. "Kay was such a believer": Carlyle, interview by Leve.

22. "We never had the feelings we weren't equal": Battelle, "Royalties Are 'Fine and Dandy.'" "I never had any trouble": K. Swift, interview by Perlis.

23. Battelle, "Royalties Are 'Fine and Dandy.'"

24. K. Weber, interview by author, New Haven, Conn., June 11, 1998.

25. K. Swift, memoirs.

26. K. Swift, memoirs. Gagliano, telephone interview by author, May 30, 2000.

27. K. Swift, memoirs.

28. K. Swift, memoirs.

29. K. Swift, memoirs.

CHAPTER 12 *Finale*

1. "She often worried": William Zeffiro, interview by author, New York, August 11, 2000, tape recording. "You must have had such an interesting life": K. Weber, interview by author, New Haven, Conn., June 11, 1998; and April Gagliano, telephone interview by author, May 30, 2000.
2. "Kay had written out from memory": Russell Warner, e-mail to author, August 24, 2001. "The students adored her": Kimball, telephone interview by author, August 13, 2001.
3. Tim Page, "Broadway Song Trove Tops Original Hopes," *New York Times*, March 10, 1987. Secaucus discovery is also described in Feinstein, *Nice Work*, 163–81.
4. Feinstein, *Nice Work*, 179.
5. "Kay Swift actually composed the verse": Feinstein, *Nice Work*, 175. "Like Ira, at times she was content": Steyn, "Kay Swift." George and Ira Gershwin, *Of Thee I Sing; Let 'Em Eat Cake*, directed by Michael Tilson Thomas (CBS: M2K 42522, 1987).
6. Warner, e-mail.
7. Zeffiro, interview. It should be noted that Bill Zeffiro has mastered an imitation of Kay Swift's voice, and as he relates stories about her, she comes to life. However, Zeffiro modestly cites Michael Feinstein's imitation of Swift as being even more realistic.
8. Videotape of Marble Collegiate Homecoming, 1985, personal copy.
9. K. Swift, invitation to serve on planning committee, KS MSS. Stephen Sondheim, letter to Kay Swift, KS MSS.
10. Robert Kimball, "Kay Swift: Fine and Dandy," *New York Post*, October 16, 1986, KS MSS.
11. Kimball, "Kay Swift."
12. Zeffiro, interview. "Kay Swift Commemorative Concert," Merkin Hall, October 14, 1986, tape recording, HSR Yale.
13. Louise Carlyle, interview by James Leve, New York, March 1, 1995, personal copy, tape recording.
14. K. Weber, e-mail to author, April 28, 2002.
15. K. Swift, memoirs.
16. Kay Swift, "Dancers in the Dark," KS MSS.
17. Zeffiro, interview.
18. Carlyle, interview by Leve.
19. Carlyle, interview by Leve.
20. S. Swift, interview.

21. Sardi's tradition is detailed in Vincent Sardi, Jr., and Thomas Edward West, *Off the Wall at Sardi's* (New York: Applause, 1991), 5. "She was so surprised": Carlyle, interview by Leve.

22. K. Weber, interview by author, New Haven, Conn., June 29, 2000.

23. Kay Levin, "Death Doesn't Play Fair," *Insight*, n.d., KS MSS.

24. "He visited her every Friday for lunch": K. Weber, interview, 2000. Short shared the story of his encounter on the street in his interview with the author, New York, June 13, 1999, tape recording.

25. Carlyle, interview by Leve.

26. K. Weber, e-mail to author, March 30, 2003.

27. "She was a wonderful, lively woman": Warner, e-mail to author, August 20, 2001. "I can only wish": Carlyle, interview by Leve.

28. "Well, I was the love of his!": Zeffiro, interview. "Kay admitted": Kimball, telephone conversation with author, April 6, 2003. "Probably the most profound influence on my life except for my father": William A. Henry, 3d, "'He Had the Universal Touch,' Recalls Best Friend," *Boston Globe*, September 26, 1973, KS MSS.

Selected Bibliography

Allen, Frederick Lewis. *Only Yesterday: An Informal History of the 1920's.* 1931; reprint, New York: Harper and Row, 1964.

Alpert, Hollis. *The Life and Times of Porgy and Bess: The Story of an American Classic.* New York: Knopf, 1990.

Appelbaum, Stanley. *The New York World's Fair 1939/1940 in 155 Photographs by Richard Wurts and Others.* New York: Dover, 1977.

Arvey, Verna. "George Gershwin: Through the Eyes of a Friend." *Opera and Concert* (April 1948): 11.

Baral, Robert. *Revue: A Nostalgic Reprise of the Great Broadway Period.* New York: Fleet, 1962.

Block, Adrienne Fried. "Dvořák's Long American Reach." In John C. Tibbetts, ed., *Dvořák in America,* 157–81. Portland, Oreg.: Amadeus Press, 1993.

Bloom, Ken, ed. *American Song: The Complete Musical Theatre Companion.* 2d ed. 1877–1995. New York: Schirmer Books, 2001.

Bordman, Gerald. *American Musical Theatre: A Chronicle.* 3d ed. New York: Oxford University Press, 2001.

Bouret, Jean. *The Life and Work of Toulouse-Lautrec: Court Painter to the Wicked.* New York: Abrams, n.d.

Bradshaw, Jon. *Dreams That Money Can Buy: The Tragic Life of Libby Holman.* New York: Morrow, 1985.

Brent, Rosemary. "A Swift Success." *Popular Songs Magazine,* December 1935, 8.

Buckman, Peter. *Let's Dance: Social, Ballroom and Folk Dancing.* New York: Paddington Press, 1978.

Cawelti, John G. *Adventure, Mystery, and Romance: Formula Stories as Art and Popular Culture.* Chicago: University of Chicago Press, 1976.

Chernow, Ron. *The Warburgs: The Twentieth-Century Odyssey of a Remarkable Jewish Family.* New York: Random House, 1993.

Citron, Marcia. *Gender and the Musical Canon.* Cambridge: Cambridge University Press, 1993.

Connelly, Marc. *Voices Offstage: A Book of Memoirs.* Chicago: Holt, Rinehart and Winston, 1968.

Damrosch, Frank. Address at Opening Ceremony. *Institute of Musical Art Lectures, Recitals and General Occasions, Oct. 11, 1905–June 12, 1906.* Lila Acheson Wallace Library Archives, Juilliard School of Music.

Davis, Angela Y. *Blues Legacies and Black Feminism: Gertrude "Ma" Rainey, Bessie Smith and Billie Holiday.* New York: Pantheon, 1998.

Engel, Lehman. *The American Musical Theater.* Rev. ed. New York: Macmillan, 1975.

Erenberg, Lawrence A. *Steppin' Out: New York Nightlife and the Transformation of American Culture, 1890–1930.* Westport, Conn.: Greenwood, 1981.

Ewen, David. *George Gershwin: His Journey to Greatness.* Englewood Cliffs, N.J.: Prentice-Hall, 1977. (Reprint of *A Journey to Greatness: The Life and Music of George Gershwin* [New York: Holt, 1956].)

Feinstein, Michael. *Nice Work if You Can Get It: My Life in Rhythm and Rhyme.* New York: Hyperion, 1995.

Forte, Allen. *The American Popular Ballad of the Golden Era, 1924–1950.* Princeton, N.J.: Princeton University Press, 1995.

———. *Listening to Classic American Popular Songs.* New Haven and London: Yale University Press, 2001.

Francisco, Charles. *An Affectionate History of the Radio City Music Hall.* New York: E. P. Dutton, 1979.

Fuller, Nancy Tatnall. *Joseph Swift: In the Wild West.* Privately published, 1997.

Furia, Philip. *Ira Gershwin: The Art of the Lyricist.* New York: Oxford University Press, 1996.

Gaines, James R. *Wit's End: Days and Nights of the Algonquin Round Table.* New York: Harcourt Brace Jovanovich, 1977.

Gershwin, George. *From Gershwin's Time: The Original Sounds of George Gershwin, 1920–1945.* Horace Heidt and His Musical Knights. Originally recorded January 26, 1939. Sony Classical compact disc MH2K 60648.

Gershwin, George, and Ira Gershwin. *Of Thee I Sing; Let 'Em Eat Cake.* Michael Tilson Thomas. CBS compact disc M2K 42522, 1987.

Gershwin, Ira. *Lyrics on Several Occasions.* 1959; reprint with preface by John
  Guare, New York: Limelight Editions, 1997.
Goldberg, Isaac. *George Gershwin.* New York: Simon and Schuster, 1931.
Gridley, Mark C. *Jazz Styles: History and Analysis.* 5th ed. Englewood Cliffs,
  N.J.: Prentice Hall, 1994.
Harrison, Helen. "Comeback of the Horse-Ridin' Romeo." *New York Journal
  America,* September 11, 1943. KS MSS.
Heller, Reinhold. *Toulouse-Lautrec: The Soul of Montmartre.* New York:
  Prestel, 1997.
Homer, Anne. *Louise Homer and the Golden Age of Opera.* New York: William
  Morrow, 1974.
Institute of Musical Art Catalog, 1907–08. Lila Acheson Wallace Library
  Archives, Juilliard School of Music.
*Institute of Musical Art Lectures, Recitals and General Occasions, Oct. 11, 1915–
  June 2, 1916.* Lila Acheson Wallace Library Archives, Juilliard School of
  Music.
*Institute of Musical Art Lectures, Recitals and General Occasions, Oct. 16, 1916–
  June 6, 1917.* Lila Acheson Wallace Library Archives, Juilliard School of
  Music.
*Institute of Musical Art Lectures, Recitals and General Occasions, Oct. 15, 1917–
  June 5, 1918.* Lila Acheson Wallace Library Archives, Juilliard School of
  Music.
Institute of Musical Art Lectures, Recitals and General Occasions, 1921–22.
  Lila Acheson Wallace Library Archives, Juilliard School of Music.
Jablonski, Edward. *Gershwin.* 1987; Boston: Northeastern University Press,
  1990.
———. "What About Ira?" In Wayne Schneider, ed., *The Gershwin Style:
  New Looks at the Music of George Gershwin,* 255–78. New York: Oxford Uni-
  versity Press, 1999.
Jablonski, Edward, and Lawrence Stewart. *The Gershwin Years: George and Ira.*
  New York: Doubleday, 1958.
Johnson, John Andrew. "Gershwin's Sketches for *Porgy and Bess.*" Paper
  presented at the joint meeting of the American Musicological Society,
  Center for Black Music Research and Society for Music Theory, New York,
  November 4, 1995.
"Kay Swift Commemorative Concert." Merkin Hall. October 14, 1986. Tape
  recording. HSR Yale.
Kimball, Robert, and Alfred Simon. *The Gershwins.* New York: Atheneum,
  1973.

Knight, Ellen. *Charles Martin Loeffler: A Life Apart in American Music.* Urbana: University of Illinois Press, 1993.

Lamb, Andrew. *150 Years of Popular Musical Theatre.* New Haven and London: Yale University Press, 2000.

Lewis, David Levering. *When Harlem Was in Vogue.* 1979; New York: Penguin, 1997.

Lindhe, Vin. "You Can't Draw a Line." *Radio City Music Hall Program Magazine,* June 17, 1935. Radio City Music Hall Corporate Library, New York.

Lockspeiser, Edward. *Debussy: His Life and Mind.* Vol. 1. New York: Macmillan, 1962.

McBrien, William. *Cole Porter: A Biography.* New York: Knopf, 1998.

Malone, Bill C. *Country Music, U.S.A.* Rev. ed. Austin: University of Texas Press, 1985. Orig. publ., American Folklore Society, 1968.

May, Lary. *Screening Out the Past: The Birth of Mass Culture and the Motion Picture Industry.* Chicago: University of Chicago Press, 1983.

Mordden, Ethan. *Make Believe: The Broadway Musical in the 1920s.* New York: Oxford University Press, 1997.

Morrison, William. *Broadway Theatres: History and Architecture.* Mineola, N.Y.: Dover, 1999.

Nichols, Roger. *The Life of Debussy.* New York: Cambridge University Press, 1998.

Nolan, Paul T. *Marc Connelly.* New York: Twayne, 1969.

Official Guide Book: The World's Fair of 1940 in New York: For Peace and Freedom. New York: Rogers, Kellogg, Stillson, 1940.

Oja, Carol J. *Making Music Modern: New York in the 1920s.* New York: Oxford University Press, 2000.

———. "Women Patrons and Crusaders for Modernist Music." In Ralph P. Locke and Cyrilla Barr, eds., *Cultivating Music in America: Women Patrons and Activists Since 1860,* 237–61. Berkeley: University of California Press, 1997.

Olmstead, Andrea. *Juilliard: A History.* Chicago: University of Illinois Press, 1999.

Perlis, Vivian. Interview with Kay Swift for Oral History, American Music, Yale University, New York, May 1, 1975. Tape recording.

Peyser, Joan. *The Memory of All That: The Life of George Gershwin.* New York: Simon and Schuster, 1993.

Reilly, Peter. "Kay Swift: Civilized Pleasure." *Stereo Review,* December 1975, 108.

Rodgers, Richard. *Musical Stages: An Autobiography.* New York: Random House, 1975.

Rosenberg, Deena. *Fascinatin' Rhythm: The Collaboration of George and Ira Gershwin*. New York: Dutton, 1991.

Rosenthal, Lynne. *Rumer Godden Revisited*. New York: Twayne, 1996.

Ryan, John. *The Production of Culture in the Music Industry: The ASCAP-BMI Controversy*. New York: University Press of America, 1985.

Sardi, Vincent, Jr., and Thomas Edward West. *Off the Wall at Sardi's*. New York: Applause, 1991.

Scharf, Lois. *To Work and to Wed*. Westport, Conn.: Greenwood Press, 1980.

Schonberg, Harold C. "Symbolism and Impressionism: Claude Debussy." In *The Lives of the Great Composers*, 452–65. 3d ed. New York: Norton, 1997.

Sharley, Jean. "Gershwin's Friend Kay Swift: 'Sounding Board' for Porgy." *Detroit Free Press*, September 29, 1959, 19.

Shirley, Wayne. "Reconciliation on Catfish Row: Bess, Serena, and the Short Score of *Porgy and Bess*." *Quarterly Journal of Library of Congress* 38, no. 2 (1981): 144–65.

Short, Bobby. *Bobby Short Is K-ra-zy for You*. 1973; Atlantic compact disc 608-2, 1990.

Skinner, Cornelia Otis. *Paris '90*. Music by Kay Swift, directed by Nathaniel Shilkret. 1952; DRG compact disc 19034, 2003.

Smith, Catherine Parsons. *William Grant Still: A Study in Contradictions*. Berkeley: University of California Press, 1999.

Susman, Warren. *Culture as History: The Transformation of American Society in the Twentieth Century*. New York: Pantheon Books, 1984.

Sweetman, David. *Explosive Acts: Toulouse-Lautrec, Oscar Wilde, Félix Fénéon and the Art and Anarchy of the Fin de Siècle*. New York: Simon and Schuster, 1999.

Swift, Gertrude Horton Dorr. Diary. KS MSS.

Swift, Kay. "April Day." KS MSS.

———. "Baseball: The Love of My Life." *Folio*. December 1975. Personal copy.

———. "Here's the Pitch." KS MSS.

———. *The Music of Kay Swift*. Liner notes by Edward Jablonski. Mark 56, 1975. HSR Yale.

———. "None but the Brave." *Black Perspectives in Music: A Birthday Offering to William Grant Still* 3.2 (1975): 188–92.

———. *One Little Girl*. Conducted by Hans Spialek. 12/33 Camp Fire Girls D-81, 1960. HSR Yale.

———. "Seven Lives So Far." KS MSS.

———. "Veltin 1915." Contribution to Veltin School Class of 1915 newsletter, 1978. Personal copy.

————. *Who Could Ask for Anything More?* New York: Simon and Schuster, 1943.

Swift, Kay, and Paul James. *Fine and Dandy.* Unpublished score. Restored and edited by Russell Warner, 1997.

Swift, Samuel. Letter to Adeline Dorr, August 22, 1905. KS MSS.

————. "Summer Music in New York." *Harper's Weekly Magazine,* June 29, 1901, 663.

Stewart, Donald Ogden. *By a Stroke of Luck: An Autobiography.* New York: Paddington Press, 1975.

————. *Fine and Dandy.* Unpublished script. Restored and edited by Russell Warner, 1997.

Tibbets, John C., ed. *Dvořák in America.* Portland, Oreg.: Amadeus Press, 1993.

Tichi, Cecelia. *Shifting Gears: Technology, Literature, Culture in Modernist America.* Chapel Hill: University of North Carolina Press, 1987.

Tick, Judith. *Ruth Crawford Seeger: A Composer's Search for American Music.* New York: Oxford University Press, 1997.

Tyng, Ed. *Making a World's Fair: Organization, Promotion, Financing, and Problems, with Particular Reference to the New York World's Fair of 1939–1940.* Introduction by Grover Whalen. New York: Vantage Press, [1958].

Warburg, James P. *The Long Road Home: Autobiography of a Maverick.* Garden City, N.J.: Doubleday, 1964.

Warner, Russell. E-mail to author, August 24, 2001.

Weber, Katharine. "Kay Swift." Presentation at conference, "The Gershwins and Their World." Library of Congress, Washington, D.C., March 18, 1999.

————. "The Memory of All That." In Mickey Pearlman, ed., *A Few Thousand Words About Love,* 15–30. New York: St. Martin's Press, 1998.

Weber, Nicholas Fox. *Patron Saints: Five Rebels Who Opened America to a New Art, 1928–1943.* New York: Knopf, 1992.

Williams, John, and Kirk D'Amico, executive producers. *George Gershwin Remembered.* BBC TV Program Development Co. and American Masters, 1987.

Winer, Deborah Grace. *On the Sunny Side of the Street: The Life and Lyrics of Dorothy Fields.* New York: Schirmer Books, 1997.

Yaroch, Patricia. "Writes with Song in Heart." Detroit, Mich. (source unclear, [1975]). KS MSS.

Index

Credits

Alma Mater, by Kay Swift. Used by Permission. Kay Swift Memorial Trust, Bethany, Connecticut

"A Boston Schoolteacher," by Kay Swift. Used by Permission. Kay Swift Memorial Trust, Bethany, Connecticut

"Calliope," by Kay Swift. © 1952 (Renewed) Chappell and Co. All Rights Reserved. Used by Permission. Warner Bros. Publications U.S. Inc., Miami, Florida

"Candles," by Kay Swift. Used by Permission. Kay Swift Memorial Trust, Bethany, Connecticut

"Can't We Be Friends?" by Paul James and Kay Swift. © 1929 Warner Bros. Inc. (Renewed). All Rights Reserved. Used by Permission. Warner Bros. Publications U.S. Inc., Miami, Florida

"Elmer's Marvelous Ark," by Kay Swift. Used by Permission. Kay Swift Memorial Trust, Bethany, Connecticut

"Etiquette," by Paul James and Kay Swift. Used by Permission. Kay Swift Memorial Trust, Bethany, Connecticut

"Fighting on the Home Front Wins," by Kay Swift. © 1943 (Renewed) Chappell and Co. All Rights Reserved. Used by Permission. Warner Bros. Publications U.S. Inc., Miami, Florida

"Fine and Dandy," by Paul James and Kay Swift. © 1930 Warner Bros. Inc. (Renewed). All Rights Reserved. Used by Permission. Warner Bros. Publications U.S. Inc., Miami, Florida